PLAY
NICE

ALSO BY JASON SCHREIER

Press Reset:
Ruin and Recovery in the Video Game Industry

Blood, Sweat, and Pixels:
The Triumphant, Turbulent Stories Behind
How Video Games Are Made

PLAY NICE

THE RISE, FALL, AND FUTURE OF
BLIZZARD ENTERTAINMENT

JASON SCHREIER

GRAND
CENTRAL

New York   Boston

Grand Central Publishing

Hachette Book Group

1290 Avenue of the Americas, New York, NY 10104

grandcentralpublishing.com

@grandcentralpub

First edition: October 2024

Grand Central Publishing is a division of Hachette Book Group, Inc. The Grand Central Publishing name and logo is a registered trademark of Hachette Book Group, Inc.

The publisher is not responsible for websites (or their content) that are not owned by the publisher.

Grand Central Publishing books may be purchased in bulk for business, educational, or promotional use. For information, please contact your local bookseller or the Hachette Book Group Special Markets Department at special.markets@hbgusa.com.

Library of Congress Cataloging-in-Publication Data

Names: Schreier, Jason, author.
Title: Play nice : the rise, fall, and future of blizzard entertainment / Jason Schreier.
Description: First edition. | New York : GCP, [2024] | Includes index.
Identifiers: LCCN 2024014052 | ISBN 9781538725429 (hardcover) | ISBN 9781538725443 (ebook)
Subjects: LCSH: Video games industry. | Blizzard Entertainment (Firm)
Classification: LCC HD9993.E452 S36 2024 | DDC 338.4/77948—dc23/
eng/20240424
LC record available at https://lccn.loc.gov/2024014052

ISBNs: 9781538725429 (hardcover), 9781538725443 (ebook)

Printed in the United States of America

LSC-C

Printing 3, 2024

For Sophie and Noah

CONTENTS

CONTENTS

PROLOGUE

November 3, 2023

On a hot Friday in November, tens of thousands of people descended on downtown Anaheim, California, best known as the home of Disneyland. But the crowd hadn't dished out $300 per ticket and flown in from around the world to ride Space Mountain or schmooze with Mickey—they were in Southern California for BlizzCon, a convention dedicated to the video game company Blizzard Entertainment.

The idea of a single company hosting a convention might seem bizarre—how much would you pay for tickets to the Cigna Expo?—but such was the power of Blizzard Entertainment and the games it had created. Fans spent hundreds of hours battling for higher *StarCraft* ranks and grinded for weeks just to get the perfect *Diablo* helmet. They played *Hearthstone* every morning in the bathroom and watched *Overwatch* short films at night.

It was one Blizzard game, more than any other, that had convinced tens of thousands of people to flock to Anaheim that weekend: *World of Warcraft*, which had hooked millions of players, inspired countless clones, and changed the way people thought about online gaming.

Throughout the weekend, attendees walked through the Anaheim convention center wearing cloaks and scarfing down massive turkey legs. The air was filled with the scent of stale popcorn and the gritty taste of smoke machines. In one hall, hundreds of fans sat in bleachers to watch top *Overwatch* players battle in intense five-on-five shooting matches, while elsewhere, attendees stood in line to get posters signed by Blizzard developers or challenge *Hearthstone* designers to duels. They held meetups for their *World of Warcraft* guilds and hugged friends they hadn't seen for years. A few devoted fans signed up to be inked with tattoos based on art from *Diablo*, while one provocateur wore a red hat emblazoned with "Make Azeroth Great Again."

Then, on Sunday at Los Angeles International Airport, a few departing attendees waited for their flights at a gaming lounge called Gameway, where they logged in to their *World of Warcraft* characters to check in with their guilds, knock out quests, and make sure they hadn't missed anything important during the days they were away.

Despite the energy, there was something different about this year's BlizzCon. Even as Blizzard's fans and employees celebrated, there were hints that the company's iconic blue frosted logo had lost some of its luster. Thanks to the COVID-19 pandemic, it had been four years since the last convention. Over those years, Blizzard had taken a series of PR hits that made some fans wonder if they were celebrating the same company they'd known and loved for three decades. There had been an international scandal over freedom of speech, a busted game release, and a set of sexual misconduct allegations that led to a cultural reckoning and the ousting of dozens of Blizzard employees.

Perhaps in part due to Blizzard's diminished reputation, BlizzCon 2023 also marked a first for the company in one other ignominious way: it was the first time since 2005, when the convention started, that tickets hadn't sold out.

■ ■ ■

In 1991, when two college students named Allen Adham and Mike Morhaime decided to start a video game company, they couldn't have imagined that one day it would spawn an event like BlizzCon. Thirty years later, their little startup had evolved into one of the largest tech companies on the planet, part of a hulking conglomerate called Activision Blizzard that would have been unrecognizable to its young founders. Then, in the summer of 2021, California sued the company for sexual misconduct and discrimination, eventually leading to the company's acquisition by Xbox as part of the biggest video game deal of all time.

Some of Blizzard's history has been documented over the years, but even the most attentive fans have been left with massive questions along the way. How did Adham and Morhaime transform Blizzard into a video game empire, with a sprawling 240,000-square-foot campus and billions of dollars in revenue? What are the real stories behind *Diablo*'s tortured development, *StarCraft*'s surge and collapse in South Korea, and the high-profile cancellation of a project code-named *Titan*?

And then there was the boardroom drama. How did Blizzard become Activision Blizzard? Why did Morhaime leave to start a new company after two decades as Blizzard's president? What role did Activision Blizzard CEO Bobby Kotick play in Morhaime's departure and in the company's cultural problems? How did a company as beloved as Blizzard—one that would drive countless men and women to line up for hours just to watch its developers talk about their next games—get entangled in a misconduct lawsuit of unprecedented magnitude?

This book will answer those questions and many more, detailing Blizzard's history, its culture, and what working there was really like. It's a story of an unbelievable run of hit games, a group of young men getting rich very fast, a hostile corporate takeover, and a culture that left many of its employees with complicated and contradictory feelings. It's also a story about money, power, and the hunt for never-ending growth.

The thirty-three-year saga documented in this book is based mostly on interviews with more than 350 people: current and former Blizzard employees, current and former Activision employees, and other people in the company's orbit, such as game makers who worked alongside or competed with Blizzard. Some executives and developers agreed to speak or participate in the fact-checking process only under condition of anonymity. Blizzard declined to comment on the record.

This book does not re-create dialogue or fictionalize scenes. Except when otherwise noted, every quote in the book was said directly to me.

■　■　■

On that BlizzCon Friday, Xbox boss Phil Spencer took the stage during the opening ceremony, declaring that "now that Blizzard is part of Xbox, we will nurture the essence of what has made Blizzard unique." To many observers, it may have seemed like a nice if toothless promise from a shiny new corporate suit. But to those who knew what had really been going on at Blizzard over the last decade, the subtext of Spencer's words was thicker than a tauren on leg day.

To understand why, we'll have to go back to the very beginning—back before Blizzard was even called Blizzard. It starts, as all good stories do, with *Pac-Man*.

RISE

ONE

MANAGEMENT BY CHAOS

Before he'd even graduated high school, Allen Adham knew he wanted to make video games. It was Southern California in the 1980s, and gaming was morphing from a curious pastime into a lucrative business. Arcades were booming, cheap home computers like the Commodore 64 were becoming living room centerpieces, and the song "Pac-Man Fever" was cresting to #9 on the Billboard Hot 100. During lunch breaks, Adham would head to his local arcade and blast through aliens in games like *Asteroids* and *Space Invaders*. At home, he and his brother convinced their dad to buy an Apple II computer, which Adham could use both to play games and to create them.

Born Ayman Adham to Egyptian parents—an engineer and a preschool administrator—he grew obsessed with the way video games functioned and how they made people feel. "He'd talk about how gaming would be the new form of entertainment, synonymous with movies and stuff like that," said a college friend. "I thought he was smoking dope." To Adham, interactivity made video games capable of evoking an unparalleled adrenaline rush: instead of just watching something happen, you could actually feel it play out.

Through a high school friend he met Brian Fargo, a charismatic, slightly older programmer who was actually paid to make video games—an absurd concept, at the time—for a company called Boone. Fargo, recognizing a smart, ambitious teenager, recruited Adham to do playtesting. "He always seemed like a really sharp kid, but he didn't act like a kid," said Fargo. In 1983, Fargo and a small group of colleagues left Boone to form a startup called Interplay Productions, and soon they were making waves in the industry with games like *The Bard's Tale*, a fantasy adventure inspired by Fargo's *Dungeons & Dragons* campaigns. Adham looked at Interplay with admiration and a little envy, wondering if he, too, could one day start his own company. He kept working with Fargo during the summers as he began attending the University of California, Los Angeles, with hopes of one day making video games that millions of people would play.

During his sophomore year at UCLA, Adham designed and programmed his first game: *Gunslinger*, a rudimentary graphical text adventure set in the Wild West. A small company called Datasoft printed the game and distributed it to stores, where prospective buyers had no idea it had been coded by someone who wasn't yet old enough to legally drink. *Gunslinger* didn't get much attention, but to Adham it was proof that he could finish and release a video game of his own—a feat about which he bragged to anyone who would listen.

One day at the UCLA computer lab, Adham took a seat next to a skinny, curly-haired student named Mike Morhaime. The two men, both bookish and soft-spoken, had shared some classes but hadn't talked much. Adham stepped out of the room, locking his computer before he left. When the computer timed out and unlocked itself a few minutes later, Morhaime decided to prank his seatmate, swinging over and typing in his own password to relock the device. Adham returned, clacked a few letters on the keyboard, and somehow unlocked the computer. Morhaime, stunned, asked Adham just how the heck he'd pulled that off. It turned out the two young computer geeks had both used the same simple password, "Joe"—a meet-cute that sparked a lasting friendship.

Morhaime, too, obsessed over video games. As a kid, he was fascinated by the insides of machinery: radios, televisions, microwaves. Whenever his family would get new electronics, he'd ignore the hardware and instead pore over the manual, curious to know the exact purpose of each port on the back of the VCR. In middle school, he and his siblings pooled together their savings to buy the Bally Astrocade, a game system that included a cartridge with the BASIC programming language on it, allowing Morhaime to write simple software and slowly figure out how games functioned. The jolt of excitement from taking things apart and reassembling them pushed him to study electrical engineering at UCLA, where he sat in the front row of every class, asking questions and trying to absorb as much as possible.

Their class of programmers was in the hundreds, but Morhaime was among the few who stood out to Adham as the best of the best—the ones who would finish their assignments early and then invent challenges for one another, battling over who could code a successful program in the fewest lines. Adham thought this fellow software-obsessed geek could be the perfect partner for the grand plan he had been formulating to make the best video game company in the world.

As the two men made their way through college in the late 1980s, the video game industry expanded at a rapid pace. The Nintendo Entertainment System, released in 1987, led to groundbreaking games like *Super Mario Bros.* and *The Legend of Zelda*. Video games were growing more complex—and more lucrative—every year. Adham's old pals at Interplay were so successful at making their own games, they also began funding and publishing other companies' titles.

In 1990, as Adham was finishing his degree, he suggested to Morhaime that they team up and start a video game company. But Morhaime, who had graduated a few months earlier, was reluctant. He'd snagged a job writing test software at Western Digital, a stable computer technology company that offered him a salary and benefits with little risk, and he specialized in hardware, not video game development. Adham persisted, laying out a lengthy case and even setting up a meeting with Morhaime's skeptical father. As computer engineers in their twenties, Adham argued, this was the best possible time to take a risk. If it didn't work out, no big deal—they could all get jobs at IBM or Microsoft. There were very few other industries in which a couple of guys could go into business with a small amount of seed money and make something that hordes of people enjoyed.

It was clear that Adham had a gift for persuasion. "People said he had Jedi powers," said one person who worked with him. "He was always calm, listening, not aggressive. Always unassuming. Then he'd start to talk and you'd get all charged up: 'Yes, I will follow you.'"

After some hemming and hawing, Morhaime agreed to take the plunge. In February 1991, the pair founded Silicon & Synapse, meant to represent a sort of synergy between computer parts (silicon) and the human brain (synapse). Each of them invested around $10,000—Adham from his college fund, Morhaime through a loan from his grandmother—and they rented out a tiny office in Irvine, California. They couldn't afford new computers, so they brought in the ones they had at home, and Adham recruited one of his other UCLA friends, Frank Pearce, to be their first employee.[1] One photo

---

1 Years later, Pearce would become retconned as a Blizzard cofounder, but at the time he took a salary rather than equity.

taken on their very first day showed Adham and Morhaime craning their necks and staring down at the camera—pursed lips, matching stubble, looking ready to conquer the world.

■ ■ ■

In 1991, the video game industry was blowing up. *Street Fighter II* dominated arcades worldwide, Sega and Nintendo battled over living rooms, and *Tetris* had become a global sensation thanks to its bouncy music and addictive block puzzles. As the money kept pouring in, companies looked to release their games on as many platforms as possible, often hiring outside contractors to help adapt a game from one machine to another. A game originally released for the DOS computer operating system might get a port—or "conversion"—to the Super Nintendo, Sega Genesis, Amiga, and more, each developed by a different contractor and packed with new features to distinguish it from the others.

Morhaime and Adham planned to one day design their own software, but to start, Silicon & Synapse would take on contract work as the company tried to make a name for itself. This was where Adham's relationship with Brian Fargo started to pay dividends: Fargo, who had received a 10 percent stake in Silicon & Synapse as an advisor (Adham had 60 percent and Morhaime had 30 percent), began giving the company a slew of these conversion contracts starting with a Windows version of *Battle Chess*, which transformed the rooks and knights into medieval warriors.

Silicon & Synapse needed more programmers to keep up with the work, so they called Patrick Wyatt, who was finishing up his final months at UCLA, where he and Morhaime had been brothers at Triangle, a fraternity of men who spent most of their time talking about code. Morhaime asked if he wanted to make video games, and Wyatt,

JASON SCHREIER

a computer science major, was intrigued. "I said that sounds like a lot of fun," Wyatt recalled. He started programming on *Battle Chess* while simultaneously finishing his degree and working another job on campus. "It was hellacious in a way because I was doing so much stuff," he said, "but it was also really fun." Soon he had officially joined Silicon & Synapse as an engineer.

As the year went on, they kept picking up conversion contracts for Interplay's eclectic suite of products, ranging from a role-playing game based on *Lord of the Rings* to an educational game that taught players how to type. "They'd fly it past us, and we'd figure out whether we could do it or not," said Wyatt. "At the time we called it the business plan du jour." Each of these contracts would take a few months at most, and each Silicon & Synapse employee would juggle several at once. "The goal at that point was just to keep alive," said Joeyray Hall, who joined the company later that year.

When they weren't completing work-for-hire projects, Silicon & Synapse's employees were fantasizing about the original games they'd make. Inspired by Adham's lofty rhetoric, they thought they could conquer the video game industry—not just because they were good programmers but because they understood video games. The industry's rapid growth had drawn interest from suited businessmen with expertise in spreadsheets and selling boxes, but not in the products themselves. In contrast, Adham and crew didn't need focus groups or market research to discern if a game was good—they could just make games they wanted to play.

Adham decided that anyone who didn't play games wasn't welcome at Silicon & Synapse. Prospective employees would be asked their favorite video games, then quizzed extensively to gauge their depth of knowledge. The team would write code in the mornings, battle one another in *Magic: The Gathering* card matches during lunch, and spend evenings playing games on the office television. James Anhalt, another engineer who had joined from UCLA, shared an apartment with Pearce, who served double duty as a programmer and the office receptionist. "It was 24/7: the people you live with, hang out with, and work with were all the same," Anhalt said. There was a constant, humming conversation about which games were good, which were bad, and what they'd all do differently.

Interplay was working on a game called *RPM Racing*, a basic driving simulator in which players steered pastel sports cars and trucks down winding tracks, and the timeline was tight. Nintendo's next console, the Super Nintendo, was planned for that fall, and it was crucial for *RPM Racing* to arrive alongside it. Fargo called in Silicon & Synapse to help develop the game and was again impressed with the team's efficiency and reliability. "I knew I could count on them, and they came through," he said.

Fargo then offered to let Adham pitch his own ideas, and by the end of 1991, Interplay had signed Silicon & Synapse to make two original games for the Super Nintendo. One was a sequel to *RPM Racing* called *Rock N' Roll Racing* that added personality to its predecessor's drab driving. There was heavy metal music, a cast of drivers with names like Cyberhawk and Snake Sanders, and an announcer offering colorful play-by-play commentary ("Let the carnage begin!"). The second was *The Lost Vikings*, a puzzle-platformer inspired by the classic strategy game *Lemmings*, in which players were tasked with keeping dozens of hapless, wandering critters alive by clearing safe passages through tunnels and over lava. But the initial concept—that the player would control dozens or hundreds of tiny Nordic Vikings—wasn't holding up because the creatures were too small to see on a television.

In the future, the video game industry would cultivate a discipline known as "game design" to solve problems like this, but in the early 1990s, the process was less rigorous. Everyone at Silicon & Synapse was either an artist or a programmer, and Adham would call them all into a room to hammer out the solution. "Everybody was allowed to say their piece," said Joeyray Hall. "There was never any animosity about it. Just pitch in: What do you think is cool?" For *The Lost Vikings*, they eventually decided to whittle down the number of Vikings to three, which felt like a good balance. Erik the Swift could run and jump, Baleog the Fierce could shoot arrows, and Olaf the Stout had a shield for blocking enemy projectiles and gliding across short distances. The player could control only one at a time but could switch between them to take down monsters or solve environmental puzzles.

All of Silicon & Synapse's employees were men, and these design meetings, fueled by caffeine and testosterone, could get rowdy. Sometimes there was screaming; sometimes there were fistfights. The burgeoning video game industry was still in the early stages of becoming an *industry*, and a ten-man game-making company like Silicon & Synapse didn't yet have legal or HR people—or even standards for how to operate. They called it management by chaos: finding the best possible option through debate. "We'd sit there and iterate on an issue until everyone was in agreement," said Jesse McReynolds, a programmer who joined later. "We could argue over something for hours and hours." The process worked in large part because Adham was so persuasive, earning him the nickname "Velvet Hammer" for his understated yet forceful approach.

The development of *The Lost Vikings* would establish design principles that the company would follow for decades to come. Everyone at Silicon & Synapse was tasked with playing the game so they all had a deeper understanding of how it functioned, and when they'd played too much and lost their sense of objectivity about what worked, they brought in external playtesters. To add levity, they gave the Vikings cartoonlike animations and added cheeky dialogue for when players died and had to restart. ("I'm tired, Erik. We've been through this level too many times! Wake me when we finish it.")

When *The Lost Vikings* came out, Adham and a few other employees gathered at a nearby store to watch people play the demo. He was elated when a teenage boy looked over at the arcade stations and went for their game. The first level aimed to teach Erik the Swift's jump move by putting Erik next to an electricity pit, and when the boy started playing, he fell into the pit and died. The boy then immediately put down the controller and moved to another kiosk. "I just thought, 'Oh my God, we killed this kid two seconds into the game and he's never going to know what an amazing game this is,'" Adham later said in a retrospective. The incident convinced him that video game intro sequences needed to be as safe, easy, and approachable as possible. "You want your players right from the start to feel heroic and powerful," he said.

Death traps aside, both *Rock N' Roll Racing* and *The Lost Vikings* were critical hits, leading one video game magazine to name Silicon & Synapse "Best Software Developer of the Year" in 1993. Interplay, which had published both games, was thrilled with the reception and hungry for more. "They were clearly one of the better developers I worked with," said Interplay producer Alan Pavlish. "They understood game design, they worked hard, and they took the time and effort to do the little bit extra that takes a game from a B or a B+ into an A or an A+."

Yet the company wasn't making much money off this success. Silicon & Synapse employees didn't earn top salaries or have much in the way of benefits, but even with expenses kept low, Adham and Morhaime had trouble keeping up. Neither *Rock N' Roll Racing* nor *The Lost*

Vikings were selling quite as well as they'd hoped. Some of the developers blamed that on the marketing, which was beyond their control. As the publisher, Interplay was funding, packaging, and selling most of their games, which also meant keeping the profits. To find real success, Silicon & Synapse would need to publish a game itself.

■　■　■

Stu Rose had grungy long hair, a perennial denim jacket, and dreams of one day becoming a cartoonist. But in the early 1990s, the newspaper industry was flailing and he realized that his dream of drawing for the daily funny pages might not pan out, so he thought he might try his luck in video games. One night while out with a friend who worked at Silicon & Synapse, Rose met Adham and other members of the team, who said they were looking for new artists. "Why didn't [my friend] say anything?" Rose remembered thinking.

Soon after getting his own job at Silicon & Synapse, Rose discovered the answer. Alan Pavlish arrived at the office to look at an expected new build for the Mac conversion of Interplay's *Castles*, but Rose's friend wasn't at the office. When they looked through his computer, they couldn't find the requisite art anywhere. "Turns out he had not really done much work," said Rose. "Allen's face almost went white when he realized."

The friend was let go and Rose took over the project, which he finished in a few weeks, helping prove that he meshed with the other type-A achievers at Silicon & Synapse. Sometime later, Rose was in Adham's office and saw a box from an educational game he had developed at a previous company. "Whoa, that's weird—you have my product on the shelf," Rose recalled saying. Adham was confused, saying he thought that Rose's friend had made it. "I think he had basically used my portfolio to get the job," said Rose. From that point on, the company formally added a new step to their interview process: live drawing tests.

Rose loved the nerdy, congenial atmosphere at Silicon & Synapse. During lunch hours, they'd gather in one of the small office rooms and pull out the Neo Geo or Super Nintendo for office tournaments. One of their big obsessions was *Dune II*, a PC game released in December 1992 by the Las Vegas–based developer Westwood Studios. Inspired by the beloved Frank Herbert novel, *Dune II* was one of the first games in a genre that would be called real-time strategy, or RTS. Rather than playing as a single character, you played as an omniscient commander with full view of the battlefield, where you could harvest resources, construct buildings, and train soldiers. Every second you'd juggle decisions about where to move your armies, how to spend your money, and what to prioritize.

There was just one problem, thought Rose and his colleagues: *Dune II* didn't have a multiplayer mode. At best, the hyper-competitive staff of Silicon & Synapse could argue over strategies and see who had the highest scores, but they couldn't battle one another directly. "Everything's better with friends" had become one of the company's core philosophies: there was nothing as thrilling as coordinating with a buddy to solve puzzles in *The Lost Vikings* or getting to declare that you were the office's best *Samurai Shodown II* player. They all agreed: *Dune II* with multiplayer could be one of the best video games on the planet.

At the same time, Allen Adham was thinking up ways to transform the company into an original game publisher. Inspired by a set of *Dungeons & Dragons* games known as the Gold Box collection because of their distinct gilded packaging, he envisioned a series with a cohesive look on store shelves. Each game would be loosely connected and take place during a different historical period, such as ancient Rome or the Vietnam War. One of the artists, Sam Didier, whose visions of big beards and giant shoulder pads would help drive the company's distinct art direction, suggested a name: *Warcraft*. Someone else pitched a high-fantasy setting inspired by *Lord of the Rings* and the *Warhammer* series of tabletop games, and soon enough they had a game idea. *Warcraft: Orcs & Humans* would be a copy of *Dune II*, with multiplayer and highly polished gameplay, set in a land of swords, spells, and monsters.

Pat Wyatt began programming *Warcraft: Orcs & Humans* in the summer of 1993, as the rest of Silicon & Synapse scrambled to stay alive by taking on as many game contracts as possible. Since there were no artists on the project yet, he started out by copy-pasting all the artwork from *Dune II*.[2] He then began devising his own innovations, like a mouse-based shortcut for selecting multiple units so the player could order them all to move or attack. "I was thinking, 'This is fun all by itself,'" Wyatt said. At first, he thought there should be no limit on the number of units that you could select, but Adham insisted that restrictions would force players to make calculated decisions instead of recruiting a massive number of knights and archers and then hurling them all at the enemy. After a few weeks of companywide "management by chaos" sessions, Adham won the argument.

Stu Rose then joined *Warcraft* as the first main artist. He drew the map interface and animations for the game's two races, the orcs and the humans, each of which had their own armies and infrastructure. The development process was so unstructured that he was also tasked with naming the heroes and cities. "I was just coming up with them in my head," he said. "Um, okay, they're going to go to a place

---

2 Later, when *Warcraft* shipped, Wyatt realized that while they'd replaced all of *Dune II's* art with their own, they forgot to change the font. They altered it for future versions, but at first, the game's text looked identical to *Dune II's*. "So yeah," he said, "we owe them a little bit of a debt there."

called Goldshire. Yeah, that's it." Later, Rose provided the voice of the human peasant, a worker minion that could mine for gold, harvest lumber, and construct buildings. "Work complete," Rose would assure the player in his flat baritone every time a new farm or barracks was finished.

Warcraft was coming together nicely, but the company's cofounders were beginning to feel the financial pressure. By the end of 1993, Silicon & Synapse had switched names—now it was Chaos Studios, alluding to their unique process—and was struggling to pay the bills. Adham and Morhaime had been covering payroll for a dozen employees on their credit cards, racking up debt to keep the company afloat. The two founders were tens of thousands of dollars in the hole—so desperate that they were getting cash advances on their Discover cards at the supermarket and then depositing that money into the company's bank account.

Although they were nervous, Adham and Morhaime didn't see these financial woes as an existential threat. The contracts were still coming in, and it always seemed like they were just a few months away from stability. Sure, they had debt, but at least they hadn't been forced to take out second mortgages or beg Fargo for a loan. It never even occurred to them that it might be time to sell the company.

TWO

DONUT THEORY

The Davidsons didn't seem much like video game moguls. Jan Davidson was a lifelong teacher who had wanted to work in education since she was a high school freshman tutoring kids after school, while Bob Davidson had a law degree, a masters in business, and years of experience in engineering. But in the 1980s, Jan designed a series of educational software programs such as *Math Blaster*, which spiced up basic equations by letting young players shoot the correct answers with a cannon. When the games grew popular, the couple started Davidson & Associates to publish educational computer software. By 1993, their company was traded publicly and worth more than $40 million, much to Jan's surprise and delight. "It's nice that I got rich," she later told a newspaper. "But honestly, it wasn't my main objective. All I wanted to do was teach kids."

As with Interplay, the Davidsons were looking for outside contractors to convert their software to multiple platforms, and one of their producers heard that Silicon & Synapse might be a good fit. Davidson & Associates was based in Torrance, California, just an hour away, so

Bob Davidson drove down to meet Adham and Morhaime in person. "We were all sitting on the floor, eating pizza and drinking Pepsi," Davidson recalled. "I was in a fraternity, so it was okay." He gave Silicon & Synapse a contract to port one of their games, *Kid Works II*, and was blown away by their speed and efficiency. "I said, 'Maybe we should go down and meet them again, see what else they can do for us.'"

Adham and Morhaime explained that they were taking outside work to pay the bills but their goal was to develop and publish their own games. Davidson thought about this for a few weeks, then came back with a shocking offer: He wanted to buy Silicon & Synapse for four million dollars. The two cofounders were baffled. Their next big projects were a fighting game based on *Superman* comics, a Super Nintendo sci-fi shooter called *Blackthorne* in which you'd mow down green space aliens with a shotgun, and *Warcraft*. It wasn't a portfolio that would fit neatly alongside titles such as *Spell it Plus* and *Reading and Me*.

The founders said they'd have to think about it. They were close to signing a distribution deal with Interplay for *Warcraft*, and Brian Fargo was still a minority owner, so the three men met to discuss Davidson's offer. "Listen, I'm a shareholder and I'm your friend," Fargo recalled saying. "I wouldn't sell. You guys have so much promise. Four million dollars is a lot, but you're going to split it up, pay taxes. You're not retiring for life here." The two cofounders agreed and turned down the offer, but the Davidsons wouldn't relent, eventually promising Adham and Morhaime that as part of Davidson & Associates, they would have the creative freedom to make games however they wished.

Then the Davidsons agreed to double their previous price, making an offer that even Fargo had a hard time declining. "As a friend, I'd rather be in business with you," he recalled saying. "But I cannot see how you say no to that." By February 1994, three years after the studio's founding, they'd come to a deal. Davidson & Associates would acquire Chaos Studios for $6.75 million, helping stabilize the company and making both Adham and Morhaime quite rich. There was just one exception to Davidson's promise of autonomy: Shortly after the acquisition, a trademark dispute forced Adham and Morhaime to give up the name Chaos Studios, and they'd switched to the way less family-friendly Ogre Studios. "I'm not sure too many moms would be too excited about that," said Bob Davidson. "They called me back a week or so later and said, 'We got a new name we like better.'"

As the story goes, Adham flipped through an electronic dictionary looking for interesting words. He ran a selection by the team and they voted the list down to a few contenders. Eventually they'd landed on a single word—one that continued to represent their chaotic processes but was anodyne enough to avoid offending even the most uptight mother. On top of that, it sounded pretty cool.

■　■　■

In January, Allen Adham and Mike Morhaime had negative net worths. A month later, they were millionaires. Their company was now Blizzard Entertainment, a subsidiary of Davidson & Associates, and they could put more resources into their first self-published game, *Warcraft*, which Davidson would package and distribute to stores.

Some of the staff, like Pat Wyatt and programmer Bob Fitch, weren't thrilled that the windfall went entirely to their bosses. Shortly before the sale, Wyatt had called a company meeting and asked for equity, to which Adham offered a resounding no. "It was a really hardcore no, and it was angry," said Wyatt. The sale did lead to perks for Wyatt and his coworkers, such as raises, 401(k)s, and health insurance.

Davidson granted Blizzard stock options, which Adham and Morhaime handed out to their most valuable employees, including Wyatt. Still, the rebels weren't mollified. Over the last three years they had put in long hours for low wages because they thought it would lead to benefits for everyone, and to see Adham and Morhaime walk away with millions of dollars while they got pieces of paper felt like a slap in the face. Furious, Wyatt declared that he was quitting to start his own company.

Adham and Morhaime spent weeks talking Wyatt down, promising him a title bump if he stayed. Truth was, his threat didn't have much muscle behind it. He had bought a house with a coworker and didn't have nearly enough money to go off and start something new. So he just kept working on *Warcraft*, pretending that the wound wasn't there. "I buried myself in the game, and had a great time doing it," Wyatt said. He was blown away by his first multiplayer match against a Blizzard colleague, "the most intense gaming experience I've ever had in my life," he recalled. Victories felt sweeter when they were against a real opponent rather than a computer, while defeats were even more painful—and more likely to lead to office outbursts and thrown keyboards.

Stu Rose brought in a friend, Bill Roper, to do some freelance voice work for a demo they'd been planning to show to fans and media that summer. Roper arrived at the company's offices and found that Glenn Stafford, the company's composer, had converted an old utility closet into his sound booth. Finding no script, Roper went on to improvise a series of lines that would later be used for the game's intro (*"In the Age of Chaos, two factions battled for dominance..."*). He fell in love with Blizzard, even writing the cofounders a letter begging to stay on. "Allen, I'll wash your car," he recalled writing. To Morhaime he promised a rare *Magic: The Gathering* card, which turned out to be unnecessary—he'd already impressed the bosses enough to get a job writing *Warcraft*'s story.

Most of Roper's narrative was crammed into the manual that would come with every copy of *Warcraft: Orcs & Humans*, along with a Blizzard-themed notepad. One of Adham's longtime beliefs was that store-goers would be more enticed to spend money on video game boxes that were heavier and therefore seemed more valuable. Rose drew the word *Blizzard* in jagged blue letters, creating a logo that they'd stamp on their boxes, discs, and merchandise for many years to come. Almost immediately, the word *Blizzard* became sacrosanct, a symbol that they were all contributing to something bigger than themselves. The first line in *Warcraft*'s credits wasn't one person, it was the company: "Game Design: Blizzard Entertainment." When Blizzard employees started to realize that they didn't want to stop playing *Warcraft* even after work hours, they allowed themselves to be optimistic about the game's chances.

In November 1994, *Warcraft: Orcs & Humans* hit store shelves. It took a little while for fans and critics to take notice, but by the end of the year, players were hooked. As one magazine reviewer wrote, "nothing in this world or any other can match the ferocity and unrelenting bitterness of two humans locked in mortal gaming combat." The game sold a hefty 100,000 copies in its first year—not enough to outpace heavy-hitters like *Myst* or *The 7th Guest* but enough to turn Blizzard from an unknown studio into a serious competitor for Westwood, the maker of *Dune II*. "I used to joke: Our game is totally different from *Dune II*," said Pat Wyatt. "You see, their minimap is in the lower right corner, and ours is in the upper left." Convinced that Blizzard had stolen *Dune II*'s code for *Warcraft*—an allegation that Blizzard employees denied—Westwood briefly considered pursuing legal action. Decades later, cofounder Louis Castle was more serene about the experience. "If imitation is the sincerest form of flattery, they were flattering us a lot," Castle said.

By 1995, Blizzard had expanded to around twenty employees and moved to bigger offices, aiming to keep growing as Adham declared they would build a video game empire. Eric Flannum, an artist, recalled Adham standing up in front of the company and detailing Blizzard's lofty mission. "He said: 'We want to make it so the Blizzard brand is so strong that we could put a bunch of rocks in a box and label it Blizzard, and people would buy it without even looking.'"

The obvious next step was *Warcraft II*, but Blizzard's staff were divided on where to take it. Some thought the next game in the series should go in a different direction, as Adham had originally envisioned, perhaps going to space or crossing military jets with fire-breathing dragons. Others thought Blizzard should take the fundamentals of *Warcraft: Orcs & Humans* and polish them, improving what didn't work and adding more, more, more. After a series of debates, the latter group won out. "We kept coming back to the unfinished business of *Warcraft*," said Bill Roper. "What we didn't get into the first game, what we would want to do. Now we can really knock it out of the park with the sequel."

Whereas *Warcraft* consisted of battles on the ground, *Warcraft II* would add the skies and the seas. Instead of just two players, *Warcraft II* would support up to eight. There would be bigger armies, crisper graphics, and a more elaborate campaign. There was a new resource, oil, and a suite of innovative new units like flying zeppelins and explosive goblin sappers. "I remember it feeling fairly unstructured," said artist Justin Thavirat. "Draw what you think is cool. A two-headed troll axe thrower? Make it." Storytelling hadn't been Blizzard's top priority for the first *Warcraft*, but this time, they wanted to make it feel like a proper world. And they had found the perfect guy for the job.

■ ■ ■

Like many future Blizzard all-stars, Chris Metzen stumbled onto the company by chance. He'd been performing in a band one night in Orange County when he ran into some Blizzard employees, who were impressed by a dragon he'd doodled on a napkin and encouraged him to come join them as an artist. When he arrived at the office, Metzen was blown away. It was geek Mecca: superhero posters on the walls, remote-controlled cars in the hallways, action figures and discarded Nerf missiles everywhere, fellow nerds battling in Super Nintendo games like *Street Fighter* and *Mortal Kombat.* "I didn't even know what they did," Metzen later said in a blog interview. "All I knew is that whatever this is, I want a piece." Metzen started off drawing and animating but found he had a knack for telling stories. He took Roper's original lore ideas and expanded them for *Warcraft II*, penning an elaborate story full of warfare, betrayal, and twisted necromancy. "He was showing some serious writing chops," said Roper.

Metzen's outsize personality set a tone for Blizzard's culture. He was brash and bombastic and could usually be found ranting about comic books to anyone who would listen. With his gravelly voice and vulgar lexicon, he was one of the most colorful characters in an office full of them. "Even on a normal day at work, Metzen smelled like cigarettes and whiskey," said David Pursley, an artist. "He'd come into your office—he didn't say hi—he'd come in and tell you a story about Thor or Captain America, one of his favorite issues, with tons of cursing, and it was super colorful. Then he'd just leave."

It was 1995, and the video game industry was growing bigger every year. Sony was about to release the PlayStation, Microsoft's DirectX software would soon make it easier than ever to play games on Windows, and the rise of more powerful computer chips was allowing consoles like the Sega Saturn to generate rudimentary 3D graphics. At the same time, most video game developers still hadn't quite become professional companies. Iconic game studios like Midway and Id Software were made up almost entirely of male nerds, living off pizza and Diet Coke as they worked and played together at all hours.

Blizzard wasn't yet attracting talented applicants from all over the world, so the company wound up primarily hiring people who its employees already knew. Almost all were men who had grown up in Southern California. Several had even worked at the same Kinko's, recommending each other for jobs at Blizzard one after another. They played pranks ranging from the innovative, like filling someone's office with empty soda cans, to the vulgar. "If you walked away from your computer and didn't lock it," recalled a tester, Ian Welke, "you'd come back to your desktop being not just pornography, but the most repugnant thing you could ever see." They wore shorts and T-shirts, jeans and flip-flops. One of their favorite pastimes was a Japanese fighting game for the Neo Geo console in which samurai warriors duked it out. "Early Blizzard was built on karaoke and *Samurai Shodown II*," said Micky Neilson, an artist. "There was beauty in the simplicity of that time."

Blowing off steam was essential because Allen Adham was pushing the company to release *Warcraft II* by the end of the year. The first game had been the longest project in Blizzard's history, taking nearly sixteen months to create, and now Adham wanted them to make a sequel in just about half the time. "A lot of it was Allen saying that we can't just rest on our laurels," said Wyatt. "We felt like we had to do it."

Adham spoke softly, with the cadence of a professional politician, and his employees left meetings feeling like they could walk on water. But he also had a temper that could emerge during periods of high stress. During one contentious meeting, Adham grew frustrated at the engineering team for trying to reel in his ambitions. Inspired by the gorgeous new Super Nintendo game *Donkey Kong Country*, he wanted *Warcraft II* to support a high resolution—640 by 480 pixels. The programmers pushed back, saying it was impractical, driving an irritated Adham to start shouting out tricks for how it might be done. "He was annoyed he was having to come up with ideas instead of the rest of the engineers," said Jesse McReynolds.

Adham would be thrilled when Blizzard employees came up with ways to make the *Warcraft* sequel feel bigger and better. In the first game, the orcs had all shared one set of vocal cords and the humans shared another. In *Warcraft II*, each soldier enjoyed its own distinct voice and suite of dialogue. In the first game, if you clicked one of the orcs too many times without giving them an order, they would yell, "Stop poking me!" For the sequel, each unit would get its own set of these "pissed lines," which Bill Roper recalled being a delight to record. "Make up your mind," Roper would growl as the human footman if you clicked on him enough times. "I *do* have work to do." The comic relief helped break up an otherwise grim story about armies at war.

To demonstrate the company's growth philosophy, Adham came up with what he called the donut theory. During meetings with staff and partners, he would wheel out a whiteboard and draw a giant donut. In the middle of the donut, he explained, was the hole—the hardcore gamer crowd. Blizzard's games needed to be deep and strategic enough to appeal to that small, dedicated audience because they would evangelize the games they liked. The ring around the donut—bigger, heftier, more significant—represented the "midcore" audience of people who maybe bought one or two games every year.

To reach those people, Blizzard's games needed to be approachable and avoid turning people off as *The Lost Vikings* had driven away that one kid at the store. In other words, *Warcraft II* had to be easy to learn, yet difficult to master.

To meet these goals and hit Adham's deadline, Blizzard's employees essentially lived at the office. When they weren't working, they'd all go out to lunch together or play card games in the hallways. Occasionally they'd go home to sleep, but even that wasn't a given—many kept sleeping bags under their desks just in case. "Our whole social life revolved around the office," said Pat Wyatt. "Oftentimes what would happen is you'd lose your friends, girlfriends, other things because of long hours at work. We called it the Blizzard Curse."

Not all of Blizzard's employees took to the intense office culture, such as Andy Weir, a programmer who hated being dropped into the pressure cooker. The day before he left on a weekend trip for which he'd provided weeks of notice, his bosses criticized him for taking off, then demanded that he leave them with a phone number. "Over the course of the weekend they probably called me twenty times," Weir said. "And I was not an important engineer." During the game's final stretch, when everyone was expected to test out the game during their spare time, Weir complained to a colleague that he was sick of doing extra QA work and not getting paid for it.

Weir became the target of endless bullying around the office. Colleagues would dismiss him, ignore him, and deride his ideas. "So many people were shitty to me, I have to assume I brought it on myself in some way," Weir said. He was criticized for delivering inadequate code that broke the game's launcher, which made things more difficult for everybody. He'd fume: How could he live up to expectations when nobody was mentoring or teaching him? There were no structures in place to help younger employees learn how to fix bugs or write better code. "We were so busy running as fast as we could, there was no culture of mentorship or training," said Wyatt. Less than a year into the job, Weir was fired for his poor performance. "This was a dream job for me, working at Blizzard," Weir said. "I was absolutely crushed."

But Andy Weir wound up doing just fine. Two decades later, he published a novel called *The Martian*, the film adaptation of which would star Matt Damon and earn more than $630 million worldwide.

■　■　■

Warcraft II: Tides of Darkness came out on December 9, 1995, just in time for Christmas. The company worked through Thanksgiving to get it done, encouraging everyone to come into the office if they could. For the first *Warcraft*, the development team had handled all the bug testing; for the sequel, Blizzard built out a team of quality assurance testers to ensure the game was as polished as possible. "In that one year we became so much more of a real company," said Jesse McReynolds.

If *Warcraft* had put Blizzard on the map, *Warcraft II* circled it with big red arrows. "Blizzard Entertainment has outdone itself," a *GameSpot* reviewer wrote. The game outperformed its predecessor exponentially, selling 500,000 units in three months and hitting one million within the year. By the beginning of 1996, the company had moved to a new office at 50 Corporate Park, smack in the middle of Irvine, and had doubled in size. It wasn't clear if the company could stamp "Blizzard" on a box full of rocks and sell it—they never quite tried that—but their star was rising. At one point, the team learned that they had to be more judicious about their conversations in public while wearing their Blizzard hoodies and T-shirts. "We went out to lunch and we couldn't just talk freely about what we were working on, because we realized that the people at the booth over realized who we were and were listening in on our conversations," said Stu Rose. "I remember that day getting this weird sense of, 'Wait, are we important now?'"

It was a different sort of milestone that helped the employees of Blizzard Entertainment realize they had truly made it. One day, a fan called in for technical support on *Warcraft II*. Nobody was available to help, so an automated message asked him to leave a voice mail. As the man talked on his headset, his wife started yelling in the background. The exchange, paraphrased from the accounts of several Blizzard employees, unfolded something like this:

"Get off that stupid game," the wife said.

"One minute, honey," said the husband. "I've just gotta get this taken care of."

"That game," the wife snarled, "is why we're not having sex anymore."

If you walked into Blizzard's offices at some point in the weeks or months that followed, chances were high that you'd hear this recording playing on the intercom. An advertisement in *PC Gamer* magazine for the *Warcraft II* expansion would cement the incident in company history. Just above "Now Available," alongside other laudatory phrases, it read:

"It's the reason we don't have sex anymore!"
—*Actual quote from the wife of a tech support caller*

THREE

CLICK CLICK CLICK

As Allen Adham and Mike Morhaime were starting a video game company, David Brevik was trying to get into one. Brevik lived in San Jose, California, just outside San Francisco, where companies like Atari and Electronic Arts had already become titans of the industry. Like Blizzard's cofounders, Brevik had grown up playing computer games and thought they were the coolest thing on the planet. His family had moved around a lot when he was a kid—Wisconsin, Georgia, and finally California—so Brevik had never been able to form many lasting friendships at school. But no matter where he relocated, the computer was always there.

Brevik was tall and lanky, with wavy hair and a coder's tan. He was blind in one eye, which hampered his depth perception and dreams of becoming a professional athlete, but he found he had a talent for programming in high school, where he finished assignments so quickly that his computer teacher started letting him help the other students. After college, his parents suggested that he might want to use his computer science degree for a lucrative career path, but Brevik was part of a small but growing group of nerds who wanted to make video games for a living. He wound up at a clip art company called FM Waves that was trying to get into the video game industry but running out of money quickly, and soon an awful feeling began to creep in: maybe his parents had been right after all.

At FM Waves, Brevik became friends with two brothers, Erich and Max Schaefer, who shared his sensibilities and complaints. Every day, they'd go out to lunch together to gripe and swap stories about the video games they were playing. As the company's instability became more apparent, the three of them began dreaming up plans to start their own video game outfit. They even gave it a code name, Project Condor, so they could talk about the secret exit without making colleagues suspicious. Ultimately, Brevik left for another game maker while the Schaefers stuck around to finish their current project, but the three stayed in touch and in the fall of 1993, they reunited to start a video game company called Condor.

Armed with some contacts that Brevik had accumulated and computer equipment the Schaefers inherited from the now-defunct FM Waves, the three new partners assumed they could find work within a few weeks—instead it took a few hours. A producer at the publisher Sunsoft who had previously been impressed with Brevik's programming skills heard about their new company and called to say he wanted to work with Condor starting that very day. Sunsoft said they could work on a game based on the band Aerosmith, the *Scooby-Doo* cartoons, or the superhero comic book series *Justice League*. Brevik ran it by the Schaefers and they instantly agreed: they wanted *Justice League*.

Condor was a few hundred miles north of Silicon & Synapse, but the two companies were on similar trajectories. Brevik and the Schaefers took on new contracts, like a football video game series called

NFL Quarterback Club, and brought in new artists and programmers to help with the workload while fantasizing about making their own original video games. In fact, Brevik had been dreaming about one specific game since he was a kid, inspired by his old *Dungeons & Dragons* campaigns and journeys through "roguelike" dungeon-crawling video games with levels that were generated by algorithms, ensuring a unique playthrough every time. His favorite game, *Angband*, was an addictive take on the formula, allowing players to collect randomized loot in a fortress from *Lord of the Rings.*

Brevik even had a title in mind for the project, inspired by an ominously named mountain near Danville, California, where his family had eventually settled. It was called Mt. Diablo.

■ ■ ■

In the early 1990s, companies like Sunsoft would show off their wares and take business meetings at the biannual Consumer Electronics Show, which was how Brevik and the Schaefers found themselves in Chicago during the summer of 1994, wandering a show floor full of refrigerators, car stereos, and brand-new video games.

Before the show, the team at Condor had fine-tuned their pitch for *Diablo*, the game that Brevik had spent years dreaming about making. It was a role-playing game set in a gothic horror fantasy world populated by demons and spiders. You'd create a character based on one of three archetypes—fighter, thief, or magician—and start off in a town above a giant mazelike dungeon with levels that would be generated by an algorithm so they were different every time. Inspired by *X-COM*, a game that had come out in March and hooked them all, the gameplay would unfold in turns as the player watched from an isometric camera, as if looking down at a chessboard. "*Diablo* captures familiar fantasy elements within a unique structure designed for maximum replayability, expandability, and versatility," the team wrote in a design document.

Brevik and the Schaefers took their pitch from publisher to publisher, expecting the dollars to pour in. But the video game industry moved in trends, and in 1994, "RPG" was considered a dirty word thanks to a string of recent *Dungeons & Dragons*–inspired flops. The executives behind game publishers were more interested in flashy platformers with big-name licenses than in a geeky fantasy dungeon crawler. "We just cold–dropped in on a whole bunch of publishers," said Erich Schaefer. "Everybody passed on it."

Dejected, the group headed to the Sunsoft booth and were shocked at what they found there: a demo station for *Justice League Task Force*, the game they were making back home, manned by an entirely different set of staff. But while their game was for the Sega Genesis, this one was for the Super Nintendo. Stunned, Brevik and the Schaefers introduced themselves to the man in charge. His name, he said, was Allen Adham. His company, Blizzard Entertainment, was working on *Justice League: Task Force* as one of many contracts they were juggling down in Southern California, where they planned to soon publish their own original games.

Once the initial feelings of shock and confusion passed, the two groups found that they had even more in common. They had explored many similar ideas for *Justice League: Task Force* and had stumbled upon some of the same mechanics for characters and stages despite working four hundred miles apart. "It was obvious right away that we had similar philosophies," said Brevik. "The way we made games, believed they should be played."

Brevik discovered that Adham, like him, was making console games but preferred to play his own games on computers, which were widely perceived as deeper and more sophisticated. Computer games were more finicky than console games—instead of just popping in a cartridge, you'd have to navigate several layers of an operating system to get them running. As a result, the people who played computer games were generally looking for more complicated experiences than their console-playing brethren. In fact, Adham said, Blizzard was showing off private demos of a computer game called *Warcraft* that they planned to release later in the year.

The Condor team followed Adham to a small meeting room, where they watched him maneuver orcs and humans on a computer monitor and were instantly sold. "I thought the game looked great," recalled Brevik, offering to playtest the game in exchange for early copies. A few months later, he called Adham to follow up and scored some *Warcraft* boxes for the Condor office. The two game designers kept talking, and eventually Brevik mentioned that they had an RPG pitch that was going nowhere. "A lot of publishers really didn't know almost anything about games," said Brevik. That was what made Blizzard seem so special to Brevik: like Condor, they were made up of people who played games and didn't just watch them with cartoon dollar signs in their eyes.

Adham said that he'd be happy to hear more about *Diablo*; they just had to finish *Warcraft* first. A few months later, in January 1995, he was flying up to the San Francisco Bay Area with Pat Wyatt to visit the studio. As soon as Brevik started pitching, he could tell that the two Blizzard executives understood the appeal. "I think we pretty much sold it in the room," Brevik said.

Adham and Wyatt took a break to talk privately and agreed: They both liked the game but wanted to make two big changes. The first was that, like Blizzard's other games, *Diablo* needed to have multiplayer. The second was that, as in *Warcraft*, the actions should unfold in real time rather than turn by turn—a suggestion that would later make Brevik bristle. "I said, 'Hell no, we can't change this,'" Brevik recalled.

But as everyone at Blizzard had learned, Adham was persuasive. By the end of January, Condor had a contract in place for Blizzard to fund and publish *Diablo*, and in the following months, Adham poked and prodded at Brevik until he agreed to at least develop a real-time prototype to see what it felt like. "The moment we changed it to real time, I knew it was the right call," Brevik said.

Diablo began to come together just as Brevik had imagined it. Gentle, unsettling strums of a guitar punctuated every step in the dark city of Tristram. You could heal your wounds and buy new gear in town, then descend into the dungeon, smashing through skeletons and beasts as you progressed through a series of randomized levels. Perhaps the game's most impressive quality was its sound design—perfectly placed *glug*s and *ching*s every time a potion dropped or a felled monster left behind a pile of glittering gold.

But Brevik and his crew were facing their own gold troubles. The contract with Blizzard gave Condor only a few hundred thousand dollars for *Diablo*—not even enough to pay their staff for a full year, let alone the two years it might take to finish the game. "We wanted to do this so badly that we signed one of the worst contracts in the history of the universe," said Brevik. When they weren't working on *Diablo*, Brevik and the Schaefers scrambled to find outside deals so they could pay their staff. But they weren't businessmen; they were game developers. The downside to keeping the suits out of the company was that sometimes the suits knew what they were doing.

By the end of 1995, the outside money was no longer coming in. They'd finished *Justice League* a few months earlier and no longer had any football games to help pay the bills. Condor was neglecting its payroll taxes—a practice generally frowned upon by the US government, whose agents sent several threatening letters. The company even failed to pay staff a few times, risking an exodus. "We were in deep, deep trouble," said Erich Schaefer. A few years earlier, the three men had watched FM Waves shut down after bouncing checks to its staff, and now they were facing the same risk. For Brevik, developing *Diablo* had been a childhood fantasy come to life, but the only thing worse than never getting to live out your dream would be watching it get cut short before it was finished.

■ ■ ■

On February 20, 1996, Blizzard employees woke up to some surprising news: A mail-order shopping club called CUC International was acquiring Davidson & Associates for more than $1 billion in stock. It was good news for anyone at Blizzard who owned stock options and confounding news for outside analysts, who had no idea why a company like CUC—best known for an annual subscription that offered customers discounts on flights and appliances—was getting into the computer software business. Analyst Jeffrey Tarter told the *New York Times* that he could think of at least "ten good reasons why this doesn't make sense."

It was also awkward news for the three owners of Condor, who had spent the last two months in their own complicated negotiations with Davidson & Associates.

After hearing about Condor's money woes, Adham, newly energized from the success of *Warcraft II*, had suggested that Brevik and the Schaefers sell their company to Blizzard. Adham felt he'd earned enough trust with Bob and Jan Davidson to get their blessing for an acquisition, particularly when *Diablo* seemed so promising (even if the gore and horror were a little much for the middle-aged couple). Soon they had the framework of a deal that seemed beneficial for everyone.

But after the CUC sale, the Davidsons had earned enough money to buy their own city, which made the Condor acquisition suddenly feel very small. "We said, 'Hey, we should ask them for more money now,'" said Erich Schaefer. He called up Davidson's finance chief to float a higher purchase price. Their response: *No.* "That was it," said Schaefer, who made the immediate calculation not to press further at the risk of losing it all. "We were worried the deal was going to fall through." By March, it was finalized. Condor would become a subsidiary of Blizzard, which itself was now a subsidiary of CUC. David Brevik, Erich Schaefer, Max Schaefer, and their top lawyer, Kenneth Williams, would all receive significant sums of money—not as much as they'd hoped, but enough to buy homes and more.

As some of Condor's staff struggled to make rent, still hurting from the bounced paychecks a few months earlier, their bosses began showing up to the office in fancy sports cars. Some employees asked for raises. Others threatened to revolt, like Pat Wyatt had in Irvine two years earlier. Brevik and the Schaefers had promised new employees that they would receive significant royalties while working at Condor but they had never materialized, and now, some of them felt screwed. Brevik was understanding, if not entirely sympathetic. "A lot of the people who joined us, it was their first job ever," said Brevik. "They didn't understand how businesses work, that the owners who take all the risk, they're the ones who get the reward... That's a harsh lesson for somebody to learn sometimes."

Adham and Morhaime had faced similar grumbling from their staff and quelled the rebellion with stock options. Brevik and the Schaefers followed suit, dangling the potential of great wealth for those who stuck around. Plus, there wasn't a lot of time to keep arguing over money—they had to finish *Diablo.* The team kept hammering away at the game throughout 1996, fine-tuning the art and arguing over design. The complexities of a role-playing game meant there were countless decisions to be made as they ironed out every detail, from the look of the inventory system to the hero's walk speed.

One of their most exciting innovations was a D&D-inspired loot system. Every piece of gear was color-coded to reflect its rarity: white for normal; blue for magic; gold for unique. When you picked up a new magical item—say, a sword or a helmet—its properties remained a mystery until you identified it with a spell or by bringing it back to town, where you might discover one of several boons. A "ruthless" sword would boost damage while a shield "of the tiger" would boost your hit points, and the stats were randomized, giving players the opportunity to hunt for the best possible version of each item. Discovering a new piece of loot led to three distinct endorphin rushes: finding the item, identifying it, and then seeing how good it really was, like a slot machine with bonus spins.

Adham pushed to make *Diablo* as approachable as possible, talking Brevik out of a system that would erase a character permanently when they died. Chris Metzen, the boisterous comic-book lover who was becoming the company's go-to for all things narrative, helped craft a story that would guide players into the dungeon with a quest to rescue the corrupted victims of the demon Diablo.

Adham knew that with two offices and dozens of people, Blizzard's traditionally chaotic approach to game development would be impossible to pull off on *Diablo*. So he put together what he called a strike team—a group of high-level employees including Wyatt, Adham, and Bill Roper—to play *Diablo* and write up their thoughts. Brevik and his staff were happy with some of this feedback, but the suggestions also created some tension. *Diablo*'s artists had filled their game's dungeon with lurid imagery including blood, gore, and naked dead bodies, leading to some arguments with the strike team, who demanded that the graphic content be toned down. Condor was now called Blizzard North: a name befitting a subsidiary rather than a partner, which raised some eyebrows among *Diablo* developers who had thought they would maintain their independence. They liked to refer to the company in Irvine as Blizzard South, but in reality the Irvine office was still just Blizzard. Adham oversaw them all.

Another point of contention became the multiplayer, which Brevik and his team had no experience developing. He had always figured they'd make it work at some point—until the Irvine office discovered that the multiplayer didn't yet exist. In the summer of 1996, months before the game was due to hit store shelves, Adham sent Pat Wyatt and another programmer up to Blizzard North's offices to crack open the game's code and implement the company's new multiplayer service, Battle.net. Wyatt camped out in a motel and began working out of Blizzard North's office, dedicating just about every waking hour to *Diablo*. "It was the hardest thing I've ever done in my life," he said. "For four months I worked more or less fourteen hours a day, sometimes sixteen. I'd go to the motel, sleep, then do it the next day, over and over and over again, for six to seven days a week."

What frustrated him was that the rest of Blizzard North didn't appear to display the same work ethic. Most of the *Diablo* team tried to work normal hours, aside from Brevik, who was the only other person in the office when Wyatt put in nights and weekends. "Here I am trying to help rescue their project," Wyatt said. "In retrospect, I was the one who was doing something foolish, right? But at the time it was like: These guys don't care about their game." (Offered Erich Schaefer: "I'm not that hard a worker, honestly. It's only a few hours before I'm kind of useless.")

By the end of the year, with a holiday deadline approaching, everyone else at Blizzard North joined Wyatt and Brevik in crunching to finish *Diablo*. Gradually, all of Blizzard's Irvine office joined the team, too, temporarily shelving their other projects to develop features and fix bugs.[3] It had become clear to everyone at Blizzard that *Diablo* was going to be great, much like the first two *Warcraft* games, when they found that they couldn't stop playing it, click-click-clicking their way through monsters, catacombs, and treasure chests. Still, there was too much to be done and not enough time to finish it all before the critical 1996 holiday season.

As Christmas approached, Adham and the other executives met with Chris McLeod, the CUC vice president now managing Blizzard. They explained that they were working tirelessly to get *Diablo* out before the holidays, but the code still had serious bugs that might make it impossible to play the game, and as a result, *Diablo* was not going to hit stores before December 25. This was a risky decision. Conventional wisdom at the time was that a game couldn't succeed unless it was featured in holiday catalogs and received prime placement on store shelves during Christmas shopping sprees.

It was here that Blizzard discovered, not for the last time, that conventional wisdom was wrong.

■ ■ ■

Technically, *Diablo* did come out in 1996. The game began shipping to stores in the final week of December, although it wasn't widely available until January. Like Blizzard's last two games, it was critically acclaimed, receiving the most glowing reviews the company had seen so far. "*Diablo* is the best game to come out in the past year, and you

---

3   Some of *Diablo*'s most distinct components emerged during this final scramble. Eric Flannum, an artist in Blizzard's Irvine office, ran into a strange, seemingly unfixable bug that caused a character named Wirt to walk with a slight limp. "I got super frustrated," he recalled, "so I just ripped his leg off and put in a peg leg." Wirt's wooden leg would go on to play a memorable role in the series, later allowing *Diablo II* players to access a hidden realm full of screaming, murderous cows.

should own a copy. Period," wrote a *GameSpot* critic. Despite missing the holidays, *Diablo* became Blizzard's newest number-one hit, selling one million copies by the end of 1997 and securing Blizzard's status as one of the top video game developers. Two years earlier, nobody had heard of Blizzard. Now it was one of the biggest hit-makers in the world.

Later, Blizzard's managers would muse that *Diablo* missing Christmas may have been one of the best things to ever happen to the company. Suddenly they had a real-life business case study for what would happen if you made a great game but missed the optimal window for sales. Although they didn't use the words at the time, this was the foundation of what would become a company mantra for decades to come: *It'll be ready when it's ready.*

FOUR

WARCRAFT GOES PURPLE

N ot all of Blizzard's bets were as successful as *Warcraft* and *Diablo*. In the mid-1990s, the company took several stabs at projects that didn't pan out, like *Denizen*, a dungeon-crawler that was shelved due to lack of resources, and *Bloodlines*, a space vampire game that didn't resonate with enough staff to justify its existence. Blizzard also tried to publish a few external games—including *Pax Imperia 2*, the sequel to a strategy game that the staff loved, and *Crixa*, a top-down arcade shooter made by a small studio in Boston, Massachusetts—but all were canceled. Later, Morhaime would estimate that Blizzard canceled around 50 percent of its projects because it would rather lose money than release subpar products.

Another game on the chopping block was *Shattered Nations*, a turn-based strategy game inspired by *Sid Meier's Civilization* that was announced in the fall of 1995. But James Phinney, the lead designer, couldn't convince Adham that a turn-based game was worth pursuing, and another, far more exciting opportunity was about to emerge. One morning, when Adham told his staff that he and Bob Davidson were in early discussions about developing a *Star Wars* strategy game, the studio began buzzing with excitement. These dreams of epic, *Warcraft*-style clashes between Jedi Knights and AT-AT walkers didn't last very long. Before they could even build a prototype, Adham came back with news that their *Star Wars* game wasn't happening after all.[4] Still, Blizzard's developers had already grown sick of fantasy and were ready to ditch elves and goblins in favor of spaceships and aliens, so they decided to stick with the idea of sci-fi strategy.

At the beginning of 1996, Adham put Phinney and his small team of programmers and artists onto a new game that they began calling *StarCraft*, aiming to finish by the end of the year.[5] With time limited, *StarCraft*'s developers decided to take *Warcraft II*'s engine—the collection of tools and technology that artists, programmers, and designers used to develop a game—and strip out all the fantasy. *StarCraft* would be set on a series of bright purple plateaus with neon green appendages floating over the inky background of space. Orc strongholds morphed into alien hives full of tentacles and pulsating eggs. It looked less like a beautiful new video game and more like the inside of a tanning bed.

The now-annual E3 video game trade show was coming up in May, and Blizzard wanted to have a big presence, so the company paid for a large booth and set up computers to demonstrate their two games of 1996. Fans were impressed by *Diablo*'s demonic dungeon crawling, but *StarCraft* left them confused. Pundits derided it as "orcs in space" or, most insultingly, "purple *Warcraft*." Exacerbating the problem was the nearby booth of game developer 7th Level, showcasing a demo for *Dominion*, a competing real-time strategy game with

---

4 Word around the office was that the deal fell apart after a dispute over putting Blizzard's name on the box. But Jack Sorensen, who was president of LucasArts at the time, said in an interview for this book that he didn't recall having any discussions with Blizzard about making a *Star Wars* game.

5 In contrast to *Warcraft*, *StarCraft*'s C was capitalized—this was to avoid any potential trademark disputes with a vehicle company of the same name.

impressive animations and hulking robots that almost appeared 3D. "We said, 'Oh man, that's better than ours,'" recalled Robert Djordjevich, an artist on *StarCraft*. By the time the show was over, they had changed most of the demo stations to play *Diablo* instead.

When the team regrouped back in Orange County, they considered three options. They could 1) resign to mediocrity and release the game for Christmas, then move on to the next *Warcraft*, 2) cancel it, or 3) reboot the game and start from scratch, creating a new version of *StarCraft* that would blow away *Dominion* and win over jaded fans. They went with the third option, only to subsequently lose the bulk of their staff to *Diablo*, which needed all hands on deck until it was finished.

Following *Diablo*'s release at the beginning of 1997, Blizzard's developers began working long hours to reboot *StarCraft*. Rather than using *Warcraft*'s top-down camera angle, this new version of the game would offer a slanted, isometric view, making buildings and units feel 3D-like, similar to what they'd seen from *Dominion*. A public display of the rebooted version of *StarCraft* later in the year left fans far more impressed than they'd been by the "purple" *Warcraft* demo.

StarCraft would be different from its predecessors in one key way: While the *Warcraft* games had two mirrored races, each with identical units, *StarCraft* would be asymmetrical. Each of the three races—the humanoid Terran, the swarming Zerg, and the high-tech Protoss—would have its own suite of innovative units and abilities that made them feel unique to play. The Terran siege tank could swap between mobile and stationary modes, trading agility for explosive power. Zerg units could burrow under surfaces, then pop out to ambush opponents. Protoss dark templars were permanently invisible and could only be spotted by detector units.

One of the secrets behind Blizzard's success was an ample, almost excessive amount of playtesting, both from outside testers and from everyone in the company. "We had days when the entire company would shut down," said Tim Campbell, who joined later. "Everyone from Morhaime to the receptionist would stop what they were doing, play the game, give feedback." On the first two *Warcraft* games, there was no need to worry about balance—every human soldier did the same amount of damage as their orc equivalent—but *StarCraft*'s asymmetrical races required far more care. If one of the three was even slightly more powerful than the others, it would skew multiplayer matches and make the game feel less fair, and therefore less fun. "We'd spend hours and hours playing it," said Jeffrey Vaughn, an artist on the project. "Polishing it, making little balance adjustments." Outsiders would come into the office and play builds, then offer near-endless lists of suggestions. "I think sometimes studios get too dismissive," said Vaughn. "Whereas at Blizzard, we'd have friends and family come in and play, and their feedback was taken seriously." Adham even hired a former Interplay producer who had become known as a top-notch RTS player, Rob Pardo, to sit with the QA team and play the game for hours and hours, offering feedback along the way.

When they weren't making serious balance decisions, Blizzard's developers stuffed the game with gags and easter eggs, from *Diablo* tributes to *Simpsons* references to shots at their top rival. Westwood, the game studio behind *Dune II*, had put out a strategy game called *Red Alert* with a main character named Tanya, so Robert Djordjevich cheekily suggested that *StarCraft* feature a commando named Kerrigan—after the rival figure skater. Sarah Kerrigan, a Terran special agent, would go on to become one of Blizzard's most iconic characters, eventually falling to the Zerg and becoming an infested supervillain.

As the year progressed, *StarCraft* began to look increasingly vibrant, with aesthetic flourishes that made it feel unlike anything else on the market: Terran buildings soaring in the sky, Zerg swarms massing on viscous gray matter called creep, Protoss soldiers warping and cloaking. Later, Pat Wyatt wound up talking to two artists who had worked on that impressive demo of *Dominion* back at E3 1996—one of the catalysts for *StarCraft*'s reboot—and could only laugh when he heard the truth. The "demo" that had made Blizzard's staff feel inadequate was actually pre-rendered footage of the game designed so the team could pretend they were playing it. Behind the scenes, the game wasn't functioning at all.

■   ■   ■

Many years later, the video game industry would reckon with its widespread culture of crunch—the act of working nights and weekends to finish a game—but in the fall of 1997, Blizzard's employees just marched along. "There was an understanding that the calendar was not our friend," said Phinney. "If you had something more to give, you'd give it. If you didn't, things were going to be worse." Blizzard employees had worked long periods of overtime on previous games, but nothing had been quite like this—a brutal process of testing and bug-fixing that required the developers to spend every possible hour at the office. One artist began living on a futon in his office—which, much to everyone's amusement, had a bearskin rug—and became known for showing up to meetings in a kimono. Crunch wasn't mandated, but it also wasn't exactly voluntary. "If you were going to be part of the group, it was just what you did," said Eric Flannum.

Blizzard's staff, almost all of whom were in their twenties, had strong and conflicting feelings about the crunch. On one hand, it could be exhilarating, and they bonded over late-night fast-food trips and intense *StarCraft* matches. Some of them didn't even want to go home—they just wanted to hang out and make games with their best friends. By crunching, *StarCraft*'s developers could rescue features that might have otherwise been canceled, like solo hero levels, which were slated to be cut until one programmer spent an entire weekend salvaging them.

On the other hand, the crunch drained their energy and destroyed their personal lives, made worse by continued promises from management that they would be finished soon. Their goal was still to release the game by Christmas, and every few weeks, Adham would assure the team that they were almost done. "We were, I think, 'two weeks away from shipping' for a year," said Bill Roper. "It just never ended." When they slipped past Christmas and entered the new year still crunching on *StarCraft*, 1997 became the first year that Blizzard failed to release a game.

After the successes of *Warcraft II* and *Diablo*, the gaming world was watching Blizzard closely. Anticipation grew so feverish for the company's next title that fans began congregating on internet forums to commiserate about the delays. They declared themselves Operation CWAL—Can't Wait Any Longer—and began writing outlandish fanfiction stories about raiding the office and stealing *StarCraft* from Blizzard HQ. A few particularly eager fans even found Blizzard's office and scoped out the parking lot, trying to gauge the game's progress based on how many cars were there and how long the lights stayed on. "In some ways it was flattering," said Pat Wyatt. "In other ways it was creepy."

In March 1998, "two weeks away from shipping" finally became reality as *StarCraft* hit store shelves. Blizzard followed it up in December with an expansion called *Brood War* that added new story campaigns and overhauled the multiplayer with additional units and balance tweaks. *StarCraft* became the best-selling PC game of 1998, selling more than 1.5 million copies and turning into another Blizzard success story. The exhausted developers weren't surprised to see *StarCraft* immediately find widespread critical acclaim and a dedicated audience. What they didn't expect was that it would become a cultural sensation thanks to an economic meltdown on the other side of the world.

As Blizzard was finishing up *StarCraft*, a financial crisis that started in Thailand had been cascading through Southeast Asia. One of the countries hit hardest was South Korea, which was also going through a series of rapid cultural changes including a pivot to democracy and a major investment in high-speed internet infrastructure. The crisis led Koreans to double down on that development, recognizing that the burgeoning communications network could play a key role in future-proofing the country's economy. By 1998, broadband internet was everywhere in South Korea. Some newly unemployed workers used the opportunity to open internet cafes, called PC bangs, where for around a dollar an hour, Koreans could spend all day playing online games with their friends. At the end of 1997, South Korea had just one hundred PC bangs; by 2000, there were 15,000.

Blizzard's Korean distributor gave copies of *StarCraft* to PC bangs across the country, knowing they'd buy more once their players were hooked. Over the next few years, *StarCraft* essentially became the national sport of South Korea, where it sold 4.5 million copies—in a country with less than 50 million people.

For the veteran Blizzard employees who had received stock options from Davidson back during the acquisition, this should have led to a major payday. But a different kind of financial catastrophe was about to make their lives much more complicated.

■ ■ ■

On April 15, 1998, just two weeks after the release of *StarCraft*, a company called Cendant announced that it was restating its earnings for the previous year due to what its president called "potential accounting irregularities." Cendant's stock plummeted 46 percent, wiping away roughly $14 billion in shareholder value.

This was a problem for Blizzard. After all, Cendant owned it.

The corporate shenanigans had started two years earlier, when Bob and Jan Davidson sold their company to CUC International. After just a year, both stepped down from the executive jobs they'd retained, saying they wanted to "pursue other interests." Allen Adham told press that he was "instructed pretty closely not to make any comments." Everything about the deal seemed strange: CUC had also spent more than $1 billion to buy the PC gaming stalwart Sierra Entertainment and tried to snag competitors Broderbund and LucasArts, which were awfully ambitious moves for a company that had nothing to do with the software industry.

Davidson would later say that he had quietly been asking questions about CUC behind the scenes, wondering why the company was taking reserves of hundreds of millions of dollars on its acquisitions. Davidson's Chief Financial Officer suspected that CUC was putting the reserves through the company's profit-and-loss sheet, which seemed potentially illegal. Davidson confronted the board but couldn't get any straight answers, so he went to a lawyer. "He said, 'Bob, you need to get off that board. There's something going on,'" recalled Davidson. "So we left."

Later in 1997, CUC agreed to merge with a hotel company called Hospitality Franchise Systems (HFS) to form a new conglomerate called Cendant. The merger came with all sorts of weird quirks, like an arrangement for HFS boss Henry Silverman and CUC boss Walter Forbes to swap places as CEO after two years. Most alarmingly, Forbes kept his company's financials opaque, shooting down Silverman's requests for nonpublic information during the merger process by arguing that if the deal fell apart, HFS might purchase one of CUC's competitors. When the merger closed and suddenly a host of new people had access to CUC's financials, the truth came out.

The US Securities and Exchange Commission (SEC) later described it as "a massive fraudulent financial reporting scheme." Forbes's company had cooked the books, using several tricks to report false income in the name of meeting Wall Street analysts' expectations and creating the illusion that CUC was growing every quarter. One of those tricks was to overstate merger reserves and then report them as earnings—hence all these seemingly senseless acquisitions.[6]

The SEC concluded that "the consequences for the company's shareholders were devastating," and some of those shareholders worked for Blizzard. After the merger, Cendant stock had traded at a high of more than $40. By the end of 1998, it was worth less than $10 a share. The earliest Blizzard employees, like Pat Wyatt, lost the most. "All of that money just—poof—disappeared," Wyatt said. "That was my first million that I didn't get."

Amidst the drama, Blizzard's staff also received some unwelcome news as management gathered the team and explained that because *StarCraft* had been delivered in 1998 rather than 1997, they wouldn't receive bonuses they had been promised, despite the game's success. "There were a bunch of people who were super pissed about that," said Eric Flannum. "Probably how pissed you were depended on

---

6 In 2006, Walter Forbes was found guilty of fraud and sentenced to more than twelve years in prison. The prosecutor was the United States attorney for New Jersey, Chris Christie, who would later become well-known for many other reasons.

how big you thought your payout was going to be." Some of these employees had taken pay cuts from previous jobs to be at Blizzard, and they knew they could be making more money at other tech or video game companies. But they'd felt like the tradeoff was worth it because this was *Blizzard*: a company that made great games and appeared to treat them well. After *StarCraft*, they weren't so sure.

The idyllic days when everyone at the company had been close friends, playing games and going out to lunch together, seemed like a lifetime ago. Now, mutiny was on the horizon.

FIVE

FUGITIVES

O n May 22, 1998, just a few weeks after the Cendant drama, Blizzard announced to the world that it was canceling *Warcraft Adventures: Lord of the Clans* after two years of work. *Warcraft Adventures*, which Blizzard had been developing in conjunction with a team of animators in Russia, was meant to be a point-and-click adventure game inspired by the likes of LucasArts' *Monkey Island*. You'd play as Thrall, an orc slave destined to start a rebellion against his human oppressors, and travel across the *Warcraft* world solving puzzles in what was meant to offer a more nuanced perspective on a seemingly bloodthirsty race.

Over the course of the game's development, Blizzard's staff realized that something about *Warcraft Adventures* wasn't feeling right: the art style seemed amateurish, and the puzzles weren't quite clicking. At one point, artist Eric Flannum was helping demo the game at a trade show when the booth was visited by *Leisure Suit Larry* creator Al Lowe, one of the luminaries of the adventure game genre, which had found a great deal of success in the early 1990s but was now losing market share to faster-paced games. Lowe came up to Flannum and told him the community of adventure-game designers was watching Blizzard closely, "because if you guys can't make this work, then who can?" recalled Flannum, who could only stammer in response. "It was not a good game," Flannum said.

As a last resort, Blizzard offered Steve Meretzky, the legendary designer behind adventure games like *Sorceror* and *Zork Zero*, a free-lance contract to help salvage the game. "They didn't think it was quite up to par," recalled Meretzky. "They asked, 'Without investing a ton more money into this, what can we do to significantly increase the quality level?'" Meretzky flew from his house in Massachusetts to Irvine for a week of intense brainstorming, then spent another week writing up design documents. His ideas impressed the team at Blizzard, but they arrived too late—a few weeks later, Bill Roper called Meretzky and told him they were shelving *Warcraft Adventures*.

The cancellation cost them hundreds of thousands of dollars, but Adham and Morhaime knew that if Blizzard ever released a product that was widely perceived as subpar, it would destroy the company's reputation. "You have all the sunk costs, all the money they put in, all the time and effort," said Flannum. "They ultimately made the very right decision to can it, and preserve the value of their brand." (Plus: adventure games weren't selling very well.) Still, for the developers who had spent months or years of their lives on games, it could be excruciating to see their work just disappear. After the Cendant catastrophe, the *StarCraft* bonus debacle, and the demise of *Warcraft Adventures*, several Blizzard staff began to fume, griping about management during car rides and lunches. Unhappiness morphed into resentment morphed into a desire to go elsewhere.

In the summer of 1998, James Phinney and Jesse McReynolds resigned, saying they wanted to start something new. They took nearly a dozen Blizzard staff with them, including Eric Flannum, Robert Djordjevich, and artist Maxx Marshall, who had decided to leave the company after trying to buy a TV at Sam's Club. He and another artist had gone up to the counter, wearing Blizzard T-shirts, when they realized they didn't have enough cash to pay for it. A woman came up to them and asked if they really worked for Blizzard. "Oh my god, you guys have made my husband so much money," she said, by Marshall's recollection. "Let me pay for the rest of the TV." It turned out the woman's husband had worked for Blizzard's parent company and was profiting greatly off their work, even as they couldn't afford to buy a television. The incident got Marshall thinking. If they could make serious money for other people, couldn't they make serious money on their own? "That was depressing," Marshall said, "but at the same time, we got a TV out of it."

Phinney and his team started a new company, Fugitive Studios, in hopes of recreating their old winning formula. "I remember it was a cool opportunity," said artist Justin Thavirat. "Let's do Blizzard again somewhere else." The exodus, which included two of the company's top developers, left a big hole in the company just as it was scrambling to finish *StarCraft: Brood War*, which would take the game to new critical and commercial heights.

At the same time, the Cendant scandal continued. There were endless investigations and lawsuits, some executives went to prison, and at the end of 1998, the battered conglomerate sold Blizzard and the rest of its video game division to a French media group called Havas that itself was the subsidiary of a French water company called Vivendi. Blizzard's new parent company became known as Havas Interactive. A few years later, it would be renamed to Vivendi Games—continuing the brand confusion. "I can't even tell you how many business cards I had," said Kathy Carter Humphreys, a marketing associate.

In just four years, Blizzard had shuffled from: 1) an educational software company to 2) a mail-order catalog company to 3) a scandal-laden hospitality company to 4) a utility provider in France. To the outside world, Blizzard was a developer on the rise—a company pumping out hit after hit. On the inside, it was pandemonium. There were corporate scandals, bitter rebellions, and, now, big vacancies.

One day during the chaos, Joeyray Hall walked into the office and found a few of the executives, who handed him an envelope and asked him to open it. Inside was a check. "It was more money than I'd made in my whole working career at that point," Hall said. For a while, Blizzard's management team had been trying to put together a profit-sharing system that would reward their employees in a more substantial way, and they'd used the Fugitive departures to muscle their new corporate owners into approving it.

Meanwhile, those who had left for Fugitive discovered that starting a video game company wasn't quite as easy as they thought it might be. Their plan to make a 3D action RPG proved too ambitious, one of their business partners turned out to be unreliable, and their desires outweighed their technological capabilities. They had decided to divide ownership equally—an idyllic move that led to its own set of issues, such as analysis paralysis. "We just were not equipped to make the kind of decisions we had to make," said Phinney. Fugitive dissolved after less than a year, driving some of the departed Blizzard employees to return. For Justin Thavirat, it was like coming home. "You step out of it: Holy cow, how abnormal was our situation," he said. "You don't realize how special Blizzard is."

Amidst the drama, Blizzard was about to face another seismic change. Adham, who had been working seven days a week since he started the company, was burnt out and ready for something new. He had always had wanderlust—while attending UCLA, he'd taken a two-year break to join the army—and he felt like he was spending way too much time managing and not enough time making games. When he told his corporate bosses he wanted to quit, they convinced him to take a sabbatical instead, with Morhaime taking over as president. Upon his return, Adham would get the title of Chief Design Officer as well as the nominal title of chairman—to show that he was in charge—while Morhaime would handle his previous responsibilities.

Morhaime had never wanted to run Blizzard—he liked programming and had even spent late nights in the trenches writing code on *StarCraft*—but he felt like there was nobody else who could take the job. He was introverted but well-liked among Blizzard's staff, and he had learned how to manage up during meetings with Adham and their string of corporate parents. He could protect the company from shenanigans and assure the bosses that the profits would keep coming if they just left Blizzard alone. Paul Sams, a manager from Davidson & Associates who had joined Blizzard a few years earlier, would become his partner, running business operations while Morhaime oversaw strategic decisions and development.

By 1999, Blizzard had avoided catastrophe and had swelled to more than one hundred employees. As the games grew bigger and more complex to make, the company was no longer able to assign each one to a few programmers and artists, and after *StarCraft: Brood War*, the company split into two formal teams, each with its own project. The first game, from Team 1, would be a sequel that the world had been awaiting for years.

■ ■ ■

It wasn't easy to play *Warcraft II* online. To battle one another on the internet, players had to jump through a series of technical hoops, using programs like Kali that were obtuse even to the most experienced computer users. Back in 1996, during the development of *Diablo*, a Blizzard programmer named Mike O'Brien went to Adham with an idea: What if they designed a multiplayer interface that would make it easy for anyone to play online, then built it into their games? "That's a tough pitch," said O'Brien. "But Allen was awesome, and if something was going to make a great game, be right for the gamers, he'd say, 'Let's find a way to do it.'"

Soon O'Brien was helming a project called Battle.net that would serve as the multiplayer infrastructure for *Diablo*, complete with a chat system and internet matchmaking. What distinguished it most from competing products was that it was completely free—an unprecedented move during an era when most other online services, like General Electric's GEnie, charged per hour, forcing addicted players to shell out hundreds of dollars if they wanted to play their favorite games every night. But Blizzard's ethos was to bring as much value as possible to players, and to Adham and Morhaime, the long-term brand equity trumped any short-term profits they could get by charging. To defray costs, they would sell ads on the platform. Over the course of a year, O'Brien wrote the code for Battle.net, working with the other engineers to get it implemented into *Diablo* on a tight timeline. "We went from zero to 'let's ship the game using this' in six or nine months," O'Brien said.

O'Brien was one of the company's strongest coders, with more network programming experience than most of his colleagues thanks to a five-year stint at a rail traffic-control software company. After *Diablo*, he kept working on Battle.net improvements for *StarCraft*, developing a custom map database and a competitive ranking system. Blizzard attributed a big chunk of both games' success to Battle .net's clean, efficient functionality, which made it simple to play the company's games online without having to input lengthy IP addresses or download sketchy middleware. O'Brien became a rising star both internally and externally and was featured in a *PC Gamer* magazine spread naming the industry's twenty-five greatest game developers— or, as the magazine called them, "Game Gods."

Adham and Morhaime were impressed with O'Brien's talents and he was eventually given the chance to pitch his own new project, which got him thinking about the appeal of strategy games. Before he'd started at Blizzard, he had been obsessed with the first *Warcraft*, in part because the armies were small and it was easier to grow attached to the characters. "I think the last thing you want in an RTS game is to feel like you're playing on a piece of graph paper," O'Brien said. "You want to get drawn into the world you're playing in." *Warcraft II* and especially *StarCraft* had grown more complex and fast-paced, with more multitasking and larger groups of units. In the first *Warcraft* you could select a group of four units at once; by *StarCraft*, the count was up to twelve. For this new game, O'Brien wanted to swing back in the other direction, making each unit more important and giving players fewer of them. Doing so would allow them to pivot to 3D without having to worry quite as much about technical restrictions, explore a new type of networking option that would help thwart cheating, and bring back some of the role-playing elements that he felt had been lost over the previous few years.

O'Brien had called the game *Warcraft: Legends*, but just before announcing it at a European trade show in September 1999, Blizzard decided to go with *Warcraft III*—a move that O'Brien later saw as a mistake because it implied an iterative sequel rather than a radical spinoff. Rob Pardo, now one of the company's top designers, explained to skeptical journalists that this game would feel different from *StarCraft* and the previous two *Warcraft* games. It wasn't "really like a traditional real-time strategy game," Pardo said in his presentation. Gameplay would unfold from a low "over-the-shoulder" perspective rather than a bird's-eye view. The buildings would all be pre-established, and instead of focusing on constructing bases and training units, you'd control a handful of heroes, each with their own small army. It was such a big departure that they even coined a new acronym to explain it: RPS, or role-playing strategy.

The magazine previews for *Warcraft III* were glowing—they usually were—but back in Irvine, Blizzard's staff started to grumble. They wanted to advance the real-time strategy genre, not develop something else entirely. O'Brien grew frustrated at what he perceived as risk-aversion from his colleagues, while Blizzard employees complained that he was dressing them down. A lighter touch, more like Adham's, might have helped him persuade the team to get on board, but O'Brien had made a few too many enemies. "I think I needed Allen more than I credited myself with needing Allen at that time," O'Brien said. "I think I was going through growing pains, and I think everyone I was working with was going through growing pains, and I think we'd lost some of the glue that connected us."

At the end of the year, a group of staff including Pardo and Metzen went to Morhaime and asked him to remove O'Brien from the project, saying they weren't on board with his vision. Morhaime consented, telling O'Brien he could find another position elsewhere at Blizzard, but to the now-former project lead, it was betrayal. After going on a long road trip to clear his head, O'Brien approached another top Blizzard engineer, Jeff Strain, with a proposal: They should start a new company. Strain liked the idea and brought it to another of Blizzard's top engineers, Pat Wyatt.

It was the winter of 2000, and Wyatt's unhappiness had been simmering for a while. He remained attached to Blizzard—he had been there for nine years, since Morhaime had called and told him they needed a programmer for *Battle Chess*—but he was also exhausted. At this point, Wyatt was both a vice president and the lead of Battle .net, which required an all-consuming amount of attention. Servers would crash, bugs would emerge, and new features needed to be implemented in a timely manner, and Wyatt was picky about bringing in new hires. *StarCraft* and *Diablo* were played by millions of people across the globe, and *Diablo II* was on the way, which Wyatt knew would require even more of his time. The last thing he wanted was to spend another three months living at Blizzard North.

Wyatt was also disappointed that the company had decided not to pursue what he thought would be a lucrative, industry-changing initiative: to turn Battle.net into a digital store for a variety of PC games instead of just Blizzard's. After all, one of the reasons they'd called it Battle.net was to keep the client independent from Blizzard so they could potentially operate it as a separate business. He, O'Brien, and a few others had pitched the idea but were outvoted by Adham, Morhaime, and the other executives, who said they wanted to focus on their own brand and products. "I thought that was a short-sighted decision," Wyatt said.

At the start of 2000, Wyatt, O'Brien, and Strain resigned to start their new company, Tri-Forge—later renamed ArenaNet. "It was such a giant relief," Wyatt said. "Day number one I'm not getting hundreds of emails I have to go and solve. I'm not on the hook for all these things."

Morhaime tapped Frank Pearce, Blizzard's first employee, to take charge of *Warcraft III*. They repositioned the camera to the traditional bird's-eye view and re-added base-building and resource gathering. Not everything was tossed—this rebooted version of the game would retain the idea of powerful hero units that could sway the course of battles—but the idea of making an RPS was mostly gone. They were putting the three back in *Warcraft III*.

But the ArenaNet departure was traumatic for Morhaime and his crew—even more painful than Fugitive because of the engineering talent they'd just lost. Blizzard's reeling and understaffed programming team had to spend the next few months crunching hard to build a demo for this new version of *Warcraft III*. They brought the game to E3 in May 2000, then went back to work, with the exponentially increasing success of every Blizzard game just adding to the pressure. The first *Warcraft* had been surpassed by the second, and *StarCraft* had blown them both out of the water. After *Brood War*, some fans considered *StarCraft* to be the perfect game—the digital equivalent of chess. "There was this energy: Can we do it again? Capture lightning in a bottle a second time?" said designer Tim Campbell.

In addition to humans and orcs, *Warcraft III* would let you play as two new races: the graceful night elves and the lumbering undead. Each race had a suite of heroes who could collect items and gain powerful abilities. The level designers stuffed each map with monsters, villages, and optional objectives. "There were probably a couple of levels we had to scrap or redo from scratch four or five times," said Campbell. "You eventually get used to that and embrace it as part of the process."

Warcraft III would tell Blizzard's most ambitious story to date, giving a lengthy campaign to each of the four races. Metzen brought back Thrall, the protagonist of *Warcraft Adventures*, to be one of *Warcraft III*'s stars and put a sympathetic face on a faction that had previously been portrayed as brutish and violent. The human hero, Arthas, would go through a tragic journey reminiscent of *StarCraft*'s Sarah Kerrigan, eventually succumbing to his darker instincts and committing atrocities at the player's hand. While most of *StarCraft*'s story had been told through pre-briefs before each mission, *Warcraft III* would feature in-game cutscenes, taking advantage of the game's 3D models to zoom in on hero characters as they talked and battled.

Warcraft III: Reign of Chaos came out on July 3, 2002, to instant critical acclaim and commercial success, selling one million copies in a month. It was another number one hit for Blizzard, which seemed destined to never fail. The achievement was especially remarkable given the shakeups they had faced over the previous few years—an atmosphere befitting a company that had once considered calling itself Chaos Studios.

SIX

RESIGNATIONS ACCEPTED

Those who work in the video game industry might bristle at the suggestion that they do nothing but play video games all day. After all, game development is a job—one in which artists, programmers, and other creative professionals collaborate to develop complex works of art. So when Tyler Thompson arrived for his first day of work at Blizzard North in the spring of 1997, he was surprised to find people doing nothing but playing video games all day.

Diablo had arrived on store shelves just a few months earlier and Thompson, an engineer fresh out of college, had gone through a rigorous hiring process including an interview in David Brevik's Porsche in which Brevik drove "like a madman" the whole way—perhaps to gauge Thompson's performance under stress. Now, he was a Blizzard employee and found that it wasn't quite what he expected. "They were still pretty burnt out and tired from *Diablo*," said Thompson. "I was right out of college, full of energy, wanting to work."

Brevik and his team had decided that their next move would be to make a sequel—a bigger, faster, more improved version of

Diablo—but they were drained. So instead they spent their days pitching, daydreaming, and playing video games, or, as they liked to call it, *competitive research*. "It was the Wild West," said Thompson. "Just do whatever you feel like you want to do."

Even as they took it easy, Blizzard's staff had big plans for *Diablo II*. Between gaming marathons and lengthy lunches, Brevik would pop out of his office and ask colleagues to bat around ideas or help him prototype features. While *Diablo* had been a vertical game, in which players descended through a dungeon one level at a time, *Diablo II* would be horizontal. It would unfold across four acts, each centering on a different town in the world of Sanctuary, which included jungles, deserts, caves, swamps, and the depths of Hell itself.

This was an opportunity to fix the problems that Blizzard's staff had discovered in the last game. Exploring *Diablo's* cavernous dungeon could feel sluggish, so for the sequel, they would add running. *Diablo's* online multiplayer was full of hacks and scams, so this time, they'd add a proper item-trading system and a sophisticated anti-cheat program. "We felt really confident in our decisions because of the success of *Diablo*," Brevik said. "These were things we really wanted to add to *Diablo* but didn't have the time to do." There would be five distinct classes, each with their own items and skills. The Barbarian, who could dual-wield weapons and spin around like a tornado, would feel notably distinct from the Necromancer, who could summon an army of wizard skeletons.

In the fall of 1997, as the Irvine studio crunched to finish *StarCraft*, Blizzard announced *Diablo II* to the world, telling press it would come out in late 1998. But three weeks later, an obstacle emerged that would endanger that release window: *Ultima Online*. Brevik grew obsessed with the new multiplayer game, which let players inhabit a virtual fantasy world, and it became common to find him playing between meetings and design jams—or hearing him yelling about loot from down the hallway. "There was a lot of that going on," said Thompson.

In some ways these hardcore gaming sessions were good for Blizzard North. Brevik would frequently lament the aspects of *Ultima Online* he didn't like, such as load times, and preach that *Diablo II* needed to do better. His long hours playing turn-based strategy games like *Civilization* and *Master of Orion* begat one of *Diablo II*'s greatest innovations: the character skill tree. Each character would gradually acquire points that could be used to unlock or upgrade their skills, which branched out to more powerful abilities as they progressed. It was a clever, malleable system that would make the game a blast to play repeatedly.

But with these long periods of relaxation, Blizzard North was taking out a time loan that it would later have to repay. By the end of 1998, *Diablo II* had missed one deadline and was approaching another. Brevik and the Schaefers had expanded their team, hiring more people for what promised to be a significantly bigger project, but, like their colleagues in Irvine, they still developed games in a chaotic, freewheeling manner. During meetings, anyone could suggest ideas, which kept Blizzard North staff feeling empowered but tore apart the schedule. "He who shouted loudest and most frequently often got heard," said designer Stefan Scandizzo.

The result of this creative chaos was a lot of overtime, and as the *Diablo II* team entered 1999 with a looming deadline, nobody was playing games in the office anymore. "It was the worst crunch of my life," said Brevik. Thompson decided to sleep at the office three nights a week so he could spend the others having dinner with his wife, but the work was so draining, he could barely think straight. "I was a zombie," Thompson said. "I'd go into restaurants, get a menu, try to read the entry, then go to the next one, and completely forget what I'd just read."

When *Diablo II* finally came out in June 2000, it sold more than one million copies in two weeks, winning a spot in *Guinness World Records* as the fastest-selling computer game ever. It also attracted a huge international audience, selling hundreds of thousands of copies across Europe and South Korea. But the game's grueling development schedule left permanent marks on many of the people who worked at Blizzard North. "It scarred me for a long time," said Brevik. "It had huge ramifications on my life, most of them pretty negative."

Diablo II's crunch put an end to Brevik's marriage and would forever mar his relationship with his two oldest daughters. Even as the game bolstered his reputation and would cement his place in industry history, it took a piece of Brevik that he would never get back. "It's really set my life up in a way that I'm so lucky to have," Brevik said. "For me to be part of that team and recognized as the leader is really special, and has really helped me throughout my entire life. But it was extremely costly."

■　■　■

By the time *Diablo II* was finished, Erich Schaefer never wanted to think about demons and barbarians again. He spent a few weeks batting around other ideas with colleagues, then decided to pack up and leave California. "I was still feeling burnt out," he said. "So I moved to Manhattan. I barely kept in touch. I just disappeared." Not everyone at Blizzard North was allowed to take that kind of sabbatical, and some openly grumbled about one of their bosses disappearing for several months when they were all just as fried.

The silver lining was that they could use this as an opportunity to step into leadership roles themselves. A small team began working on what would become *Diablo II*'s expansion, *Lord of Destruction*, while others broke off to follow whims that never materialized, like a version of *Diablo* for Nintendo's Game Boy. At this point, Blizzard North had grown to a company of more than sixty people, but its bosses still operated with the same philosophy they had when they'd started Condor back in 1993: Let people do whatever they want. "Some people were more burnt out than others; some were better programmers than others," said Brevik. "Some had their own agendas and were really ambitious, and all of those things kind of collided." When two different groups of programmers each decided independently to develop their own 3D engine—a move that many staff pointed out was a massive waste of resources—nobody stopped them. "There was this power vacuum, mainly because a bunch of us, like myself and Erich, weren't there very much," said Brevik. "Everyone's trying to step up."

By now, *Diablo II* was played by hundreds of thousands of people every day, but just like their colleagues in Irvine, the staff of Blizzard North were clashing behind the scenes. Long-time employees were still sore that their bosses had sold Condor for millions; bonus checks from *StarCraft* and *Diablo II* had been substantial, but not enough to ease the strife. "There were major cracks in the social fabric of the company," said Peter Hu, a programmer. "There were people who absolutely did not get along and refused to work on projects with each other."

After *Lord of Destruction*, the bosses split Blizzard North into two groups: one to make *Diablo III* and the other to build something new that the team began calling Project X. It wasn't yet clear what that second game would become; they just didn't want to make more *Diablo*.

Both projects floundered for different reasons. Project X transformed into a different game every few weeks or months, pivoting any time Brevik decided he didn't like an idea anymore. At one point it was about kung-fu fighting, then pirates, and then team-based super-hero strategy. "I was burnt out and struggling to come up with what our next project was going to be," said Brevik.

This went on for two years—a cycle in which very little work got done—until Brevik and Erich Schaefer gathered their team one morning for an impromptu meeting. *Enough*, they said. They were going to stick with one game: *Starblo*. "The whole team cheered," said Julian Love, a technical artist. "In that one word, we understood the game we were making." The idea, which had been bouncing around the studio for years, was a sci-fi take on *Diablo*. Instead of exploring gothic fantasy towns, players would hop in a spaceship and travel between planets, collecting new guns and battling aliens as they traversed the stars.

The *Diablo III* team had devised a more concrete plan: *Diablo II* with way more people. Inspired by *Ultima Online* and its successors, the developers decided to make *Diablo III* a massively multiplayer online role-playing game, or MMORPG. In the previous two games, players could only team up in small groups—this time, hundreds if not thousands of people would be able to interact and play together. "You'd have these towns everyone could congregate in, but then go out to separate instances," said artist Anthony Rivero. "It was very pie-in-the-sky." Blizzard North had decided that for *Diablo III* they would switch to 3D graphics because few games in the early 2000s were still using 2D, and their colleagues down south had already made the shift. But the company was still working on two 3D engines at once, and neither was established enough for *Diablo III*'s development.

By 2003, it had been two years since Blizzard North had released any new games. The staff were fractured, the office was in chaos, and neither of the company's two projects had made much progress. And their next game might still be years away.

■ ■ ■

There had always been an uncomfortable tension between Blizzard and Blizzard North. Over the course of *Diablo II*'s development, the two companies had fought the same sorts of battles they'd fought on the first game—over code, art, and aspects of the game that the Irvine managers found objectionable. "Our argument was, again, 'Fuck that, we'll do what we want here,'" said Erich Schaefer. "We won most of those." Technically the northern unit reported to Irvine, but they believed that the *Diablo* games contributed just as much to the company's success as *Warcraft* or *StarCraft*, so why should they be treated like a subordinate?

Matt Householder, a senior producer on *Diablo II* and one of Blizzard North's oldest developers, felt that an insurmountable philosophical chasm had erupted between the two companies. "Blizzard North was more freeform, exploratory game design," Householder said. "Whereas South was more linear, less welcoming of random chance." One of the biggest pressure points was bug fixing. The developers in Irvine believed that a game should be near-perfect on release, while Blizzard North was more willing to address problems down the road through patches and updates, as they had with *Diablo II*, which remained unstable for weeks after it came out.

Despite their differences, the two game studios were allied against a common adversary: corporate overlords who seemed to barely know they existed. During the Cendant scandal, the three bosses of Blizzard North had partnered with Allen Adham, Mike Morhaime, and Paul Sams to form a committee that would deal with whichever company owned them that year, which had helped both Blizzard offices get along even during times of stress.

Bill Roper, the early Blizzard employee who had gone from

writing impromptu *Warcraft* dialogue to producing games and even serving as PR spokesman, had worked as Irvine's liaison on *Diablo II*, helping to finish the game during those difficult final months. After the game's release, as Brevik and the Schaefers began discussing expanding their own leadership team, Morhaime thought it might be a good idea to send Roper up north to bridge the gap between the two studios. Roper moved to the San Francisco Bay area, where he was promoted to vice president and installed as one of Blizzard North's new bosses.

But Roper's presence did not entirely solve the company's communication issues. By 2003, rumors were floating around that a struggling Vivendi was looking to sell its video game division. In January, press reported that Microsoft, which had just entered the gaming industry with its Xbox console, was close to buying Blizzard and the rest of Vivendi's game studios. The rumors were false—although Microsoft had considered an acquisition, nothing was imminent—but they still shocked Blizzard North's bosses, who were upset to hear the news at the same time as the public. When staff asked what was going on, Roper and crew didn't have much of an answer. "It felt like every week there was some new big life-changing possibility that could occur," said Roper. "It becomes really hard to run a studio in any stable way under that kind of environment."

In June 2003, the four Blizzard North executives, frustrated with the rumors, wrote a stern email to Vivendi asking for financial protections, better communication, and inclusion in the sale process. If the corporation wouldn't acquiesce to their demands, they wrote, the four executives would resign. "We said hey, unless we resolve this, we can't be here," Brevik said. The threat of resignation was a tactic they had used effectively in the past, and one they had been discussing for months. Morhaime and Adham had been part of some of these conversations, although the two ultimately decided not to participate. "It was less of a bluff and more: we want to show you how serious we are," said Roper.

They already had reason to be sour toward their corporate owners. When *Diablo II* had made it into *Guinness World Records*, Vivendi sent emails to Brevik and the Schaefers to congratulate them, only to misspell each of their names in different ways. "Erich was spelled 'Etlich,' which we always kid him about," said Roper. "There was something about it that didn't sit real well."

They emailed Vivendi on a Friday, assuming they'd hear back the following week. Roper was relaxing on a weekend getaway with his wife when he got a frantic call from Brevik asking him to return right away. The four of them then convened at the Schaefers' house, where they got some disturbing news.

On Monday, June 30, Blizzard North employees filed into work and noticed something bizarre: a contingent of executives from Blizzard South, including Adham and Morhaime, was in their office and meeting with the four bosses in one of the conference rooms. Brevik then gathered the staff and explained what had happened: Vivendi had accepted their resignations, effective immediately. David Brevik, Erich Schaefer, Max Schaefer, and Bill Roper were all gone.

Morhaime told Blizzard North that as part of this transition, they would be laying off staff, canceling *Starblo*, and refocusing on *Diablo III*. The staff, reeling from the news that their leaders had just resigned, now had to interview for their own jobs with managers that they barely knew. Executives from Irvine probed each Blizzard North employee about the studio's problems, potential solutions, and what they wanted to see the company do next. "They'd ask you about certain people: yay, nay, or neutral, then compare that against everybody," said artist Anthony Rivero. "It was brutal."

On Friday, employees received emails directing them to one of two conference rooms, which they quickly realized was a culling: one room was for good news; the other was for bad. Designer Stefan Scandizzo was one of the first people in his room, and as more and more people joined him, he started to realize that they were all about to be laid off. "Everybody groaned as the next person walked in," Scandizzo said. "Oh, you're with us too." Blizzard North lost a third of its staff, shrinking to around forty employees, and any illusions that it had been an equal partner to Blizzard Irvine were now completely shattered. Although Morhaime picked a new studio head—Rick Seis, an engineer who had been with the company almost since the beginning—it was clear that he didn't have the same clout as Brevik.

Perhaps the implosion was inevitable. Blizzard had always struggled to work with external studios, and its perfectionist programmers had grown frustrated with Blizzard North's laid-back ethos. Morhaime had proposed several times that Brevik and the Schaefers relocate to Irvine so they could all work together, only to be rebuffed, and installing Roper as a liaison hadn't bridged the gaps. During that chaotic final week of June, Morhaime and Adham pulled aside Brevik and asked if he would stay, but he turned them down.

Brevik and his vice presidents decided to start a new video game company—Flagship Studios—and began plucking employees from Blizzard North to join them. For some former *Diablo* developers who had already been at one another's throats over the last two years, it was an easy decision. "There were some people I liked working with better than others," said Tyler Thompson, who went along with the founders.

For those who stayed behind, there were reasons to be optimistic. It had been two years since the release of *Diablo II: Lord of Destruction*, and they'd failed to make much progress on new projects. There were political battles and baffling decisions, like the engine debacle, which had left even Brevik and the Schaefers wishing they had intervened. Now, those who remained at Blizzard North had a clean slate. "It felt like they had asked the right people, who were the positive forces for change in the studio, to stay," said writer Joe Morrissey.

Although it hadn't been Morhaime's idea to send Blizzard North's founders packing, he had accepted their resignations without pushing back. For all of their talents, it had become clear that the studio was too toxic and unproductive to remain intact. This was one of the first times that Blizzard would make big changes to overhaul cultural issues. It certainly wouldn't be the last.

SEVEN

A BOYS' CLUB

The two Blizzards always had one thing in common: They were both made up almost entirely of men. To commemorate Blizzard's tenth anniversary in February 2001, a couple of years before the catastrophe up north, veteran artist Joeyray Hall had put together a video about the company's history that encapsulated this atmosphere—a goofy, lighthearted documentary that described the work environment as "thankfully more like a frat house than a business."

You could interpret that sentence in a few different ways. One was as a reflection of Blizzard's freewheeling office, a place where the staff wore T-shirts and flip-flops rather than button-downs and khakis. They played games, formed roller hockey clubs, and sang karaoke on the weekends. Another interpretation involved their status as video game industry rebels. "What that meant was it's fraternal," said Bill Roper. "It's us against them, especially when you look at what was happening in the industry at the time." Big corporations—including CUC and Vivendi—were looking to get into video games because they were lucrative, not because they were fun.

Yet the term also conjured the image of booze-soaked couches, testosterone-fueled antics, and hazing rituals. As they developed games like *Warcraft* and *StarCraft*, most of Blizzard's staff were in their twenties. They had either just graduated college or had skipped it to come work at Blizzard. "This was a bunch of young guys who were making some money, having a good time, not knowing what to do," said artist Justin Thavirat.

For most of Blizzard's employees, this was an atmosphere that facilitated success and made them love going to work every day. But for the few women who worked there, or those who might have wanted to? The frat house image was much more complicated.

■　■　■

The best-selling PC game of 1996 was *Myst*. At number two was *Warcraft II*, with just over 835,000 copies sold. And ranked sixth, with 351,945 sales on CD-ROM, wasn't *Command and Conquer Red Alert* (#7) or *Doom II* (#10), but a game called *Barbie Fashion Designer*. The unexpected success of this *Barbie* video game—which allowed players to create doll clothing and even print out their designs—helped kick off a wave of "girl games" and disproved the common thesis that only boys liked to play on the computer. In subsequent years, new games like *The American Girls Premiere* (which let players create historical stage plays) and a series of mysteries based on *Nancy Drew* also found commercial success from a generation of young women who wanted to inhabit virtual worlds but didn't care all that much about shooting demons. Behind these games were a handful of female developers—designers, artists, and even programmers—who wanted to make games that they enjoyed playing.

There were certainly women who played Blizzard's games, but the company made little effort to draw them in. Most of the characters and units in *Warcraft* and *StarCraft* were men, and when women did show up in Blizzard games, they were frequently sexualized, like *Diablo*'s bare-breasted succubi. "You get the fans you go after," said Mary Kenney, author of the book *Gamer Girls: 25 Women Who Built the Video Game Industry.* "You can make games that appeal to women without having any women on your team, but you can't make games that feel authentic, thoughtful, and reflective of women's experiences without giving them the power to make or break creative decisions in production."

Some women would trickle into Blizzard over time, starting with office managers in both locations who were often described as the company's den mothers. Others joined to work in sales, marketing, and PR, either directly as Blizzard employees or alongside the company from one of its various corporate owners. By 2000, there were women working in development positions at Blizzard, such as art and quality assurance, but even the utilities reflected their scarcity. "There were two bathrooms upstairs—both men," said designer Kris Zierhut.

Later, one person who worked as a hiring manager at Blizzard said that their applications came almost entirely from men and that the gender imbalance "wasn't a matter of purposeful discrimination." It was true that the world didn't have as many female programmers. In 1984, 37 percent of computer science majors were women, but by 1995, that percentage had plunged to nearly 25 percent. An NPR report found that this decline corresponded with the rise of personal computers, which were marketed largely to boys, as well as a glut of films propagating male geek culture, such as *Revenge of the Nerds.* "A colleague called us unicorns," said Leigh Bauserman, an engineer who worked on *Barbie Fashion Designer.*

Bauserman, who considered herself to be a casual gamer, said she wouldn't have wanted to work for a company like Blizzard, but even if she'd had the desire, it might not have been an option. Since the beginning, Blizzard's ethos had been to hire only hardcore gamers, and its interview process reflected that, probing prospective developers on everything from their favorite *Street Fighter* character to which creatures inhabited the darkness in *Zork*. The goal was to ensure that all of Blizzard's employees played video games, but it was also one of the main reasons so many of them looked the same.

Some Blizzard executives suggested that they, like their peers at many other video game companies, didn't even consider the ramifications of being a male-heavy studio. "We never sat and thought: Are we being inclusive enough; are we making sure there's enough diversity," said Bill Roper. "That just wasn't in our young-to-late-twenties vocabulary." But others remembered colleagues saying, half-jokingly, that women would ruin the vibe. Jason Hutchins, a QA tester, recalled days when it felt like they were working in a locker room. "Every Friday, people would post pornographic pictures and we would talk about it, vote on the best one," he said. In one instance, a tester took down the office server because "he was trying to see how much porn he could send," said artist David Pursley.

Of course, Blizzard wasn't the only video game company that was mostly made up of men. A survey by the International Game Developers Association in 2005 found that just 11.5 percent of industry workers identified as female. Women who grew up wanting to make games like *Barbie Fashion Designer*—or even *Diablo*—would have to tolerate this gender imbalance if they wanted to pursue their dreams.

■ ■ ■

Kathy Carter-Humphreys liked just about everyone she'd met at Blizzard. She was part of the marketing team at Davidson & Associates, where she helped put together what would become iconic, influential box art for each game. Inspired by the box of an old adventure game called *Suspended*, which featured a striking image of a white plaster face, Carter-Humphreys and the rest of her team leaned toward big, bold imagery. *Warcraft* and its sequel featured side profiles of snarling orcs and humans, while *Diablo* drew in buyers with the menacing visage of a horned demon. Carter-Humphreys appreciated the artistry at Blizzard, although she sometimes grew frustrated with her colleagues' obstinance. "We always had little challenges," she said. They planned to release *StarCraft* with three different box covers—one for each race—and Blizzard's artists wanted to put a cigarette in the Terran marine's mouth. "We kept sending it back, saying, 'Sorry, Walmart is not going to take that,'" Carter-Humphreys recalled. "They'd take it out. Then when we got the final art from them, they'd put it back in. So we had to pay a film house to retouch it out."

Carter-Humphreys was engaged to one of Blizzard's developers, so she often found herself visiting the company's office. "On an individual basis I really liked most of the guys I worked with," she said. "But the overall culture was definitely a boys' club." Hazing was a regular part of welcoming new employees at Blizzard, as were nerf gun fights, dirty jokes, and elaborate pranks. "There was a social pecking order that was enforced regularly," said Pursley. Some developers maintained collections of smashed keyboards and controllers in the office—relics of competitive video game matches gone awry.

These antics weren't uncommon in the video game industry during the 1990s, but even veteran game developers felt like Blizzard's culture stood out. One night during the development of *StarCraft*, Pursley recalled falling asleep on a couch in the office, waking up in the middle of the night, and finding one of his colleagues vomiting in the hallway, having just returned from karaoke. "David, how's it going?" asked the colleague in between heaves. Pursley then went upstairs and found a drunk Chris Metzen, who challenged him to a few angry rounds of *Samurai Shodown 2*. Back downstairs, Pursley ran back into the colleague, cleaning up. "Stuff like that happened all the time," Pursley said. "No other place was like that or probably will be again."

Metzen, one of the company's biggest partiers, helped drive much of the chaos and testosterone. He was loud, charismatic, and easy to talk to, which made him popular among Blizzard's staff. People loved soaking in his comic book stories and were impressed by his work envisioning iconic characters like Sarah Kerrigan and Grom Hellscream. But his partying could also lead to office mishaps. During an office party the night that Blizzard finished *StarCraft*, he and artist Scott Abeyta were drinking heavily and began to push one another. "We started fucking around like people do," Abeyta said. "Wrestling. It just got a little out of hand."

What started as friendly roughhousing turned into a brawl across multiple rooms of the office after one shoved the other into a door, breaking it off the hinges. Soon other people got pulled into the fray, and someone knocked out Metzen cold. The next day, when they found out what had happened, executives at Blizzard's parent company demanded that both men be fired. "I heard later it was lucky for me that this was with Chris Metzen," said Abeyta. "Had it been any lesser soul, they would've fired us both. But they could not fire Chris. And because they could not fire Chris, they could not fire me." The incident led Blizzard to ban alcohol at the office—for a while, at least.

Anyone who worked at Blizzard for more than a few months found that their work and social lives became intertwined. "Everyone I knew at Blizzard became my circle," said Josh Kurtz, a designer. "It became my support structure, my family. I did everything with them." It became clear—especially in later years, as the company expanded—that the best way to succeed at Blizzard was to befriend the top employees. Cigarette breaks with executives. Barbecues at the founders' houses. And, as the money began rolling in, trips to Vegas strip clubs with the boys.

Adam Maxwell, who bounced between various roles at Blizzard, recalled sitting down for his first interview at the company and being shocked when a colleague walked in with a six-pack of beer, which set the tone for his three-year stint there. "When we did E3s, every night we'd go out and drink all the alcohol we could find," Maxwell said. "You'd hear the stories: 'Oh, so and so is in trouble because he maxed out all his credit cards at the strip club.' It was absolutely that kind of culture." Once, Maxwell recalled, after hitting a big milestone to finish *Diablo*, a group of Blizzard staff decided to hop in a car and take the four-hour drive to Las Vegas "because none of the strip clubs in Orange County were open, but the ones in Vegas are always open."

These Vegas trips became a company tradition for game launch celebrations and staff bachelor parties. Some of Blizzard's developers considered themselves straight-edge and preferred to stick to the arcades and slot machines, while others were big partiers, unwinding from the stressful development of *Diablo* and *StarCraft* with tequila shots and lap dances. When the female employees tagged along, many of the male staffers tried to make them feel welcome. "We looked out for each other," said Jeffrey Vaughn, who worked in tech support. "It may have been a boys' club, but at least when I was there, I wouldn't have called it hostile."

This party culture wasn't limited to Sin City: The E3 trade show, which normally took place in Los Angeles, spent 1997 and 1998 in Atlanta, Georgia, where Blizzard's staff took the opportunity to patronize some well-known local strip clubs. During one of these excursions, the dancers talked a group of Blizzard staff into moving to the back room for some private activities. They were then shocked to receive a bill for thousands of dollars—per person—which led to some marital strife when they returned home.

Melissa Edwards, who worked in business development, said she never felt uncomfortable working at the company. "Yes, it was a bro culture," she said, "but I had a great time in that culture." Edwards enjoyed the work—testing games, facilitating logistics, bringing in family and friends on New Year's Day to stuff envelopes full of *StarCraft* beta discs—and she loved her colleagues. Edwards also dated several Blizzard coworkers—a trend that was growing common thanks to the demanding workload.

These relationships were consensual but could set an uncomfortable tone. Up at Blizzard North, a newly divorced Brevik began dating and eventually married a female programmer, which led to tension among their colleagues. Similar situations unfolded at the main Blizzard office, where high-level Blizzard employees would date and even compete over subordinates. Paul Sams, who would become vice president of business development and eventually Chief Operating Officer, dated and later married the company's head of PR. Rob Bridenbecker, who started in technical support before working his way up to director and, later, vice president, was engaged to one woman at Blizzard and wound up marrying a different one.

Not every woman who worked at Blizzard during this period felt safe or respected. Some had to deal with unwanted sexual advances or worse. One woman, who had joined the Irvine office as a QA tester on *Diablo II*, was asked a series of horrifying questions by her manager: what her favorite sexual position was, what color underwear she was wearing, and so on. "She had long black hair and was very pretty," said Michelle Elbert, another tester. "There was this parade of people coming downstairs to welcome her." The woman left Blizzard after just a few months.

As Blizzard's games became more successful, the fratlike behavior of the company's developers had wider effects. Sometimes their antics were harmless. Sometimes they were harmful. And sometimes they led to the company getting banned from a hotel.

■   ■   ■

In the spring of 2000, Blizzard was riding high: *StarCraft* was selling millions, *Diablo II* was set to be another big hit, and *Warcraft III* was beginning to get back on track after the big reboot. At the Game Developers Conference in San Jose, California, Blizzard's staff were rock stars of the industry, and they took advantage of every open bar they could find.

One night, Duane Stinnett, one of Blizzard's top artists, drunkenly stumbled back to his hotel with the colleague who was sharing his room. Both felt sick and began to vomit—on the floor, on themselves, on each other. Stinnett's coworker brought him to the shower, began running the water, and started to take off both of their shirts. Stinnett wasn't quite lucid, but when he noticed what was happening, he freaked out. "I was thinking, 'I don't know what's going on, but I don't want to be here,'" he said.

Shirtless, drunk, and covered in vomit, Stinnett stumbled out of the room and wandered upstairs. "I didn't know what rooms the others were staying in, so I just started knocking on random doors," he said. "Then I passed out in the middle of the hallway." Several Blizzard staff recalled stepping over a half-naked Stinnett and laughing as they returned to their rooms. One pair, pitying him, decided to carry him to their own room, where Stinnett woke up the next day, confused and "feeling like shit," he said. He groggily rode the elevator back down, trying to remember exactly what had happened, when a stream of water came rushing in and he noticed firefighters standing outside, the floor completely submerged. "So of course I close the elevator doors and go back to the fourth floor without saying a word," Stinnett said.

Later, he learned what happened. After Stinnett left the room, his roommate passed out in bed but forgot to turn off the shower, and the drain was clogged with their vomit, so the tub began overflowing. Stinnett's pounding and yelling led a guest to call security, who barged into the hotel room only to find his passed-out roommate. On one of the nightstands was Stinnett's wallet, which was bulging with cash he'd brought for strip clubs and happened to contain a spare copy of his wife's driver's license. "They found a dude's wallet with a girl's ID and a bunch of cash in it," said Stinnett. "They thought he had killed this chick and stolen her money."

As security grabbed the roommate and began escorting him downstairs, he managed to spurt out that they were from Blizzard, and an infuriated Morhaime was called to come to the lobby in the middle of the night and explain. Nobody was arrested, but Stinnett's roommate was reprimanded and had to pay for the property damage. Some remembered being told that Blizzard Entertainment would now be permanently banned from the hotel, and the company enacted a new policy: no more sharing rooms on trips.

Stinnett flew home with a hangover, a colleague's jacket, and a story he'd go on to share for the rest of his life—one that might have been embarrassing for Blizzard and Morhaime, but at the end of the day, didn't lead to anyone getting hurt. "In today's world, we would've been fired on the spot," said Stinnett. "Back then the reaction was: 'Don't ever do that again. But that was really fucking funny.'" Professionalism would come later.

EIGHT

NOMAD

W hen he wasn't passing out in hotel hallways, Duane Stinnett was making movies. He grew up shooting films with his friends on an eight-millimeter camera, then landed a series of computer jobs before joining Blizzard as an animator in 1994. As he rose through the ranks, Stinnett grew obsessed with the idea of filling their games with short films—pre-rendered videos called cinematics that could depict more elaborate graphics than the games themselves.

At first, these movies were mostly there to set the tone—humans and orcs battling it out—but by the time they'd started developing *Diablo*, Stinnett wanted to use them to tell a story. He hired his best friend from grade school, Matt Samia, and they crafted a provocative closing cinematic that transformed *Diablo's* hero into a villain. On their next game, *StarCraft*, Stinnett asked Blizzard's bosses if they could start a proper cinematics department rather than dragooning whichever artists happened to be free at any given time. After some initial resistance, Adham and Morhaime agreed—in part because competitors, like Westwood, were also making short films for their games. This fledgling Blizzard cinematics department started with just a few artists making *StarCraft* videos but would eventually grow into the envy of the industry.

In 1998, after *StarCraft* came out, Blizzard split into two teams. Team 1, under Mike O'Brien, began working on *Warcraft III* while Team 2 would be led by Pat Wyatt and Stinnett, who departed the cinematics department to pitch a game that he called *Nomad*. Inspired by a tabletop game called *Necromunda* that was set in a violent, postapocalyptic world, *Nomad* would be a...well, it wasn't really clear. Stinnett didn't have Adham's gifts for design and persuasion, and he struggled to articulate how the game would feel from moment to moment. "I didn't have it fully baked in my head either, exactly what the gameplay was and how it was supposed to work," Stinnett said. Different people came away from meetings with different ideas of what *Nomad* was meant to be. Was it postapocalyptic *X-COM*? *Diablo* with a team of multiple characters?

Previous Blizzard projects had easy points of comparison: *Warcraft* was *Dune II* in a medieval fantasy world, *Diablo* was a real-time roguelike game, and *StarCraft* was *Warcraft* in space. "*Nomad* was its own thing," said Stinnett. "And I didn't know how to encompass that in a package that was presentable." There were elements of the project that impressed Blizzard and even their corporate owners at Vivendi Games, like outlandish concept art featuring surreal depictions of turtles and ostriches, but after months of development, the basics still weren't clear.

At the same time, several of Blizzard's employees had grown obsessed with a different video game: *EverQuest*, which let them inhabit a giant, persistent online fantasy world. Each *EverQuest* player would start off by creating a character based on the classic archetypes—warriors, rogues, clerics—and could then explore, defeat monsters, and gain levels. Everywhere they went, they'd run into other players whom they could battle or befriend.

Kevin Beardslee, who worked on the *Nomad* team, was one of Blizzard's earliest *EverQuest* obsessives, but he also hated many aspects of the game. The most frustrating part, he thought, was that defeated bosses wouldn't regenerate until a server reset, which happened once a week. "I kept thinking: Who would go to Disneyland if a ride closed after one group rode it?" Beardslee said. He began cataloging aspects of *EverQuest* he disliked in a document, which eventually transformed into a pitch for a new game.

It almost seemed too obvious. Blizzard was obsessed with *EverQuest*, but the game was full of flaws. Why were they still bothering with this *Nomad* thing when they could make their own *EverQuest* instead?

■　■　■

In reality, people at Blizzard had been talking about making an online game like *EverQuest* for years. The new Sony game was just the latest iteration in a long-running genre that had started in the late 1970s, when two British university students created a text-based online game called *Multi-User Dungeon*, or MUD. An offshoot in 1991 called *Diku-MUD* brought in Tolkienesque fantasy and D&D-style level mechanics, building the foundation for many online games to come. One of the most popular of these games, which would eventually be called Massively Multiplayer Online Role-Playing Games (MMORPGs), was 1997's *Ultima Online*—the game so good it had nearly derailed the development of *Diablo II*.

Allen Adham had also become obsessed with *Ultima Online*, declaring after his first all-nighter that Blizzard was going to make a game like it one day. From the beginning, one of Blizzard's core philosophies had been that video games were at their best when they were social, and this was the ultimate manifestation—a living world that never stopped existing, even when you stopped playing. But while *Ultima Online* felt antiquated, with its 2D graphics and rudimentary interface, *EverQuest* brought those same killer ideas to a massive 3D world.

People who tried to play *EverQuest* on their own didn't typically have a great time. *GameSpot* reviewer Greg Kasavin wrote that "the combat may be a little boring, the manual may be horrible, the quest system half-baked, and the game not without its small share of miscellaneous bugs." But, he added, find another player and "all of a sudden *EverQuest* stands to become one of the most memorable gaming experiences you've ever had." Some, like Joeyray Hall, didn't understand the appeal, mocking colleagues as they spent hours waiting for friends to log in to the game. "It was just a lot of standing around," Hall said. But most of Blizzard's employees were hooked on the game that the world started calling *EverCrack*, and they often talked about developing their own MMORPG. Blizzard had a universe that might be the perfect fit: *Warcraft*, which had familiar tropes yet oodles of unique lore and history thanks to Chris Metzen's wandering imagination.

Soon, *Nomad*'s leaders were meeting to talk about whether they should cancel the project and pivot to making a Blizzard *EverQuest*. "We all took a vote," said Stinnett. "I was the only one who said no." He tried to push back, arguing that they'd already put months of hard work into *Nomad* and they were already making *Warcraft III*. "I don't want to spend my life working on the same franchise or two," he said. But it was futile. Momentum had already turned against him.

Stinnett was replaced by another senior developer: Adham, who was so excited about the new project that he decided to end his sabbatical and become lead designer. Following his *Ultima Online* obsession,

Adham had picked up *EverQuest* and concluded that it might be the best video game ever made. Like Beardslee and others on the team, he thought that sanding off the rough edges could introduce casual players to a genre that was perceived to be only for the hardcore, bringing in both the donut hole and the donut. Whereas *Nomad* had struggled due to a muddy vision, this was crystal clear. "We knew what the game was," said Beardslee. "We're making a better *EverQuest*."

They were going to make a *Warcraft* MMORPG.

NINE

EVERQUEST, BUT BETTER

Nobody really knows who first came up with the name *World of Warcraft*. It just seemed like a natural fit—one of those titles that emerged organically from the creative morass of game development. Fans had always imagined what it might be like to inhabit the forests and swamps of Azeroth. Now, years after the release of the first *Warcraft* game, it could be a reality.

As *Nomad* wound down toward the end of 1999 and Blizzard officially broke ground on *World of Warcraft*, Adham and the team began mapping out the universe, building tools, and brainstorming how they'd improve on the game that inspired them. One of *EverQuest's* biggest problems, they believed, was its loose, open-ended structure. Some areas of the game were perpetually empty while others, the ones that dropped the best loot, were always crammed full of players waiting for monsters to appear. The game's quests offered a bit more guidance, but they were opaque; to trigger one, you'd have to talk to one of the game's computer-controlled characters and figure out the correct phrase to input.

Blizzard's solution was to design *World of Warcraft* like a guided museum. You would start off in a beginner area like the lush Elwynn Forest or the arid Valley of Trials, where you'd find a handful of characters with big yellow exclamation points over their heads, signaling that they would send you off to collect rabbit pelts or clear out a kobold camp. After a few of these quests, your character would gain a level, unlocking even more quests. A rebellious player could ignore these tasks and roam aimlessly, but following the path was the most efficient way to progress through the game. "You basically spiraled out of a quest node until you needed to go to a new quest node," said Kevin Beardslee.

Where *EverQuest* felt like a dangerous world that would annihilate anyone foolhardy enough to travel alone, *World of Warcraft* would aim to make every player feel like a superhero. Characters in *World of Warcraft* were split into two factions: the Horde and the Alliance, each featuring a suite of classes that were powerful enough to take on groups of enemies by themselves. "It was all about minimizing the barriers for fun," said Alen Lapidis, an artist. "In games like *EverQuest*, you'd get your cake after a lot of vegetables. *World of Warcraft* wanted to be all cake all the time."

After a year, the *World of Warcraft* team expanded to more than twenty people. Blizzard didn't want the outside world to know about the project—both for competitive strategy and to maintain an aura of mystery—so they kept it secret even from new recruits. David Ray, a programmer, joined the company in January 2001 with no indication of what he had been hired to make. On his first day, the team said they were taking him out to lunch. "They still hadn't told me what the project was," Ray said. "They asked, 'Any questions before we go out to lunch?' Yeah, what game am I working on?"

Ray had been a hardcore *EverQuest* player and was delighted to hear that they were making a *Warcraft* MMORPG. He became one of the engineers in charge of the game's tools—the internal software that would allow artists and designers to build chunks of the game. He grew to love his time at Blizzard, where the team regularly listened to his feedback—"It was just a really good working environment," he said—although he also cultivated a reputation for shutting down requests that he thought would be a waste of time. When artists and designers would barge into his office asking for tools and features, he would look at them with a grin and tell them to go away. "My nickname at Blizzard was Dr. No," Ray said.

Blizzard's aura of secrecy could backfire, potentially costing them veteran developers who weren't interested in committing to a mystery project. And new recruits weren't always as jazzed as Ray had been. Matt Mocarski, a 3D artist who joined Team 2 in the summer of 2001, had been hoping to work on a sequel to *StarCraft*. "I was so upset," said Mocarski. He took a five-figure pay cut to join Blizzard and was disconcerted when he first showed up for work and found what looked "almost like an abandoned office space." Blizzard's building was in a generic office park on UC Irvine's campus with no indications that the company was located there. Inside, the carpets were stained with alcohol and dried food and it was impossible to avoid the scent, a pungent mixture of liquor and body odor. The monitors were old and cheap, and some of the furniture was missing parts. "You protected your chair with your life," Mocarski said. "Over half the chairs in the studio were broken. You couldn't roll them, or you'd sit down and they'd tip over."

It was a bizarre contrast: here was a video game company that was at the very top of its field, with games that sold millions of copies, yet people had to hoard their office equipment like they were living in a postapocalyptic wasteland. Despite his initial misgivings—and the decrepit conditions—Mocarski found working on *World of Warcraft* to be more satisfying than anything he'd done before. "I knew that whatever Blizzard did, the art was going to be phenomenal," he said. Because there was so much work to do and the team was so small, their process was loose and unstructured. They would convene to talk about what the game needed, sketch out some basics on big whiteboards, then go off and build levels however they saw fit.

On September 4, 2001, Blizzard put an end to the secrecy, officially announcing *World of Warcraft*. Journalists were impressed with early demos, praising the straightforward quest system and visual flourishes. Few people were shocked that Blizzard was making an MMO, as the business model was too lucrative for any game company to ignore. To play *EverQuest*, you'd have to buy the box for $40 and then, after a monthlong free trial, dish out another $10 per month to keep playing. By the end of 2001, *EverQuest* had 400,000 players, which meant a gross revenue of roughly $4 million per month—a hugely profitable enterprise even after server costs.

But within Blizzard, there was skepticism that *World of Warcraft* would be all that successful. *Warcraft III* was the higher priority, and *World of Warcraft*'s story even changed several times due to decisions that Team 1 was making. "There was this feeling on the team that the rest of the company felt like we were going to fail," said Ray. "Nobody cared what we were doing. It was just Adham's pet project, whatever." Even their official name, Team 2, reflected a lesser place in the company's hierarchy. "We were the second-class team," said Beardslee.

Video game development was always an uncertain process, and Blizzard had never done anything like *World of Warcraft*. The company's previous games had all existed in 2D spaces and even *Warcraft III*, which had 3D graphics, unfolded across top-down battlegrounds with limited verticality. *World of Warcraft* would let the player character walk around, jump, and explore vast landscapes in ways that Blizzard had never tried. The developers had to learn how to design 3D levels and create elaborate animations, all while building the biggest game they'd ever made—and making it possible for thousands of people to play together. Success seemed far from a sure thing, and at the turn of the century, 3D technology was advancing so rapidly that every month Blizzard's artists would discover new tools or techniques. "That's what makes the video game industry challenging in a unique way: You always feel like you're behind the curve," said Mocarski. "At a certain point you can't be upgrading graphics. You have to cut it off, say no more, this looks good enough."

The team was still relatively small, and there was a lot of work left to do. During E3 in the summer of 2002, when fans and journalists asked about *World of Warcraft*'s release date, Blizzard staff in their black-and-blue jackets and T-shirts would always give the same answer: *It'll be ready when it's ready.*

■　■　■

Quality assurance testers at Blizzard worked on the floor below the development team. "It was cold and it was dim," said tester Michelle Elbert. Testers at Blizzard, like at most other video game companies, were at the very bottom of the corporate ladder. They were tasked with playing games like *Diablo II* and *Warcraft III* endlessly, experimenting with every possible character class or unit combination to try to find the bugs. It was a critical job, but it was also perceived as low-skill work, so testers across the industry were paid poorly—often as little as $8/hour. They were told not to talk directly to the developers and almost always had to work long shifts. "There was one point where I forgot what it looked like to get to work during the daytime," said Elbert. "Because I'd get there really early and leave really late. So one time I drove to work during a normal morning hour and almost got lost."

The dangling carrot that helped testers look past these conditions was the promise of becoming a game developer. Morhaime liked to promote from within Blizzard and had found some success bringing up testers like Shane Dabiri and Chris Sigaty, who were now two of the company's top producers.[7] As development on *World of Warcraft* progressed and the team began to grapple with the fact that this game was going to be larger than anything they'd made before, they decided to bring in more artists to construct the farms and mountains of Azeroth. One day, designer Eric Dodds—also a former tester—went down to the QA pit and made an announcement: Team 2 was looking to promote at least one tester to work on the game. Applicants would have to use the *World of Warcraft* map editor to design their own 3D environments, and the best ones would get promoted.

Blizzard hired four new artists in this round, and more would follow. "I felt like a bunch of Skittles rained down on me," said Matt Sanders, who got the gig alongside three of his friends. Testers and customer service agents would play "Movin' On Up," the theme from *The Jeffersons*, as they said good-bye to their former colleagues. "People would sing the song as you moved upstairs," said engineer Twain Martin. Cultivating homegrown talent was a big win for Blizzard—it kept the testers motivated, raised morale, and helped fill their ranks with cheaper talent.

World of Warcraft grew so massive that the team had to double in size, expanding to more than forty people as Blizzard swelled to the hundreds. Company meetings outgrew the office and had to relocate to

---

7   This created an odd dynamic for some veteran employees, who sometimes found it frustrating that former testers were now their bosses. "There was no upward movement for the people who were doing the development," said Stu Rose, who left in 2003 in part because of this trend.

a nearby movie theater. Team 2 had hoped to finish *World of Warcraft* in time for the 2003 holiday season, but it became clear that would be impossible. Early hopes of using art assets and models from *Warcraft III* hadn't panned out, and the amount of content in the game was ballooning, while every new MMORPG announcement built up the pressure. The team was particularly scared of the upcoming *Star Wars Galaxies* and *EverQuest 2*, both of which were developed by *EverQuest* creator Sony Online Entertainment and seemed positioned for market dominance.

There were two camps within the upper ranks of Blizzard. One believed that *World of Warcraft* was going to be the next big thing; the other thought it was going to fail, piss off Blizzard's corporate parents, and cost the company its autonomy. *World of Warcraft* was an expensive project thanks to its growing team size and the hefty cost of external servers, which were essential for supporting a massive player base. Adham and Morhaime were both bullish on *World of Warcraft*'s prospects, but when Paul Sams and his team built financial models for the game, they had no idea what to expect. Previous Blizzard games had all followed the same pattern, with sales spiking on release and declining from there, but *World of Warcraft* was a big question mark.

At the same time, Vivendi was drowning in debt thanks to huge media investments made by CEO Jean-Marie Messier—later convicted for misappropriating funds—that weren't panning out. Vivendi hired a new CEO and began looking to divest from many of those investments, including gaming. Throughout 2003, the French executives talked to US game publishers like Microsoft, Take-Two, and EA about potentially buying their video game division, but Blizzard was just about the only profitable part of the Vivendi Games portfolio, which had grown bloated with flops thanks to various mergers over the years. A few publishers asked if they could carve out Blizzard, but Vivendi was only interested in selling the whole package.

The uncertainty helped lead to Blizzard North's implosion over the summer and hung over *World of Warcraft*'s development as Team 2 set out to finish the game. Morhaime, Adham, and Sams considered finding investors and buying the company back for themselves, but it wasn't a practical option. "We're used to having more control over our destiny," Morhaime told a reporter, "and now we're just waiting."

In the fall of 2003, they finally got an answer: they would stay with Vivendi, which wound up selling off the other parts of its entertainment division but hung on to the struggling games business, bringing in an executive named Bruce Hack to whip it into shape. Hack was charming and congenial but came from the music business and didn't know anything about the video game industry. Poring over the portfolio, Hack found that Vivendi had three seemingly redundant MMOs in development: a Marvel game, a *Lord of the Rings* game, and *World of Warcraft*. As he set out to understand the video game business, he commissioned several analyses to map out what made a hit (the answer: usually sequels) and try to figure out just what was up with this Blizzard company. One analysis tallied the average review score of every PC-focused studio's output for the last decade. "Blizzard ranked number one," Hack said. "It became unmistakable to me that it was an extraordinary studio."

When Hack met Morhaime and Sams, he was impressed. For years, the pair had successfully convinced their higher-ups that if they gave Blizzard autonomy—and allowed them to slip past a deadline or two—they would be rewarded with hit games, and Hack didn't want to mess with a working formula. Blizzard owned its IP, had cultivated a successful relationship with customers through Battle.net, and was probably the most beloved brand in PC gaming. One of Hack's first moves as CEO of Vivendi's video game division was to cancel the other two MMOs in favor of *World of Warcraft*.

Suddenly, the stakes had become very high. What had once been perceived within Blizzard as Adham's weird experiment was now one of Vivendi's biggest bets.

■   ■   ■

Veteran Blizzard employees never wanted to repeat *StarCraft*'s terrible crunch again. Long hours were one thing; spending evenings and weekends at the office for months on end was quite another. When development began on *World of Warcraft*, the team's management concocted a new plan: Rather than working every hour for months at the end of production, they would start doing overtime early. Starting in 2001, Team 2 began staying late for two nights a week on a regular basis in hopes of avoiding far heavier overtime toward the end of development.

By 2003, with *Warcraft III* out the door and deadlines approaching, it became clear this strategy was a failure as the *World of Warcraft* team entered true crunch mode. Nights and weekends became company time, and the team ate so much pizza that the taste became unbearable. Several potential revolts were quelled by Blizzard management with promises of title bumps, profit-sharing checks, and bonuses upon the game's completion. "My kids called themselves *WoW* orphans," said Twain Martin. "You wanted to see Dad, you came to work."

Adham, who had already left the company for a year because of burnout, found the schedule taking a toll. Many of the game's ideas went through him, and every week he'd host meetings in the designer bullpen to discuss how items would work, how magical spells would be handled, when player vs. player combat would be allowed, and much more.

In January 2004, Adham made a stunning announcement: He was leaving Blizzard again. He had passed his day-to-day management responsibilities to Morhaime, but his role on *World of Warcraft* had been instrumental. He was the company's design guru and the safeguard that many of them relied on to ensure their games were great. Although he could be abrasive and had aggravated some colleagues—he didn't always live up to the nickname Velvet Hammer—he was widely considered to be the linchpin of Blizzard's games. But once again, he was burnt out. He'd met a woman, and wanted to raise a family, not screw up his relationship by continuing to work seven days a week. His disciple, Rob Pardo, would take over as lead designer of *World of Warcraft*. Pardo and Metzen were also both promoted to vice president, helping fill the void in management.

Adham's sudden absence didn't make a huge difference to *World of Warcraft*. Many of the key design decisions had already been finalized, and Pardo had already been quietly making a big impact behind the scenes. If anything, waiting on Adham's approval had been such a bottleneck that his departure came as a relief to some of the designers—but his shadow would hang over *World of Warcraft* for years to come. Much later, designer Kris Zierhut would remember asking about specific decisions in the game only to be told they were "Allen features" and were not to be touched.

Blizzard's previous games had been ambitious, but none compared to *World of Warcraft*. It had hundreds of monsters, thousands of items, and dozens of unique zones and dungeons. There were nine classes, each with a host of abilities that required design, visual effects, and audio. As the game's world expanded, Team 2's artists and designers began to realize in horror that they had too much space and not enough stuff. Regions like the Barrens, a massive desert full of aggressive creatures like centaurs and quilboars, looked beautiful but felt incomplete, so the team decided to bring in more people to fill in the gaps.

Christine Brownell was one of four women in Blizzard's QA testing pit when she'd started a year earlier, and she immediately took the opportunity to apply to be a quest designer. She impressed the bosses when, in response to a job listing that asked applicants to write five quests, she instead wrote five entire quest chains, each comprising missions across Azeroth. By February 2004, she was part of the burgeoning quest team, assigned to create content for all of *World of Warcraft's* vast areas. With some loose story guidance based on Metzen's lore, the designers were given almost complete autonomy. "I don't know if I've experienced anything that gave me that degree of creative freedom," Brownell said. By the end of the process, they'd come up with more than one thousand new quests.

During the final months of 2004, it was easy for Team 2's developers to fall into despair about how much work was left to do and how little time was left to finish it all. But there were also reasons to be optimistic about the game's potential success. A public beta in March 2004 built up some buzz, as did a series of closed tests the team held throughout the rest of the year. At one point, a few months before *World of Warcraft's* release, producer Shane Dabiri felt compelled to get on the office intercom for a team intervention. "He said, 'Hey guys, we know you love the game, but if you don't get off the beta server and go back to work, we're going to cut off access,'" said Brownell.

John Smedley, the president of Sony Online Entertainment and one of the minds behind *EverQuest*, hadn't spent much time thinking about the competition. He was too busy trying to get *Star Wars Galaxies* and *EverQuest 2* out the door. "We were living the good life with *EverQuest*," he said. "I'd say we got arrogant. We thought, 'Oh my god this ride's going to go on forever.'"

Then he played the *World of Warcraft* beta. "It was like: 'Ruh roh.'"

TEN

CONSOLIDATION

O n the evening of November 22, 2004, just a few nights before Thanksgiving, a group of *World of Warcraft* developers drove to Fry's Electronics in nearby Fountain Valley, California, to celebrate the release of their game. What they saw was confounding: endless traffic, pillars of smoke, and a teeming black mass. As they got closer, they realized that the blob was in fact a horde of thousands of people. "I parked like a mile away," Paul Sams told the *New York Times*, "and when I get there the line is looped around the building, and then looped around the parking lot."

Blizzard's staff took seats at a long row of black-clothed tables in the center of the store, wearing matching shirts and bomber jackets as they signed *World of Warcraft* boxes, notebooks, and other paraphernalia. "It was like we were a rock and roll band," said Alen Lapidis. Early in the morning, Fry's ran out of copies of the game, so Morhaime sent a crew back to the office to grab all the boxes that had been earmarked for employees. Roughly five thousand fans showed up, waiting for hours just to meet the game's makers.

Morhaime had told Blizzard's staff that they were hoping to hit half a million *World of Warcraft* subscribers within the first year, matching the whopping success of *EverQuest* in one-fifth the time. Adham had been even more optimistic, telling prospective business partners before he left that he thought they could reach one million people in a year. Both had been way off. "Nobody really anticipated how big it was going to be," said Stuart Massie, a tester. "Or how it was going to change Blizzard."

World of Warcraft sold more than 240,000 copies in a day, breaking every computer game sales record in existence. By the end of November it had hit 350,000 copies. It was on track to reach one million players not in a year but in just two months.

As they popped champagne on the lawn to celebrate the game's success, Blizzard's employees began to feel a storm of emotions: exhaustion, elation, and pure terror as they realized what this meant. *World of Warcraft* ran on servers—computer farms that processed data and transferred information between the game and its players—and each one could handle only a limited number of players at once. Overload them and the game would buckle, like a horse trying to carry too many riders, triggering log-in errors and preventing customers from playing. Within twenty-four hours, the available servers were full and Blizzard's engineers were scrambling to stand up new ones so players could get online without interruption. "All the equipment, the servers we had planned to deploy, meticulously planned every month—we deployed them all," said producer Shane Dabiri in a documentary released later.

By March, *World of Warcraft* had 1.5 million subscribers. Morhaime and Sams told the operations department to stop shipping new boxes to stores because they didn't have the capacity to support more players. For Blizzard's leaders, the game's resounding success proved to be even more stressful than development had been: Now, there were hundreds of thousands of players disappointed whenever they couldn't play, and when the servers did get back online, everyone would try to log back in at the same time, clogging the pipes. It was as if their own players were inadvertently conducting an attack on Blizzard's servers.

To keep up with this demand, Blizzard would have to hire throngs of new people: engineers, customer service representatives, community management, and so much more. It would have to transform into a new company.

■   ■   ■

One afternoon amidst the chaos, Jeremy Masker knocked on the door to Blizzard's offices and waited for someone to buzz him in. After dropping out of law school in Colorado, he had driven to California on a whim to apply for a job at Blizzard. "At the time, I was playing *World of Warcraft* a lot," he said. "I was thinking: 'I'm doing this every waking moment. I should see if I can get paid for it.'" He'd packed his two cats in a van, sold his possessions, and hunted down Blizzard's nondescript office, where the receptionist told him there were customer service positions open. He filled out an application, slept in Blizzard's parking lot as he learned he was rejected, and remained there as he applied again.

Eventually Masker convinced Blizzard to hire him as a customer service agent, where he would be one of hundreds of *World of Warcraft* "game masters" responsible for fielding questions and complaints. Every day, he'd arrive at 3:00 p.m. and grab a computer—the seats were all swappable—where he'd sit and try to hit his quota of tickets before his shift ended at midnight. Their area was run-down and dirty, full of old monitors and clacky keyboards, but it was always buzzing with activity. Everyone in the customer service department was in their late teens or early twenties, much like the whole company had been a few years earlier. They'd slam back free soda, argue over games, and go to lunch at one of the two cheapest options available: the burger joint Carl's Jr. or a sandwich shop on UC Irvine's campus. Every week the company hired dozens of new customer service agents who crammed into the office and tried to keep up with the influx of *World of Warcraft* players. "We used to have a joke," Masker said. "If you had a pulse and knew anything about *Warcraft*, we'd put you on a keyboard."

Blizzard had always tried to offer decent customer service—once, in the early days, Jesse McReynolds and Mike Morhaime himself had driven to a nearby customer's house to debug a sound issue—but now, expectations were different. Players had spent $50 to buy *World of Warcraft* and were now paying $15 per month to play it, which drove them to demand 24/7 support. The company went international, opening offices across Europe and Asia. "Normally when we ship a game it is basically done," Morhaime told the *New York Times*. "In the case of *World of Warcraft*, we worked really hard and we shipped the product, but in some ways the work was just beginning."

Rather than move to a new game, Team 2 kept working on *World of Warcraft*. The developers released bug fixes every few weeks and new content every month or two. Kris Zierhut, a former high school teacher who had joined the team as a designer, would spend hours talking to his colleagues about what they liked and disliked about the game, even though it had been out for months. "There was just so much excitement within the team for what we were doing," he said.

Blizzard built an entire team devoted to community management—people who would read through the company's online message boards to collate feedback and interact with players. Eventually,

Blizzard would begin investing in analytics, using data to pinpoint exactly what people were doing in the game, but during *World of Warcraft's* first year they had to rely on the loudest voices and their gut feelings.

Two of these new community managers, Paul Della Bitta and Matt Kassan, went to the executives with an unorthodox pitch: a fan event dedicated to Blizzard games. If the Fry's midnight launch had attracted that many people, they thought a Blizzard-hosted convention could do even better, drawing in fans from all around the world. As an experiment, they put up an advertisement on the *World of Warcraft* launcher so players would see it as they logged in to the game. A day later, tickets were sold out.

On October 28, 2005, thousands of people gathered at the Anaheim Convention Center to attend the first BlizzCon. Attendees received Blizzard-themed swag, like T-shirts and playing cards. They dressed up as their favorite characters and lined up to watch *Warcraft III* matches, participate in jousting tournaments, and play demos of the company's future games. Mike Morhaime, wearing khakis and a loose black-and-blue bowling shirt with a *World of Warcraft* logo on the lapel, thanked the crowd for coming and teased the announcement of the game's first expansion, *The Burning Crusade.* "I had no idea that one day I would be standing up here, welcoming almost eight thousand people to our very first BlizzCon," he said, pacing the stage in what seemed like a mix of wonder and awe. "We just wanted to make some great games."

■ ■ ■

Not everybody was as elated as Morhaime. Kevin Beardslee, who had been the lead animator on *World of Warcraft,* had grown increasingly unhappy during the game's development. The grueling overtime had taken a heavy toll on him and his colleagues, and now there were rumblings that they might have to crunch again to release *The Burning Crusade*. Blizzard's management had resisted their attempts to push back against the intense schedule in the past, and Beardslee was skeptical that the company would pay them enough to justify the workload.

Toward the end of *World of Warcraft*'s development, Beardslee had quietly been talking to colleagues about leaving Blizzard and had even reached out to other video game publishers as a backup plan. "Hey, I represent twenty people from the *World of Warcraft* team," he recalled saying. "We think the game's going to be amazing; we're just not sure we're going to be taken care of." The most positive response came from the Korean video game publisher NCSoft, which specialized in MMORPGs and was also funding the first game from ArenaNet, the studio founded by Pat Wyatt and other Blizzard refugees.

After *World of Warcraft* launched, Beardslee and his crew watched in amazement as the subscription numbers climbed. Almost everyone at Blizzard had been promised hefty profit-sharing bonuses to make up for the long hours and lack of overtime pay. Over the previous two years, as the company had burned through money without releasing any games, those bonuses had been all but nonexistent, but now they were hopeful that their hard work might be rewarded with fat checks. When the bonuses arrived a few months later, their excitement morphed into befuddlement and then outrage. "Everybody was just livid," said Matt Mocarski, who remembered receiving a check for less than $2,000. Exacerbating the insult, the bonus was split into two payouts. The second would arrive later that year as an incentive to ensure that employees stuck around—which meant that they'd have to keep crunching. "I remember that felt shitty," said Beardslee. His wife had given birth the previous year and he'd barely seen the baby.

Beardslee went to Frank Pearce, Blizzard's first employee and now an executive, to explain that people were unhappy, saying that he and his colleagues had been expecting to double their salaries after *World of Warcraft*'s incredible success.

"This is kind of a slap in the face," Beardslee recalled saying. "'You could potentially lose a lot of people over this.' Frank's response was: 'You should be happy you work for Blizzard. You should be doing it out of pride, not for money.'"

In a separate meeting, Mocarski recalled Pearce scoffing that employees should be happy that they had received any sort of bonuses. "It just rubbed everybody the wrong way," said Mocarski.

An almost identical situation had played out seven years earlier, when James Phinney and crew had left to form Fugitive Studios, which perhaps offered some solace to Blizzard's management— Fugitive had failed and many of its employees had returned to Blizzard. But in 2005, the industry was larger, healthier, and growing every day. That spring, Beardslee and nine other *World of Warcraft* developers resigned to form Carbine Studios, a new video game company funded by NCSoft. More would follow in the coming months and years, and unlike Fugitive, Carbine had longevity.

Around the same time, Blizzard laid off a small group of employees, which also seemed like an astonishing move. Alen Lapidis, an artist on *World of Warcraft*, was called into a meeting with the company's human resources representatives and told he was being let go. "It was really shocking, considering the success of the game and how it had become such a force," Lapidis said. Maxx Marshall, who had left Blizzard for Fugitive in 1999 and then returned in 2003 to help finish *World of Warcraft*, was surprised when he and several other veterans lost their jobs. "There was a feeling about the layoffs that all they were doing was firing people for money," Marshall said. His hypothesis seemed to be proven true a few weeks later, when he got an email asking if he'd be interested in returning to Blizzard for about $15,000 per year less than he had been making before.

Blizzard had just created one of the biggest games of all time—one critic described it as "a stunning achievement that will make you feel privileged to be a game player"—and yet the company was operating like a cash-strapped startup. Between the exodus and the layoffs, it felt like a large chunk of the people who had delivered *World of Warcraft* were no longer around. "We had this team photo and we did the *Back to the Future* thing," said Mocarski. "Every time someone would leave, we'd white them out. And slowly the team was getting whited out." One small group of employees even filed a class-action lawsuit against Vivendi for unpaid overtime, although the company settled before it went to court.

Morhaime and Sams responded to the drama by convincing Vivendi to let Blizzard once again revamp its bonus system, using the Carbine departures as leverage to secure better profit-sharing as well as a "phantom equity" plan that would give top employees a financial stake in the company's success. Those who stuck around were rewarded with big checks that would only get bigger over the next few years. James Chadwick, a designer on *World of Warcraft*, had been in the hospital for a month with a nasty case of diverticulitus. "When I got back, half my friends had already left," he said. When he saw his first bonus check, he just laughed. But shortly afterward, when the system was revamped and he received $25,000, Chadwick decided to stay. "Pretty soon my bonus checks were outpacing my actual pay," he said.

As *World of Warcraft* approached its one-year anniversary, it reached five million subscribers, eclipsing *EverQuest* tenfold. Blizzard began building systems to improve morale, like an employee opinion survey and more sophisticated procedures for monitoring and responding to *World of Warcraft* server outages. The game single-handedly turned Vivendi's video game operation into a massive profit center, which was now leading to rewards for the entire development team. "We were making a lot of money," said Vivendi Games boss Bruce Hack. "It was a beautiful thing. There's a joy about it that's associated with success. The entire organization felt it."

■　■　■

Matt Uelmen didn't consider himself to be an angry or violent person. He was the composer behind *Diablo*'s iconic guitar strums and a beloved if eccentric colleague who had worked at Blizzard North since the beginning. So he was surprised to find himself, after hearing news that David Brevik, Erich Schaefer, and Max Schaefer had all departed the company, throwing a tiny glass bottle of Calistoga mineral water against the wall of his office, where it left a permanent mark. "I was pretty enraged to find out that tensions I'd observed in the office came to a head very fast," said Uelmen. "I was the kid who wanted to keep the family together as much as possible."

It was the summer of 2003, and Uelmen had watched the founders depart Blizzard and start something new with many of his longtime colleagues. He didn't feel financially comfortable enough to go off and join their startup—he was raising a family and helping to pay for his wife's law school—so he found himself stuck at Blizzard North with only a dent in the drywall to keep him company.

Over the course of just one week, Blizzard North had been completely transformed. The bosses were gone. A large chunk of staff had either quit or been fired. Their *Starblo* project was canceled, and the few dozen remaining employees were told to keep working on *Diablo III* with strict supervision from Blizzard HQ. Those who survived the culling were left with the impression that this was their last chance to prove that the project was still viable. For the next few months, the *Diablo III* team worked on a vertical slice—a small chunk of the game meant to demonstrate how it would feel to play. They built some monsters, some items, and a few dungeon levels to explore. Under Brevik, they had been working on a massively multiplayer iteration of the game; now, they would scale back the ambition and develop something that steered closer to *Diablo II*.

Finally, after all that dysfunction, the team at Blizzard North felt like it was clicking. Morhaime and the other Blizzard bosses were relieved when they saw the first *Diablo III* build. *World of Warcraft* was in the thick of development and sucking up most of the company's resources, and with no idea how successful it might be, it was nice to have a new *Diablo* game on the back burner just in case. Morhaime gave Blizzard North the green light to keep working on the game and then turned his focus to Irvine's other projects. But as time went on, the *Diablo III* team began to run into new problems. Blizzard executives like Metzen would come in and offer direction that sent *Diablo III*'s staff scrambling, there were tensions on the team between those who wanted to follow the formula of *Diablo II* and those who wanted to explore new ideas, and the game wasn't making progress in key areas. "Qualitatively, the game never improved," said artist Julian Love. "We made a lot more content but it never got more fun. In fact, it kind of went backwards."

In the summer of 2005, as *World of Warcraft*'s popularity skyrocketed, Blizzard North studio head Rick Seis (who had replaced Brevik) called artist Anthony Rivero into his office and warned him that bad news was about to hit. In an eerie reflection of what had happened two years earlier, Morhaime and a group of other executives were planning to fly out to Blizzard North's office the following week. "It's not looking too good," Rivero remembered Seis saying. "So just be ready."

Back in Irvine, the executives had evaluated *Diablo III*'s progress and decided that Metzen, Pardo, and the company's other creative leaders would need to supervise more closely. But with *World of Warcraft* vacuuming all of their resources, nobody at Blizzard had the desire or bandwidth to move to San Francisco just to oversee Blizzard North's developers. As a result, Morhaime explained to the forlorn group of staff, they were relocating the development of *Diablo III* to Irvine. The good news was that many of the staff would get the chance to re-interview for their jobs and stay on the team. The bad news was that if they wanted to keep working at Blizzard, they'd have to move to Southern California. After twelve years and two big hits—one of which was widely considered to be one of the best video games ever made—Blizzard North was shutting down.

It took a little while before Uelmen heard what had happened. His wife had gone into labor that morning, and he was in the hospital when his colleagues learned that the studio was closing. When he finally got to sit down with Morhaime and crew, they made him a generous offer, and he decided to move to Irvine along with a handful of other Blizzard North staff.

When he arrived at Blizzard HQ, Uelmen wasn't shocked to learn that his first assignment was to write music for *World of Warcraft*. He understood their new business reality. "The money it was making was obscene," he said. Sooner or later, *World of Warcraft* would come for them all.

ELEVEN

"THAT KIND OF LOOKED LIKE ME"

Robert Huebner and his friends used to call LucasArts, the venerable video game company started by *Star Wars* creator George Lucas, "Lucas University." It was a great place to learn how to make games, but the pay was subpar, so most people quit after a couple of years. As they worked on projects like *Star Wars Jedi Knight II* in the 1990s, Huebner and his colleagues would daydream about finding fame and fortune by starting their own company. In 1997, when Huebner was ready to depart, his friends weren't yet willing to take the startup plunge, so instead he relocated to Irvine for a job at Blizzard, working on *StarCraft*.

A year later, Huebner's old pals were ready to go indie, so he moved back to San Francisco to start a new company called Nihilistic Software. After successfully developing a role-playing game called *Vampire: The Masquerade—Redemption* for the publisher Activision in 2000, they began talking about their next project. Huebner reached out to Morhaime for a casual chat—"wouldn't it be cool if we made a game together?"—that gradually grew more serious. Blizzard was focused on PC games, while Nihilistic had experience making games for consoles. What if Huebner's team developed a Blizzard game for the next generation of consoles? What if it was a third-person shooter? And what if it was set in the *StarCraft* universe?

Shooters, or games in which the action centered on guns, had grown popular in the early 1990s, when a Texas-based studio called id Software released a string of hits called *Wolfenstein*, *Doom*, and *Quake*, all of which used a first-person perspective, putting the camera where a character's eyes would be. As video games moved into 3D spaces, the "third-person shooter" emerged, giving players an over-the-shoulder perspective that offered a broader view of each game's world. By the twenty-first century, the genre had proven lucrative and every big publisher was getting in on the action.

By 2001, Nihilistic and Blizzard had struck a deal for the project, which they called *StarCraft: Ghost*. Whereas most video game contracts only paid developers once they'd hit specific goals, known as milestones, this was a looser arrangement, with Blizzard writing checks to Nihilistic every month to keep iterating and prototyping the design of the game. "At the time it seemed like nirvana," said Huebner. "Who wouldn't want to be able to spread your wings? Flex muscles, try things."

Starcraft: Ghost's main character would be Nova, a lethal agent with a suite of powerful abilities. She could see through walls, zip around with supersonic speed, and pick up weapons straight out of *StarCraft*, like the firebat's flamethrower. When Blizzard announced the game in the fall of 2002, fans were as hyped as they'd ever been, gobbling up every magazine preview and screenshot. But the loose, iterative process that had been great for early production made it tough to lock down ideas as the game entered proper development. Producers at Blizzard, who checked in with the project regularly, offered strict and sometimes confusing directions. *StarCraft: Ghost* oscillated between stealth and action, shifting every few months as the vision changed. "We were always chasing the cool thing," said Huebner.

After years of delays and what appeared like an endless amount of discarded work, it became clear that *StarCraft: Ghost* wasn't working out. On June 22, 2004, Blizzard abruptly announced to the press that Nihilistic had halted development on *StarCraft: Ghost*. To Huebner, it was almost a relief. "We'd been at it so long," he said. The good news was that unlike some other victims of cancellations in the video game industry, Nihilistic wouldn't be shutting down. Huebner, anticipating that the project might go awry, had tracked down some other contracts as a failsafe. Nihilistic would live on—and so would *StarCraft: Ghost*.

■ ■ ■

Two weeks after Blizzard shared that it had parted ways with Nihilistic, the company made another surprise announcement: it would partner with a company called Swingin' Ape Studios to make several games, starting with *StarCraft: Ghost*. Swingin' Ape, founded in 2000, had released a shooter called *Metal Arms* that impressed Morhaime and the other decision-makers at Blizzard. And, perhaps more importantly, they were based in Aliso Viejo, California, just a twenty-minute drive from Blizzard's offices. Many of the conflicts between Blizzard and Nihilistic had emerged because they were four hundred miles apart, which exacerbated communication difficulties—much like it had with Blizzard North. By contrast, many of Swingin' Ape's staff were already friends with their counterparts at Blizzard. "It was kind of fun when a business relationship started to form as well," said Matthew Bell, an artist at Swingin' Ape.

Blizzard took the code and art that Nihilistic had developed and handed it over to Swingin' Ape, whose developers discarded it and decided to start from scratch. "Some of the things just weren't up to Blizzard standards," said Bell. To avoid running into some of the mistakes that their predecessors had made, the new development team prioritized multiplayer, looking to *Halo* for inspiration and creating a demo that would let classic *StarCraft* units battle in ground-level shooter combat.

Morhaime seemed impressed by the new team's work and on May 16, 2005, Blizzard announced that it was acquiring Swingin' Ape and folding its forty employees into a newly formed console division. "They said, 'Hey guess what, good news: we're going to be Blizzard,'" recalled Bell. "Everyone was excited." But while the multiplayer portion of *StarCraft: Ghost* received rave reviews in internal playtests, the single-player mode wasn't shaping up. "We just had a lot of trouble finding the fun," said engineer Mike Schweitzer. More alarmingly, a new generation of consoles was about to arrive.

Over the last two decades, the video game industry had split into two parallel tracks. There were computer games, which had been Blizzard's primary focus, and there were console games, which were generally perceived as easier and more approachable. To play games on a console, you didn't have to worry about Windows, DirectX, or whether your graphics card was compatible with your motherboard; you just needed to insert the disc. The tradeoff was that consoles were locked pieces of hardware and could only run games that were designed specifically for those machines. As graphical technology evolved, console makers released new iterations of their hardware—Nintendo went from the NES (1985) to the Super Nintendo (1991) to the Nintendo 64 (1996) and so on—that were referred to as "generations."

By the early 2000s, there were three main entrants in the console space: Nintendo's GameCube, Microsoft's Xbox, and Sony's Play-Station 2, but the next generation was on the horizon: the Wii, Xbox 360, and PlayStation 3. This presented a problem for *StarCraft: Ghost*, which was being developed for the older consoles and risked feeling graphically obsolete by the time it was finished. Plus, big-box retailers like Walmart weren't interested in giving premier shelf space to games from the previous generation, in large part because they retailed for ten dollars less.

In March 2006, Blizzard decided to shelve *StarCraft: Ghost*, announcing to the world that the game was "indefinitely postponed." In a press release, Morhaime said that the company would be holding a review period to explore potential future console games. The developers at Swingin' Ape—now Blizzard's console division—spent the next few months in R&D mode, prototyping all sorts of ideas, such as creating a different *StarCraft* spinoff. But the gravitational pull of *World of Warcraft* was inescapable, and by the end of 2006, as the MMO prepared to hit an astonishing eight million subscribers, Blizzard decided to close its console division.

Morhaime and the other executives interviewed each of the Swingin' Ape employees one by one, like they had at Blizzard North years earlier. Some moved to the *World of Warcraft* team, where they would help finish up *The Burning Crusade*. Others moved to other projects, were laid off, or decided to quit. Over the next decade, Blizzard would repeat the same stock answer whenever asked about *StarCraft: Ghost*—that it wasn't canceled, just postponed—perhaps because they were still holding out hope that it might come back one day. But that would never happen. The unfathomable success of *World of Warcraft* had transformed the company in irrevocable ways, and it was only getting started.

■ ■ ■

Ben Vinson and Ben Schulz met in middle school, where they started playing video games together and never stopped. They spent long nights in the 1990s competing in *Doom* death matches and binged on every Blizzard game that came out, pulling pranks on opponents. Vinson had a video capture card, so they could record the mischief—what today might be called "trolling"—as they violated the rules of sportsmanship to infuriate their fellow *StarCraft* players with annoying tactics. Vinson and Schulz would ramp things up by pretending to be clueless newcomers, asking ignorant questions in chat. "We'd really piss them off," said Vinson.

They got hooked on *World of Warcraft* in college, starting a guild called PALS FOR LIFE that became infamous on their server for goofing on more serious groups of players. One day, they started joking about an area called the Rookery, which was full of dragon eggs that would spawn hostile whelps if players got too close. It was a trivial obstacle that made Vinson and Schulz wonder: Were there actually people who couldn't get past this part of the game?

On May 11, 2005, they posted a message on the *World of Warcraft* forums titled "UBRS (vid) ROOKERY OVERPOWERED!" with a link to a video. They wrote that this was their seventh time trying to get past the encounter and begged other players "to give us constructive criticism on our tactics and how you beat this room."

In the video, their group of characters convenes just outside the Rookery, discussing the battle in weary tones, as if they've been at it for hours.

"These eggs have given us a lot of trouble in the past," says Vinson before laying out the plan. "What do you think, Abdul, can you give me a number crunch real quick?"

"I'm coming up with 32.33—repeating, of course—percentage of survival," deadpans Abdul.

"That's a lot better than we usually do," Vinson says.

"All right, chums, I'm back," says a character named Leeroy, played by Schulz. "Let's do this." His character then runs straight into the Rookery, stomping on every egg he sees. "LEEEERROOOOYYYYY JENNNNKINNNNS!" he yells.

Dozens of dragons appear on screen and attack the party, wiping them out in a few seconds. "Leeroy, you are just stupid as hell," Vinson says.

It was clear to most *World of Warcraft* players that the video was a joke, but it spread well beyond fans of the game. It brought in exponentially more traffic than any other video on WoWmovies, the hosting website they'd used, and soon it began popping up on a little-known video streaming website called YouTube that had been founded just three months earlier. The Leeroy Jenkins video racked up millions of views and became one of the first viral videos in internet history, in part because so many people didn't realize it was staged. "We never thought anyone was going to think it was real," said Vinson.

Later that year, Vinson got a call from his mother, informing him that Leeroy Jenkins had been part of a clue on *Jeopardy!*. In the coming years, the name would be referenced on television shows like *The Daily Show* and *How I Met Your Mother*. Schulz was interviewed by NPR, contacted by talk show host Jimmy Fallon, and even received a request from an assistant of the actress Jennifer Garner asking him to record a video for her then-husband, Ben Affleck, who was a big fan. "I said, 'Okay, pay me $500,'" Schulz recalled.

"Leeroy Jenkins" became shorthand for rushing into a situation with no thought or preparation. It also put millions of new eyeballs on *World of Warcraft*, helping sustain its unlikely path to becoming one of the biggest video games in history. After all, nobody was making viral videos about *EverQuest 2*.

■ ■ ■

If you were to try to pinpoint the exact date that *World of Warcraft* became a cultural phenomenon, one strong contender would be October 4, 2006, nearly two years after the game's release. Once, many years earlier, Joeyray Hall, Blizzard's crusty, foulmouthed cinematics artist, had gathered the staff of Silicon & Synapse to watch a video called *Spirit of Christmas*, about four young boys who build a snowman that comes to life and attacks them. The video grew so popular among Hollywood executives that its creators, two Colorado filmmakers named Trey Parker and Matt Stone, secured a deal with Comedy Central to bring its characters to television for a show that would be called *South Park*.

By the fall of 2006, *South Park* was up to its tenth season and many of its animators had developed addictions to *World of Warcraft*. When Parker learned about the game, he was inspired to write an episode of the show about the kids playing an MMORPG and came up with an ambitious idea: What if half of the show took place in the animated cartoon world of *South Park* while the other half was set in a 3D recreation of *World of Warcraft*? *South Park*'s producers and animators knew that building *World of Warcraft*'s models from scratch would be near impossible, so they asked Blizzard if the two companies could collaborate.

Soon, Hall and his small team of video makers were driving up to South Park Studios to work on the episode. They built custom characters and shot footage within *World of Warcraft* based on Parker's vision. The plot: *South Park* foursome Kyle, Stan, Cartman, and Kenny are all hooked on *World of Warcraft* but grow frustrated when a seemingly invulnerable "griefer" repeatedly kills them, halting their progress. After months of level-grinding and with the assistance of some Blizzard executives, the boys defeat the griefer and save the day.

On the last night of production, Joeyray Hall was reviewing some footage of the in-game scenes when he glimpsed the "real-life" version of the griefer—a large, acne-ridden man with stubble, a wrist brace, and orange crumbs dribbling down the front of his shirt. "Just for a second, the character flashes up and down," Hall said. "I go: 'That kind of looked like me.'" He asked the lead animator, who confirmed that they had based the villain on Hall.

Hall was disconcerted until it sank in: he was one of the main characters on an episode of *South Park*, one of his favorite shows of all time. "I didn't think I made that much of an impression on people," he said.

The episode "Make Love, Not Warcraft" was watched by millions of people and even won a Primetime Emmy Award—the first "machinima," or film production made from computer graphics, to take the honors. It became a symbol of *World of Warcraft*'s cultural potency and helped lead celebrities like Vin Diesel and Mila Kunis to talk openly about their obsession with the game. Although the episode only referred to the antagonist by the moniker He Who Has No Life, a FAQ on the *South Park* website later revealed his real name: Leeroy Jenkins.

■　■　■

In 2004, before *World of Warcraft* launched, Blizzard had employed around five hundred people. By 2007, Blizzard boasted nearly three thousand employees across the world, with satellite offices in France, South Korea, and China, as well as a supplemental customer service office in Austin, Texas. *World of Warcraft* now had nine million subscribers—a boon for Vivendi, which still wasn't exactly sure what to do with its video game division. Blizzard was generating a tremendous amount of money, but other parts of Vivendi Games were still lagging. Previous attempts to sell the unit had fallen through, but now, as the proprietor of the most lucrative video game in the world, Vivendi had more leverage.

In 2006, executives at Vivendi began talking to Activision, which had grown into one of North America's biggest video game publishers. Activision had found a great deal of success with console games like *Tony Hawk* and *Guitar Hero*, while Vivendi had dominated the PC market thanks to Blizzard's magic. The two companies concluded that with some sort of collaboration, they could even surpass Activision's top rival, Electronic Arts. After a year of negotiations, they struck a deal: Vivendi would buy a controlling stake in Activision. Then, Vivendi would merge its video game division into Activision to create a new publicly traded company called Activision Blizzard.

Morhaime gathered Blizzard's employees to announce the news. When they asked what this merger would mean for them, he responded with a few solemn words. Blizzard was doing well. *World of Warcraft* was printing more money than the US Treasury. Nobody at Vivendi or Activision wanted to do anything that might stop the golden goose from laying eggs.

Nothing was going to change.

PART

2

. . .

FALL

TWELVE

BOBBY

Robert A. Kotick liked to go by Bobby, a childlike nickname that belied adult sensibilities. In truth, he came out of the womb ready to generate revenue for shareholders. Growing up in Roslyn, New York, Kotick all but learned how free markets functioned before he could walk. Kotick's mother, a teacher, told a *Forbes* reporter that she caught him selling one of her ashtrays when he was three years old. Later, as a curly-haired teenager with an impish smile, Kotick launched business after business, buying items and selling them for slight profits: wallets, candy, sandwiches, and whatever else he could get his hands on. In high school he rented out music halls in Manhattan for parties and hired limos to chauffeur classmates in from Long Island. It didn't matter to Kotick what he was selling—only that he was making money.

In 1981, Kotick began studying at the University of Michigan in Ann Arbor. He had never been a big fan of school and skipped classes to pursue entrepreneurial endeavors, much to his lawyer father's dismay. Through a friend he met Howard Marks, a computer geek from

France who was like him in many ways. Although they had distinct hobbies, both were blunt and unafraid to say exactly what they meant. "We clicked nicely," said Marks. "He was very interested in business. I was very interested in computers."

The two became roommates—Kotick on the top bunk, Marks on the bottom—and soon began talking about starting a company together. After an initial venture involving electric printers didn't work out, they devised a new plan. It was clear to Marks that computers were powerful devices capable of changing the world, but they were impenetrable to all but the geekiest programmers, so he planned to design a graphical interface that made them more approachable—easy enough, Kotick would joke, to be used even by someone as computer-illiterate as him. Their new company, Arktronics, would sell the interface as a package containing a word processor, spreadsheets, and other convenient tools.

But first they needed seed money, so they called up Kotick's dad, who connected them to a wealthy investor who was willing to meet with the pair. The investor was skeptical—Kotick and Marks were college students with no real experience—and began rattling off a long list of conditions to which they'd have to agree for him to make the investment. That was when Kotick showed his early negotiating chops. "Bobby stands up and says, 'We're done,'" recalled Marks. "He was so stunned that these young kids stood up to him."

Soon enough, another opportunity emerged. One of their friends was headed to Dallas, Texas, for an annual fund-raiser called the Cattle Baron's Ball, where moguls in cowboy hats gathered to watch live country music and raise money for cancer research, and Kotick figured he'd tag along to network. There he was seated next to the man who would change his life: Steve Wynn, a Las Vegas casino magnate with big hair and a bigger personality, who ran the iconic Golden

Nugget and was close friends with the likes of Frank Sinatra. The next day at breakfast, Wynn asked if Kotick wanted a ride to New York on his private jet—an invitation that no ambitious college student would ever decline. On the way, Wynn explained that two decades earlier, a Las Vegas banker had become his mentor and given him the investment capital he needed to enter the casino business, on the condition that Wynn one day find a young businessman to take under his own wing. Wynn would go on to unlock previously impenetrable doors for Kotick, granting him a social network and access to investment capital. Wynn became Kotick's sherpa, his rabbi. "Like my dad," Kotick would say years later.

Thanks to Wynn's subsequent $300,000 investment, Kotick and Marks were able to build Arktronics into a proper company. By 1984, they had more than twenty employees, including Michigan graduate students and even a few professors. Marks handled the software and operations, while Kotick, who dropped out of school, ran marketing and met with investors. He wasn't an organizational expert, but he had a natural charisma that could make serious businessmen forget they were talking to a teenager. "I think my talent is being able to get things done very quickly, very easily, just by a simple negotiation," Kotick said in an interview with PBS at the time. "I can go in there and put on a smile, say, 'I'll be your best friend, I'll play with you every day,' and people are more apt to give in to something like that."

Arktronics was too small to keep up with the soon-to-be-released Apple Macintosh and Microsoft Windows and went out of business shortly afterward, but the failure only inflamed Kotick's ambitions. He changed the company's name to International Consumer Technologies, looking for new ways to enter the computer industry. He tried to purchase Commodore International, the floundering company behind the Amiga computer—"the wildest of wild ideas," recalled Marks—but he couldn't convince the board to sell. Instead, Kotick and a group of partners, including Wynn, bought a controlling stake in a licensing company that helped market Nintendo games like *The Legend of Zelda*. Kotick didn't spend a ton of time playing video games—he'd later say in various interviews that he avoided them due to an "addictive personality"—but he was fascinated by the burgeoning industry. And in 1990, he and his partners stumbled upon a potentially promising opportunity: a nearly bankrupt video game publisher called Mediagenic that was better known by its old name—Activision.

■ ■ ■

In 1979, a group of programmers at the video game company Atari rebelled against their bosses over what they saw as exploitative work conditions, then started a new company whose name came before Atari in the phone book. Activision found quick success with hits like *River Raid* and *Pitfall!* but struggled when a wave of imitators began flooding the market with cheap games, causing what would later become known as the great console video game crash of 1983. Revenue plummeted, the founders departed, and the company downsized. To turn its fortunes around, Activision brought in a new CEO named Bruce Davis, a former lawyer who decided to rename the company Mediagenic and expand into other areas of software. Within a few years, as the console market bounced back thanks to the Nintendo Entertainment System, a slow and steady recovery seemed possible.

But Davis knew there was an existential threat on the horizon—a patent infringement lawsuit filed by Magnavox, maker of the first video game console. Magnavox had pounced on several big video game companies based on a series of broad patents that engineer Ralph Baer had filed in the early 1970s that encompassed just about any electronic sports game, such as Activision's old tennis and ice hockey titles. Incredibly, the courts all ruled in Magnavox's favor, granting some $100 million in judgments and leading top Nintendo executive Howard Lincoln to grumble in one 1989 interview that "Magnavox isn't in the business of making video games. They're just in the business of suing people."

Davis tried to start settlement conversations with Magnavox's lawyers but was rebuffed, which he later assumed was so they could get more favorable terms from the significantly larger Nintendo. Magnavox defeated Mediagenic in court and then won again on appeal, and the ruling came down in March 1990: Mediagenic owed a total of $6.6 million in damages and attorneys' fees, a death sentence for a company that was already struggling to stay afloat. The ruling set off a chain reaction: Lenders pulled back, customers slashed their orders, and the cash-strapped video game publisher suddenly couldn't pay many of its partners, including an Orange County–based studio called Interplay. "They were very close to putting us out of business," said Brian Fargo, who estimated that Mediagenic stiffed his company out of at least one million dollars.

For Bobby Kotick, this was an opportunity. He and his partners, including Marks and Wynn, called up one of Mediagenic's biggest investors, a Canadian company, and offered to buy their 25 percent stake for around $440,000. The price tag suggested that Mediagenic was worth less than $2 million—a staggering plummet for a company that just a few years earlier had generated $158 million in revenue—and they were astonished when the company said yes. "It was a fluke," said Marks. "We didn't know they would sell."

Then, Kotick reached out to Davis. "He says, 'I've bought an interest in the company and I'd like to take it over,'" recalled Davis. "I said, 'Well, I don't want to do that right now, but thanks for your interest.'"

But Kotick didn't relent. With help from Steve Wynn—and

Wynn's high-priced lawyers—he began what Davis considered a hostile takeover. "It wasn't a fair fight," said Davis. "I went to a gunfight with a knife." After some negotiations and the promise of a cash infusion, Davis handed over the keys. And in February 1991, just as Allen Adham and Mike Morhaime were assembling desks, Bobby Kotick became CEO and chairman of Mediagenic. The company's financials were still a disaster, and salvaging it would be a tough order, but Kotick recognized that there was an asset in Mediagenic that Davis had essentially discarded: its old name. Kotick planned to file for bankruptcy, reorganize the company under the Activision brand, and pay off as much debt as possible with equity, transforming creditors into shareholders with vested interest in the company's success.

Now they needed to figure out what to do with the Magnavox lawsuit. As Kotick tells the story: He, now twenty-seven years old and a newly minted CEO, walked into a conference room full of executives and lawyers from Philips Electronics—Magnavox's parent company—and proposed that they convert their $6.6-million debt into Activision stock as part of the bankruptcy restructuring. Philips said it wasn't interested, so Kotick took out his office keycard and left it on the conference room table, wishing them luck with their new assets. A few minutes later, by Kotick's account, Philips called him back in and accepted the offer. Davis believed that Wynn's influence played a far bigger role than Kotick's negotiating skills, but whatever ultimately swayed the lawyers, Philips agreed.

Kotick filed for bankruptcy, laid off most of the staff, and relocated the company now again called Activision from San Francisco to Santa Monica. He rereleased classic games in new packages and rebuilt the company from scratch, recruiting people with no video game industry experience—perhaps to get fresh perspectives, or perhaps because they couldn't convince experienced game developers to work for them—which meant an office full of architects, lawyers, and engineers right out of college. "It was effectively a startup," said Tim Morten, who joined in 1994.

Armed with some $40 million in capital from Wynn and other investors, Kotick set out to return to profitability. One of the company's biggest bets was *MechWarrior 2*, which would use 3D graphics to create high-speed battles between hulking robots. "There was absolutely no confidence at that time that it was going to be a hit," said Josh Resnick, a Wharton business school graduate who became a producer on *MechWarrior 2*. Faced with a tight deadline and significant technical constraints, a small team of artists and engineers scrambled to get the game out the door. "It was a race to the finish," said Resnick. "We went days without sleeping, lived in the office."

MechWarrior 2 shocked the gaming industry by becoming Activision's first smash success since the 1980s, selling half a million copies in just three months. Kotick liked to reward people who delivered hits: Resnick received a pay bump and was promoted to a management role. "He'd give you a big leash and let you run with it," said Resnick. "If you kept hitting a wall and not performing, he wasn't a sentimental guy: You were done. But if you performed, he gave you the resources and support you needed."

Over coffee one day, a colleague named Andrew Goldman approached Resnick with an intriguing proposal: They should start their own outfit and develop games externally for Activision. "This was a moment when they were very forward-thinking," said Resnick. "They could have been petty, emotional, given us a bad deal. Instead they gave us a very generous transition."

Kotick and his team figured that, rather than drive entrepreneurial-minded top talent to competing publishers, they should embrace the opportunity. When Goldman and Resnick started their new company—Pandemic Studios—Activision gave them a publishing deal for two games. The pair was allowed to bring along furniture, equipment, and even game technology from Activision. "We didn't have to raise any money," Resnick said. "We were able to stand up as a studio within five minutes." But at the last minute, Kotick decided to renegotiate their agreement. "At the eleventh hour, he said, 'Hey Josh, I'm going to feel weird if you guys take off and become a huge success and I don't own a piece of you,'" Resnick recalled. "'So as a prerequisite of this deal, I'm going to take 5 percent of the company.'" Kotick wrote a check for $100,000 in exchange for this equity, but Resnick still wasn't thrilled about the last-minute rug-pull.

Over his tenure, Kotick became known as demanding but unexpectedly generous—the type of guy who would both reprimand employees for making typos in emails and surprise them with thoughtful gifts, like secretly paying for their vacations. He was a ruthless competitor and grew obsessed with beating his rivals. "He wanted Activision to be the biggest video game publisher in the world," said Keith Moore, one of his early partners. He also had a reputation for being litigious and could show a vindictive side to people he believed had wronged him. "He doesn't shoot, but he points guns," said Marks. "There's a tendency to really go aggressive on people." In a PBS documentary aired in 1984, a young Kotick talked about meeting with a company whose executives told him they had entered the software business because it was a load of fun. "We're in it for the fun, too," Kotick said. "But we're in it really for the money."

By 2000, Activision was generating more than half a billion dollars in revenue every year and growing rapidly. Kotick continued investing in external game developers and acquired the ones that seemed most lucrative, such as Raven Software, the maker of popular shooter games, and Neversoft, the company responsible for the hit

Tony Hawk's Pro Skater. He said he believed in letting game companies make their own strategic decisions and maintain their autonomy, in contrast to Electronic Arts, which Kotick described as a hotbed of "Death Star culture" due to its tendency to homogenize game development teams.

At the same time, Kotick surrounded himself with people who had expertise in selling packaged goods. In contrast to Blizzard, Activision's executives weren't video game fans—they were businessmen who had worked for companies like Procter & Gamble and knew how to sell chocolate and laundry detergent. "If you want to run an institutional-level company, having people who know how to run businesses is in many respects a lot more valuable than having people who know how to make video games," Kotick would later tell a reporter. His strategy was to treat video games like commodities, and when a game like *Tony Hawk* turned out to be a hit, Kotick would use every possible resource to turn it into a franchise, with regular sequels and spinoffs. "It was made very clear to us: If it did not have an opportunity to be a billion-dollar-plus franchise, don't consider it," said Dusty Welch, a top Activision executive.

Later, Kotick would be vilified for this approach and criticized by players for running franchises into the ground. One comment to investors, which Kotick later said was meant to be a joke, would hang over him for the rest of his career. "The goal that I had in bringing a lot of the packaged-goods folks into Activision about ten years ago," he said, "was to take all the fun out of making video games."

■ ■ ■

As Kotick's star rose in the video game industry, he schmoozed with just about every other mogul in the business, including an educational software guru named Bob Davidson. The two first met in 1994, shortly after Davidson had spent around $7 million to buy a little-known company called Silicon & Synapse. "I was thinking it was mind-boggling that he could have spent that much," Kotick later recalled. More than a decade later, as Kotick began meeting with Vivendi Games CEO Bruce Hack to talk about a potential merger, that $7 million seemed like one of the best investments in business history.

The conversation first started in 2006, when Vivendi executives got in touch with Kotick and asked if he was interested in adding *Warcraft* to his portfolio of franchises. He and Hack began dining regularly and realized that their two companies complemented one another perfectly: Blizzard was the most revered PC developer in the world, while Activision had dominated the console space. Next up was Morhaime, who arranged to meet Kotick at Morton's Steakhouse in Costa Mesa, California, right near Blizzard's offices. In a cavernous private room removed from potential prying eyes, the two spent hours talking about their respective goals and business philosophies.

Later, Morhaime went back to his executive team and confessed that he had been charmed. Kotick had said all the right things, assuring Morhaime that he had no problem with Blizzard's mission to be player-first and to refuse to release games until they were ready. Kotick promised that he didn't want to damage what made Blizzard such a big success. Morhaime told his lieutenants that he thought this would ultimately be a win for them, providing stability after years of turbulence under Vivendi. He saw Activision as an efficient, well-run company with several successful franchises that could help fill out the calendar in case Blizzard had to delay a game. He was also impressed by Kotick's Rolodex of contacts across the world, from politicians to celebrities. Kotick, meanwhile, was enticed by the growing appeal of Blizzard in China, one of the world's largest markets and an untapped audience for most of the video game industry.

The deal was in place a year later. Activision would merge with Vivendi's video game unit to form Activision Blizzard. Kotick would become CEO of the entire outfit while Morhaime would be CEO and president of Blizzard Entertainment. Vivendi would own 52 percent of the new entity, which was valued at $18.9 billion.

It seemed inconceivable, after rescuing Activision from bankruptcy all those years earlier, that Kotick would agree to relinquish control of his company. But the allure of *World of Warcraft*—which by the end of 2007 was approaching ten million subscribers—proved too strong for him to resist. He told press at the time that he couldn't figure out how to re-create Blizzard, so instead he would have to acquire it. *World of Warcraft* was a path to what Kotick appeared to value dearly: steady, predictable revenue growth.

Blizzard also gave Kotick access to more franchises with Hollywood potential. A decade earlier, Kotick had reluctantly moved Activision down to Los Angeles because that was where the talent was—"It sure wasn't for the quality of life," he told the *New York Times* in 1993—but in the years that followed, he appeared to grow enamored of the City of Angels. He befriended Hollywood moguls such as Dreamworks CEO Jeffrey Katzenberg and would later give an unexpectedly compelling performance as a baseball team owner in the movie *Moneyball*. "I fundamentally believe it was a core driver of Bobby, wanting to be a player in the Hollywood space," said Dusty Welch.

Kotick promised that Blizzard would retain its autonomy. In 2008, as the merger closed and he took his seat as CEO of Activision Blizzard, he said he believed his job was to give each of their subsidiaries the freedom to be creative. "If you look at any of the studios we have anywhere in the world...they all retain their own culture and identity," he told a reporter.

At the same time, observers couldn't help but notice that Kotick's business philosophy seemed to be diametrically opposed to the values that Blizzard had been preaching since the Silicon & Synapse days. Paul Reiche, founder of the game studio Toys for Bob, which Activision acquired in 2005, described it as an explicit divide. "That was really a fundamental, understood concept at Activision," Reiche said. "We weren't doing this for art, for the player first. We were creating a product to make money."

THIRTEEN

GROWING PAINS

n March 2008, just a few months after the merger was announced, Blizzard Entertainment packed up and left behind its UC Irvine offices for a new campus on Alton Parkway. Whereas Blizzard's previous offices had been muted and unadorned, this campus had a guarded entrance topped with a large iron gate featuring the company's name. Later, the mayor of Irvine would grant it a fitting new address: 1 Blizzard Way.

The move had been in the works for several years. After the release of *World of Warcraft*, Blizzard began running employee surveys and saw a consistent theme: Their games were so successful, so why was their office so bleak? In the past, Morhaime and his leadership team had been frugal when it came their workplace, but now it was clear that they needed an upgrade to retain talent.

The new campus was 240,000 square feet, lined with trees and gray office buildings flanking a gym, a volleyball court, and two basketball courts. Blizzard's executives set up a library and even a private museum that included the company's huge selection of awards, script pages from the *World of Warcraft* episode of *South Park,* and a letter from a soldier who had played the game while serving in Iraq. Later, Morhaime framed the 1991 loan agreement that he had struck with his grandmother: $15,000, interest free, to help him and Adham start Silicon & Synapse.

In the seventeen years since then, Blizzard had become the sprawling empire that the two of them once dreamed about. Since the release of *World of Warcraft,* the company had expanded into the thousands—not just in game development but in sales, marketing, finance, cinematics, and the countless customer service operatives who worked nonstop shifts to address players' problems. Less than a year after the move, executives were even dreaming up plans to design yet another, more sprawling campus. "We were supposed to be in those three buildings for five to ten years," said one person who worked there. "We outgrew them in three months."

As the company reckoned with its bulging head count, a group of Blizzard's top executives and managers gathered for an offsite meeting with a lofty goal: Figure out what Blizzard stood for. Under the guidance of an outside management guru, Morhaime and his team whittled down the company's philosophy to eight core values, each represented with a short and catchy phrase:

1. Gameplay First
2. Commit to Quality
3. Play Nice; Play Fair
4. Embrace Your Inner Geek
5. Learn & Grow
6. Every Voice Matters
7. Think Globally
8. Lead Responsibly

The values began to drive conversations throughout the company, leading developers to stamp "Play Nice; Play Fair" on top of a presentation or argue that they were correct about a design decision because they were committing to quality. That summer, Blizzard installed what would be the centerpiece of the campus for years to come: a twelve-foot, two-ton bronze statue of a snarling *Warcraft* orc riding a wolf, his axe held high. Circling the statue were eight plaques, each stamped with one of the values. *Gameplay First. Commit to Quality. Every Voice Matters.* Even the most cynical Blizzard employee would get nerd chills when they saw it.

Since reluctantly taking over as president of Blizzard ten years earlier, Morhaime had grown to embrace the role. He joined a CEO support group, meeting with cadres of chief executives from other industries to talk about strategic and personnel challenges. He pushed staff to embrace a single guiding mantra—if you serve players first, the profits will follow—and set up an "email Mike" program for employees to reach out with questions. "Mike Morhaime is as awesome as everyone says he is," said Jeremy Masker. "It didn't matter if you were associate QA or an executive producer. He treated everyone well."

Even as his role expanded, Morhaime continued to lean on Paul Sams to run the non-development parts of the company. During the merger process, the pair negotiated clauses in their contracts that would prevent them from being fired except under egregious circumstances, such as criminal activity, which they figured would help them protect Blizzard from corporate pressure when they were inevitably late on a game.

On July 10, 2008, the merger was finalized and Blizzard Entertainment became a subsidiary of Activision Blizzard. Veteran staff who were lucky enough to have equity received significant paydays, and everyone began eyeing Bobby Kotick, now their corporate boss, wondering what he had planned. Blizzard's employees weren't sure what to make of this shrewd businessman, but they did know they could rely on Morhaime and Sams to maintain the company's values. "It seemed like upper management at Blizzard was able to stave off any control or changes that'd happened when we got bought out before," said Jay Hathaway, an animator. "Besides, they're buying us because we're good. Why would they want to change anything?"

The answer was: they didn't. As Blizzard's employees grew into their new digs, few even noticed that they had changed corporate parents. "It was very hands off for a while," said Alex Brazie, a designer on *World of Warcraft*. Even if Activision's executives had wanted to come in and tear up the carpets, they were busy—the company's latest big game, *Call of Duty 4: Modern Warfare*, had been a monumental success, selling more than ten million copies and turning into the best-selling game of 2007. Soon Kotick would be involved in a nasty legal dispute with *Call of Duty*'s creators, whom he fired after accusing them of breaching their contracts, which occupied much of his attention.

There was no need to get involved with Blizzard because *World of Warcraft* remained, by some estimates, the most lucrative video game ever made. By the end of 2008, eleven and a half million people were paying monthly to play *World of Warcraft*. In other words, the land of Azeroth had a larger population than countries like New Zealand, Norway, and Greece.[8] During the four years that *World of Warcraft* had been in operation, the game had become a second home for its players, who met friends and future spouses, raced to complete new raids, and organized in-game protests when they weren't happy with Blizzard's decisions.

---

8   Every time the game surpassed the population of a new country, *World of Warcraft* designer John Staats would send out a taunting email. "In your face, Estonia!" he recalled writing. "Suck it, Switzerland."

Despite taking place in a realm full of orcs and sorcerers, *World of Warcraft* became a hotbed of real-life sociological and economic questions. The in-game currency, gold, became so valuable that outside websites popped up to facilitate buying and selling it for real cash—a violation of the game's terms of service, but there were too many offenders for Blizzard to possibly quash them all. A string of companies, mainly in China, hired workers to spend all day battling monsters for gold that they would then sell to other players, mainly in the United States. These so-called gold farmers became a perpetual presence in *World of Warcraft* for many years, despite Blizzard's attempts to whack-a-mole them.[9]

Epidemiologists also had a field day with *World of Warcraft* thanks to a raid boss that could infect players with a contagious, debilitating virus. The effect was meant to be contained within the raid, but a programming oversight led to the disease escaping, leaving corpses strewn across Azeroth. "People were scrambling to deal with it," said programmer David Ray. Much later, the United States Centers for Disease Control and Prevention would contact Blizzard for their data on how people behaved during this in-game pandemic—after all, *World of Warcraft* was a more useful case study than any mathematical model.

In the past, Blizzard had developed games the traditional way: finish a product, then move to the next one. But because players were now paying a monthly fee, they expected *World of Warcraft* to receive a never-ending stream of content: new dungeons, monsters, areas, and stories. The first expansion, *The Burning Crusade*, came out in January 2007 to critical acclaim. By the time they had moved to the new campus, Team 2 was in the thick of development on *Wrath of the Lich*

---

9   One gold-farming company, IGE, was briefly helmed by the right-wing firebrand Steve Bannon, who would later play an outsize role in US politics as a strategist to Donald Trump. One IGE operation profiled in *Wired* magazine was said to force its employees to work eighty-four hours a week for about $4 per day.

King, an expansion that would continue the story of Arthas, the fallen hero of *Warcraft III*. For many of Blizzard's developers, *Wrath of the Lich King* represented the company at the peak of its powers. "At that point we had everything figured out," said Kris DeMeza, a designer on the game. "We were more confident in making expansions and knowing what they could be."

Each new update brought in more subscriptions, and Team 2 turned into an ivory tower on Blizzard's campus. As the money rolled in and the numbers went up, *World of Warcraft*'s top designers and producers became geek celebrities. Every fall at BlizzCon, which was growing larger every year, fans would come up to *World of Warcraft* developers to ask for autographs and share stories. "When people come up to you and tell you how the game has changed their life or saved their life, you really feel a missionary kind of experience," said Chris Kaleiki, a designer.

But this newfound fame and fortune also impacted some of Blizzard's staff in less virtuous ways. "Success like that has the power to change people," said Shawn Carnes, a designer. "When millions turn into billions, everything changes."

■　■　■

Blizzard in the 1990s had felt like a frat house: almost entirely men, working together during the day and playing games or partying at night, occasionally getting into drunken antics or fistfights. By the mid-2000s, Blizzard had evolved: now it was more like a whole college campus.

The renowned video game company entered a tweenlike state of maturation as it aimed to become a proper company, with codified HR policies and more women joining every day. Within the next few years, women would make up about 20 percent of Blizzard's staff, which was also the industry average. "It is the sad reality of this industry," said DeMeza, one of the few women on the *World of Warcraft* team. "It is no secret, and everybody will tell you, that Blizzard was a boys' club at the time."

Still, both men and women felt like there was nowhere else like Blizzard—and many of them were thrilled to come to work every day. New employees would walk onto the campus and declare that they would spend the rest of their lives there. If you were a geek who had grown up in the twentieth century, when comic books and video games were associated with misfits and social outcasts, working at Blizzard was like finding your tribe—a place where you didn't have to hide your nerdy pastimes to maintain your place in the social hierarchy. If anything, the opposite was true: Having an encyclopedic knowledge of *Final Fantasy* lore or a massive collection of *Batman* comics was a sign you were one of them. "There used to be a saying," said one customer service representative. "A bad day at Blizzard is better than a good day everywhere else."

Employees frequently wore T-shirts and hoodies emblazoned with the blue Blizzard logo. At the office they gathered for D&D nights, workout sessions, and art groups, and then on weekends they met up for barbecues and surf clubs. They were granted custom trophies based on their tenure at the company. At five years, they'd get a sword and an elaborate ceremony that felt almost like an initiation. Ten years was a shield; fifteen years was a ring; and later, when the company turned twenty, employees who had spent two decades of their lives at Blizzard would score an ornate crown modeled after the Lich King's helmet. Loyal employees had an expression—"bleed Blizzard blue"—that was easy to imagine being chanted at a college football stadium. Some staff would even rent out apartments within walking distance of the office that they called the Blizzard dorms.

But this dedication to the brand could also be weaponized, and new employees were expected to put up with practices that they might not have accepted at other shops. Blizzard often hired people one rung on the corporate ladder below where they might land elsewhere in the industry, telling them that a senior developer at, say, Ubisoft was the equivalent of a midlevel developer at Blizzard. Salaries were still lower than those at competing companies, with the promise that profit-sharing checks would help close the gap, but the bonus system was opaque and byzantine. "To this day I couldn't tell you the process," said Shawn Carnes, "and I was a fucking manager."

Later, in a push for more transparency, the company began telling employees their target bonus numbers ahead of each year, and many who received five- or six-figure checks found themselves even more loyal to Blizzard. But they also found a culture that was stratified into two tiers: game developers and non–game developers. Those who worked on *Warcraft* and *StarCraft* received better perks and swag than their colleagues on support teams, while people in divisions such as Battle.net or marketing found that their priorities were secondary. This classification was by design—Paul Sams liked to say that nobody under him would even have jobs without the developers—but it also led to bitter feelings. "An effective caste system emerged," said business manager Vlad Coho. "It was a real division between developers and everyone else."

And, as on a college campus, hormones raged across Blizzard, where it seemed like the entire company was part of one big incestuous relationship. A practice discouraged in other corporate atmospheres seemed to be rampant in Irvine. "Everyone was either married to or dating someone else at Blizzard," said one woman who joined the company around this time. "Why would you mix the two?"[10]

Nearly every top executive at Blizzard was involved with someone

---

10 So many Blizzard employees dated and married one another that while reporting for this book, I would interview someone who worked there only to then learn that I had already talked to their spouse, who also worked there. This happened on three—three!—different occasions.

lower than them at the company, including Morhaime, Sams, and Metzen. The executives and their partners signed paperwork, called love contracts, declaring that the relationships were consensual and that they would avoid conflicts of interest. But in some cases, these relationships still became messy for everyone involved. Frank Pearce, Blizzard's first employee and now one of the company's senior executives, split with his wife, who also worked at Blizzard, and dated a woman in customer service, many rungs below him. He and Lisa Pearce, a manager in the business department, divorced in 2007. She would wind up staying at the company for another four years, maintaining what she said was "a good working relationship" with her ex-husband once they'd finalized their divorce. But, she said, "it was awkward for a lot of different reasons." Years later, Frank Pearce would wind up partnering with a third woman at Blizzard.

Women at Blizzard sometimes found themselves fending off unwanted advances when they were trying to do their jobs. Conventionally attractive women would be greeted by lines of men waiting to introduce themselves while managers, especially in lower-level departments like QA and customer service, felt comfortable hitting on employees who directly reported to them—after all, they argued, the bosses had done it.

The company was hiring more women but seemed to have trouble treating those women equitably. It would be years before the company implemented standard policies like parental leave and lactation rooms. And sometimes, as one couple learned, the blurring of professional and personal life at Blizzard could have severe repercussions.

■　■　■

Anissa Housley and Jeremy Wood first met in a *World of Warcraft* guild for Blizzard employees. Wood, the guild leader, was a programmer who had worked on the game during the early days, while

Housley didn't work at Blizzard but was married to J. Allen Brack, *World of Warcraft's* top producer. Housley and Wood found that they had a lot in common: they both liked rock climbing, they were both introverted—during parties at Brack's and Housley's house, they would go off and play *Guitar Hero* while everybody else was drinking—and they were both unhappy in their marriages. After realizing they had feelings for each other, Housley and Wood made plans to leave their spouses—an ugly situation rendered even uglier because Wood's wife was pregnant.

It was a messy personal knot that might have been left to divorce proceedings and friend-circle gossip if not for the fact that Brack was one of Blizzard's most powerful developers. Wood said he suddenly found himself iced out at work and that he was placed on a Performance Improvement Plan for failing to produce results, "which was completely drummed up," he said. Colleagues who had worked with him for years would avoid making eye contact when he passed them on campus, he said. He was advised by a family lawyer not to leave the company for financial reasons, so he stuck around, trying not to contact Brack. "While I think what he did was reprehensible, his anger and resentment were understandable," Wood said. After floundering for two more years, Wood was fired.

The event was indicative of the uglier side of Blizzard's culture, where wronging a powerful person outside of the office could make it more difficult to sustain a career. There were other complicating factors: Wood had a reputation for being abrasive and a history of being rude to colleagues, and some friends undoubtedly cut ties with him because he left his wife while she was pregnant. But the couple also believed that Wood's career at Blizzard was derailed because of their relationship choices. "It's the fact that our normal human issues became a Blizzard professional issue that made it weird and damaging," said Housley.

■　■　■

On November 13, 2008, Blizzard released *World of Warcraft: Wrath of the Lich King*. It was critically acclaimed and became the fastest-selling computer game of all time, moving 2.8 million copies in just 24 hours. (The previous record, 2.4 million copies, was set by *The Burning Crusade*.) On an earnings call a few months later, Bobby Kotick bragged about the company's ability to weather the ongoing global economic recession with "predictable and stable franchises that have served us well over long periods of time." For Blizzard, that would mean a brand-new release just about every year, mostly involving the company's tentpole franchises: *Warcraft*, *StarCraft*, and *Diablo*.

The video game industry was growing exponentially. Back in 1997, games generated around $5 billion in revenue; by the end of 2008, they had leaped to $21 billion, according to data from analysts at the NPD Group. For a thriving Blizzard, it made sense to work on as many projects as possible. Team 1 was developing a sequel to *StarCraft*. Team 2 moved right from *Wrath of the Lich King* to the next *World of Warcraft* expansion, which would be called *Cataclysm*. Blizzard formed Team 3 to work on *Diablo III* after Blizzard North shuttered and the project moved down to Irvine, and a new unit, the mysterious Team 4, was quietly incubating a secret game called *Titan*.

But Blizzard's "when it's ready" philosophy seemed to be holding up games for longer than ever before, in large part because *World of Warcraft* was sucking up so many of the company's resources. Back in the 1990s, Blizzard had developed a reputation for taking as long as necessary to make video games—but that meant missing Christmas by a week or shipping in March instead of December. Now it could mean slipping for years.

FOURTEEN

BASEBALL 2.0

I n South Korea, *StarCraft* wasn't just a video game—it was a national sport. Koreans frequently gathered to watch the best players compete—first in small groups, then in packed arenas and even on television. Companies like Samsung sponsored professional *StarCraft* teams, while a player named Lim Yo-hwan, best known by his handle, BoxeR, became the Korean version of Michael Jordan. "These players were the equivalent of K-pop stars," said Elaine Di Iorio, a director of business development at Blizzard. "Girls were yelling and screaming. It was crazy."

Back in 2004, this success had presented the developers on Blizzard's Team 1 with an odd dilemma. From a financial and creative perspective, a sequel to *StarCraft* made sense, but how could they possibly live up to a game that players considered perfect? "It would be extremely difficult to surpass those expectations, and not ship something that was disappointing," said Tim Campbell, a designer. At first they hoped to put together a quick sequel, but just as *StarCraft II* began development, Team 1's programmers and artists were pulled over to help out with *World of Warcraft*, grinding momentum to a halt. For the next two years, *StarCraft II* remained on Blizzard's back burner as the company scrambled to fix bugs and churn out content.

By the end of 2006, Team 1 was back intact, working on a new graphical engine for their sequel that would improve on what *Warcraft III* had accomplished. "Games were looking so different by then that we couldn't just make it look like the original," said Jay Hathaway, an animator. "We have to do it in 3D but it still has to feel like *StarCraft*." One of the team's first tasks was to remake the original *StarCraft* in the new *StarCraft II* engine so they could get a feel for the technical differences. They realized that they could now play around with depth and height, creating units that would never have been viable in the first game, like the colossus, a hulking robotic walker that could plod up and down cliffs. "There was a lot of tech that just wasn't possible in a 2D game," said artist Phill Gonzales.

The *StarCraft II* team had no shortage of ideas for new units, but experimenting too much risked alienating *StarCraft* obsessives. Under Blizzard vice president Rob Pardo and director Dustin Browder, the team came up with a handful of mantras for the game. One tenet, adapted from legendary *Civilization* designer Sid Meier, was that one-third of the units should return from the old game, one-third should be modified versions, and one-third should be brand-new. But some members of the team—whether they were Blizzard veterans or younger employees who had grown up playing *StarCraft*—struggled to make decisions that moved too far away from the first game. In meetings, Pardo liked to tell the team that what baseball was to the United States, *StarCraft* was to South Korea. What they were making, then, was baseball 2.0. They needed to make an even better version of one of the most iconic games of all time. Good luck.

In the spring of 2007, executives and developers flew to Seoul,

South Korea, for the Blizzard Worldwide Invitational, a smaller-scale, international version of BlizzCon. They took over the Olympic Park, where attendees could line up for developer signings and take rides on hot air balloons adorned with *World of Warcraft* art. Thousands of fans swarmed the arena to watch a short teaser trailer, which spotlighted a gruff Terran marine putting on his gear and proclaiming what everybody in the crowd was thinking now that it had been nearly a decade since the first *StarCraft* came out. "Hell," he said. "It's about time."

■ ■ ■

Security was tight when Adam Hayes first showed up at Blizzard's campus a year later, in the summer of 2008. He had to check in at the guarded steel gate, walk to the front office building, and then wait for his new boss to come down and escort him to his desk. When he looked around and saw that the lobby's walls were covered in snapshots from Blizzard's history, he choked up. Hayes had spent countless hours playing *StarCraft* in college—conquering the campaign, battling other players in high-stakes duels, and even creating his own maps using the game's robust editor, which made him realize that maybe he could be a professional video game designer. He'd spent six years at Electronic Arts working on real-time strategy games that aimed to be as influential as *StarCraft*, and now he was standing on campus at Blizzard Entertainment, about to become a level designer on the sequel. He looked over at the photos and realized that some were from the original release of *StarCraft* ten years earlier. "I remember getting goose bumps," Hayes said.

When he arrived at the Team 1 building, Hayes was blown away. At his last job, they had put up a few video game posters—here, the walls were completely painted with scenes from *StarCraft*, hand-drawn by longtime Blizzard artist Sam Didier. "Walking through the halls for the first time was exhilarating," said Hayes. "You could tell they were very proud of what they'd created." Hayes learned that *StarCraft II*'s multiplayer was in solid shape, mixing old units like Terran siege tanks with new ones like the Protoss stalker, a quadrupedal robot that could teleport short distances. There were very few single-player missions completed, but there was plenty of time for that. "The philosophy was: Let's nail the multiplayer, then we'll build the campaign," said Hayes. The only problem was that Chris Metzen had come up with way more story than could fit in a single game, and there were plans for upward of thirty missions per race—three times the scale of the first *StarCraft*. "When I got there and saw what they had planned, I'm thinking: There's no way we're going to do this for all the factions in one game," said Hayes.

Inspired by Valve's smash hit *Half-Life 2*, leadership proposed that they split *StarCraft II* into three games. The first, *Wings of Liberty*, would include the Terran campaign and a handful of other features, like multiplayer and a map editor. Then they'd put out the Zerg campaign with *Heart of the Swarm* and conclude the trilogy with the Protoss in *Legacy of the Void*. It seemed like a natural split, and each new release would be an opportunity to continue refining the multiplayer and other features. Players weren't pleased when they first heard that they'd have to wait years for the complete experience, but the developers knew that the only other options were either scaling back their ambitions or working impossible hours. "Splitting it was the right decision," said designer Jason Huck.

By the mid-2000s, video game storytelling had evolved in significant ways. Games like *Mass Effect* boasted detailed 3D models for their characters, who could now demonstrate hand gestures and crinkled eyes as they spoke. Blizzard wanted to take a similar approach for *StarCraft II*, so the company's ever-growing cinematics department was tasked with building elaborate short films that would unfold during the game. Between *Wings of Liberty* missions, cutscenes would show a cigarette-smoking Raynor chatting with members of his crew or banshee jets firing missiles at swarms of menacing Zerg. This led to some painful growing moments as the *StarCraft II* team and the cinematics department learned how to work together—a tension that would become increasingly common at Blizzard. The filmmakers in cinematics wanted to make their shots look as visually striking as possible, even if that meant building units that didn't look exactly like their in-game counterparts. "We'd have this pushback with the cinematic department over their designs," said Phill Gonzales. "You got rid of the archon's blades? What's going on?"

Newcomers to the *StarCraft II* team had to navigate these politics, but they also quickly found out what made Blizzard stand out from other companies: a willingness to let games simmer, like chili sitting on the stove, as Browder described it. Blizzard's developers would iterate over and over, polishing some ideas and discarding others. Jason Huck, who had previously worked at companies that prioritized hitting deadlines, found it difficult to acclimate to an atmosphere where he didn't just have one chance to design a mission. "I had to develop the confidence to say, 'No, this sucks, I'm going to start over,'" Huck said. "It's easy to get really attached to something, to guard it until it's perfect... It's more important to get your ideas out quick, iterate. That's really how you refine stuff to the quality level we were aspiring for."

In the summer of 2009, *StarCraft II* was nearing the finish line when another obstacle emerged: Battle.net 2.0, the next iteration of Blizzard's online service, which was planned to coincide with *Wings of Liberty* but needed more time. Engineers from across the company relocated to the Battle.net department to help finish the service, while

StarCraft II's artists and designers were suddenly granted months of extra time to polish the game.

When Morhaime called Kotick to tell him that Blizzard planned to delay the next *StarCraft* a year, he was shocked when the new boss asked how he planned to make up for the missing revenue. Back in the Vivendi days, slipping a year might not have been a huge deal, because Blizzard had been such a small part of the broader conglomerate, but now, the bump could have a significant impact on Activision Blizzard's stock price. It was like Blizzard had gone from small fish in big pond to big fish in small pond—except the pond was full of investor piranhas who expected revenue growth every quarter.

Morhaime had to offer an explanation to shareholders and analysts. "We recognize that we only get one chance to make a first impression," Morhaime said on a quarterly earnings call in August 2009. "While we could rush into beta and launch an inferior game and service experience this year, fixing that experience over time, our track record has proven that there is a far greater value for us and for our players in making sure that the experience is great right from the start."

Executives at Blizzard knew delaying the game was the right decision, no matter how Wall Street reacted. In February 2010, *StarCraft II: Wings of Liberty* received a public beta that lasted several months, allowing players to mess around with multiplayer and build excitement for the full release. "Everyone expected Blizzard's 'when it's ready' philosophy to pay off in terms of polish and consistency and the beta is proof that this approach can pay real dividends," wrote an IGN critic. When *StarCraft II* came out that July, it sold three million copies in a month and was widely praised for feeling innovative while at the same time retaining what made the first game great.

In South Korea, Blizzard put on a marketing blitz, advertising the new game on television and even, in one ostentatious move, on the side of two 747 jet planes. But something about the release felt off. *StarCraft II* didn't seem to be resonating with Koreans as much as its predecessor. In 2000, you'd have found people playing *StarCraft* in every PC bang in the country; a decade later, Koreans were flocking to other games. In the months following the release of *StarCraft II: Wings of Liberty*, it became clear that it hadn't even come close to surpassing baseball. Many Koreans were still sticking to the first game.

Perhaps Blizzard should have seen this coming. After all, it was locked in a cold war against one of South Korea's most powerful organizations.

■　■　■

Ten years earlier, with *StarCraft* on the rise, South Korea's government created an official division called the Korea e-Sports Association, or KeSPA, with the authority to regulate competitive leagues for video games. For the next few years, as *StarCraft* evolved into South Korea's national pastime, KeSPA handled the game's professional scene as it saw fit. Blizzard, preoccupied with *World of Warcraft*, didn't pay much attention—Morhaime and crew were just thrilled to see how many people were buying and playing *StarCraft*.

But in 2007, the landscape changed when KeSPA signed a deal with Korean cable networks, reportedly worth around $1.3 million, to broadcast *StarCraft* matches on television. The money was insignificant for a company as large as Blizzard, but the deal sparked other concerns. Video game broadcasting existed in a legal gray area that didn't yet have clear precedent either in Korea or the United States, and Blizzard's executives wanted to ensure that *StarCraft* didn't somehow fall into the public domain. They'd already seen the trademark for their online platform, Battle.net, get rejected in South Korea, where it was used as a generic term to refer to playing games online.

The executives commissioned the consulting firm McKinsey to conduct some research, and the recommendation helped solidify their perspective: They should charge a licensing fee for TV broadcasts. It was too late for *StarCraft*, but they would not allow South Korea to have free rein with *StarCraft II*. For the next three years, Blizzard and KeSPA held a series of on-and-off negotiations that grew increasingly contentious, peaking during one meeting where, according to several attendees, a representative for KeSPA looked at Blizzard's Paul Sams and declared: "We're FIFA. You guys are just the fucking soccer ball."

From KeSPA's perspective, Blizzard's demands made no sense. Why would anyone try to copyright a sport? Did the inventor of basketball get royalties from the NBA? KeSPA had built the *StarCraft* scene in South Korea—and nobody was really making all that much money from it in the first place.

In 2010, shortly before *StarCraft II*'s release, negotiations reached a standstill. Morhaime wrote an open letter to Korean gamers declaring that they had cut off talks with KeSPA because the organization "did not recognize our intellectual property rights." Instead, Blizzard signed a deal with a different company, called GOMTV, for the broadcast rights to its games in South Korea. KeSPA fired back that Blizzard's demands had been unreasonable and began blitzing the company in the Korean press, even forbidding its professional *StarCraft* players from competing in the sequel. South Korea gave *StarCraft II* a restrictive "Adults Only" rating, which Blizzard executives suspected was also the work of KeSPA. The two organizations entered a legal dispute, and Sams sniped in one press conference that it was "unfortunate that the esports industry in Korea is lagging behind other industries in recognition of intellectual property rights."

In 2012, five years after the battle began, Blizzard and KeSPA finally made peace, negotiating a threeway deal with GOMTV to collaborate on tournaments and TV broadcasts, but the damage was already done. *StarCraft II* sold millions of copies but would never hit the same highs as its predecessor in South Korea, preventing it from truly meeting the company's expectations.

Yet it was still a great game, and to the people who ran Blizzard, that was what mattered most. Everything else would take care of itself, Morhaime believed.

FIFTEEN

THE CURSE OF SUCCESS

S tarCraft II wasn't the only Blizzard game to struggle under the shadow of its predecessor. In the mid-2000s, as Team 1 tried to figure out how to make a sequel to baseball, a new team was facing a similar challenge.

When Morhaime and his executive circle decided to shutter Blizzard North in the summer of 2005, they started what would be called Team 3, an internal Irvine group dedicated to making *Diablo III*. They needed a new director—someone who could fill Dave Brevik's shoes—so Rob Pardo tracked down Jay Wilson, a veteran game designer with a diverse résumé. Wilson had started off as a hobbyist, then bounced around several game studios before winding up at Relic Entertainment in Vancouver, Canada, where he led the design of *Warhammer 40K: Dawn of War*, a strategy game that many of Blizzard's staff loved.

When Pardo reached out, Wilson was flattered but reluctant. Relocating his family from Canada to California would be a huge pain, and he wasn't confident enough in his abilities to think that he could be a lead designer at Blizzard. In response, Pardo suggested that he and his family come down to Orange County for BlizzCon. Blizzard flew them all out and paid for Wilson's wife and kids to visit Disneyland while he was wined and dined. He met Chris Metzen, who had already become a bona fide geek celebrity, with his rock 'n' roll outfits and gravelly voice. Metzen looked at him and boomed: *Jay Wilson? Come work for us.* "I didn't know he knew who I was," recalled Wilson, "much less that he was excited about me coming to work here."

In January 2006, Wilson started at Blizzard and inherited an unusual situation—an unfinished project that had been in development elsewhere, along with a handful of artists and engineers who had been forced to relocate four hundred miles to continue working on it. "It was a culture shock," said Anthony Rivero, one of those artists. "Blizzard North was pretty freewheeling, with a very flat structure. Blizzard South was definitely more corporate." Wilson was shocked to find that former Blizzard North employees were accustomed to offering feedback on just about everything. "They came down with this idea that everything we do must be a unanimous vote," said Wilson. "I'm thinking: 'How did you guys do anything?'"

Perhaps the biggest difference between the two companies was how they approached art direction. Blizzard North's artists generally leaned toward gloomy aesthetics with lots of shadows and dark colors, while the developers at Blizzard preferred lighter, stylized graphics. During the development of the first two *Diablo* games, this had been an ongoing point of contention—Blizzard North would push hard in gritty directions, often making lurid artistic choices, and Irvine would reel them in. Now, as Wilson joined Team 3 to begin conceiving and creating a playable prototype for *Diablo III*, the former Blizzard North artists went with what they knew: grays and browns. "Our first dungeon really had no color in it whatsoever," said Wilson. "I wasn't crazy about that, but I was also fine with it."

Wilson and the *Diablo III* team spent six months working on this dungeon—a dingy labyrinth full of skeletons and beasts. Then they took the game to a Blizzard company show-and-tell, where a room full of developers observed the footage with apathy. "The feedback we got from the company was: 'I think this looks boring,'" said Wilson. "My concern at the time was not even: Are we going to be able to make a better game than *Diablo II*? It was: *My god, are we going to be able to make a game at all?*"

Wilson, who had just overhauled his entire life to work on the next *Diablo*, now had to figure out how to prevent the game from falling apart. The team brought in a new art director with the goal of creating a distinct visual style for *Diablo III*, eventually coming up with a look that featured more colorful monsters and vistas—not quite as vibrant as *World of Warcraft*, but brighter than the first two *Diablo* games. The team built a new prototype showcasing the wizard class and brought it to another Blizzard show-and-tell, this time leaving their colleagues impressed.

On June 28, 2008, Blizzard announced *Diablo III* to a crowd of hollering fans at an event in Paris, France. Although people were generally excited for the game, they grumbled that the art was too bright and cartoony. One internet petition, signed by some fifty thousand people, begged Blizzard for "a true sequel to *Diablo II* that is graphically coherent with the *Diablo* universe it belongs to." What fans didn't know was that *Diablo III*'s art style had become the fulcrum of a bigger political battle within Blizzard. For many veteran employees, including some of the company's top executives, making it feel different was the whole point. Now that Blizzard North was gone, old-timers like Pardo, Metzen, and Didier had an opportunity to fashion a *Diablo* game in their own style—no matter what fans, or even their own artists, thought. "I think it was a massive mistake," said Chris Haga, a former Blizzard North artist who moved south for *Diablo III*. "It was not smart to completely pivot on the art style."

Later that summer, *Diablo III*'s new art director quit, but the aesthetics were already in place and wouldn't change again. To Blizzard, the internet complaints were just noise—they weren't going to make a *Diablo* game that was nothing but drab grays and browns. "The game we had before, the unhappy people on the internet probably would've liked the look more," said Wilson. "But that game would have never been made."

■ ■ ■

In the years since its release, *Diablo II* had become enshrined in the pantheon of video game history, ranking in the top of just about every magazine's "greatest game" list. What was remarkable was its longevity—on a random day in 2009, nearly a decade after its release, you might find tens of thousands of players going on Mephisto runs or hunting for Stones of Jordan. But the exact secret behind *Diablo II*'s success was difficult to pinpoint.[11] *Diablo* almost felt like a chemical formula: every atom, from the dank atmosphere to the *clink* of gold, seemed integral to the final product, and if you took one element away, it might become something else entirely. This presented a problem for a team of artists and designers who were tasked with making a sequel. Every design conversation became a debate: How did *Diablo II* do this? Shouldn't *we* do it that way, too?

Diablo III's art team, now a mix of new artists and ex–Blizzard North employees, was particularly vociferous in pushing back against many of the things Wilson wanted to do. There were arguments over

---

11 Even Blizzard North's founders, Brevik and the Schaefers, couldn't replicate their old hits. After their dramatic resignation, they went on to release a spiritual successor to *Diablo* called *Hellgate: London* that was criticized for feeling undercooked and monotonous. Later, they found more success with a series of *Diablo*-like games called *Torchlight*, but none of them resonated with people quite like *Diablo II*.

what monsters were allowed to be in the game (only demons, some argued), whether there should be magic (no), and whether humor should be banned (yes). A frustrated Wilson found himself digging up screenshots from *Diablo II* to prove to his staff that the classic game had dark humor, plenty of humanoid enemies, and, yes, even some bright colors. "It was very hard to make decisions because somebody always had a reason it wasn't *Diablo*," said Wilson. Yet he could sympathize with his colleagues, who had been dropped into an impossible situation. "You put them in the double-boiler pressure pot of: you have to do better than *Diablo II* and you also are an employee at Blizzard, where every other person in the company is also the best in the world at what they do," he said.

Chris Haga, the former Blizzard North artist, was frustrated for another reason: He had played a ton of *Diablo II* while many of his colleagues hadn't. He would grow agitated in meetings when designers made suggestions that felt at odds with what he had loved about the first two games. "You can play *Diablo II* for ten hours and feel like you understand it," said Haga, "but you don't." When Blizzard brought in potential new hires to interview with the *Diablo III* team, Haga would nix anyone who wasn't a fan of the series. "They eventually stopped asking me to come to interviews," he said.

In 2011, as *Diablo III* approached beta, members of the team realized in horror that it had been in the works for a decade. To some degree this sluggish pace was unavoidable—each of the game's five classes took an entire year to finish—but they were also still haunted by the specter of *Diablo II*, which made every creative decision take longer than anyone could have possibly anticipated. "My argument was always that the best, fastest way to ruin something is stagnation," said Wilson. "If you just make a copy of *Diablo II* that's in 3D, that's not going to be better than *Diablo II*—it's going to be worse."

There were two big aspects of *Diablo III* that Wilson suspected might be controversial. One was that the game would be online-only, in contrast to its predecessors, which had featured both online and offline modes.[12] In subsequent years it would become more common for video games to require an internet connection, but in 2011, it was a shocking notion.

The second controversial decision revolved around trading. For *Diablo II*, Blizzard North had created an in-game bartering system, but there was no standardized economy, and cheats were rampant. To try to solve these problems, players created third-party marketplaces, but the scams only grew more pervasive, and Blizzard couldn't control or stop them.

Diablo III would offer an official solution: an auction house in which players could buy and sell items on Battle.net, which the company could keep secure. To put it together, Rob Pardo called upon his strategic initiatives department, a group of business experts responsible for special projects and analyses throughout the company—sort of like an in-house version of McKinsey.

Vlad Coho, a Wharton business school graduate, was the analyst tasked with the auction house. As he read through economic books and mapped out a plan, he began to suspect that having an in-game currency wouldn't be enough. If players could buy and sell items exclusively using *Diablo* gold, a third-party marketplace would inevitably emerge to allow those players to swap that gold for real money—the same phenomenon that had spawned gold farming in *World of Warcraft*. "Real money became a necessary part," said Coho. The company would take a small fee from each transaction, which

---

12 *StarCraft II: Wings of Liberty* also faced controversy when it ditched local area network (LAN) connections and went online-only for multiplayer (although you could still play the single-player mode offline). During one notable tournament, a dropped connection led to the rowdy crowd chanting, "We want LAN! We want LAN!"

"was not meant to be a moneymaker for Blizzard," Coho said. "It was just meant to solve the problem of trading."

Coho spent a year and a half working on the project, studying economies and researching anti-money laundering laws in different countries. He was proud of what he'd accomplished—"the first game ever to offer an open-loop commerce trading system"—and when *Diablo III* came out, he thought players would eventually grow to appreciate the auction house. Maybe some of them would even make a few bucks.

■ ■ ■

Diablo III was released on May 15, 2012. As throngs of players across the world eagerly tried to log in to the game and start slashing through demons, they were greeted by a vague message: *The servers are busy at this time. Please try again later. (Error 37)* Nobody knew what "Error 37" meant or why they kept seeing it, but it soon became an internet meme—a symbol of the greed and obstinance of making a game that was online-only.

Like with *World of Warcraft* eight years earlier, Blizzard had again underestimated how many millions of people were going to play the game on launch. "We put a queuing system in at the beginning," said Jeremy Masker, who had once camped out in Blizzard's parking lot to get a customer service job and had now worked his way up to be *Diablo III*'s producer of live operations. If the authentication servers were overloaded, people would be placed in a line, and then they'd be gradually allowed into the game. "Problem was, there was a cap on the number of people who could be in the queue," Masker said. "When we filled up the queue, we crashed the system, and caused even more problems for ourselves."

Masker and the rest of the live-ops team spent the next few days in crisis mode. Blizzard brought in cots so they didn't have to leave campus between shifts in the company's war room, a giant office full of server monitors and metrics, where they gathered engineers to try to fix the many technical issues that had gone wrong. The energy was high, the team was focused, and the mood was surprisingly jovial. In the war room, they didn't have to battle over creative decisions or worry about the weighty expectations of *Diablo II*—they just had to find and fix problems. "It's almost like an Apollo 13 sort of atmosphere," Masker said.

After a week or so, Blizzard's team had fixed most of the server issues. But as the game became more accessible, players began to realize that it had more fundamental problems. The difficulty system, which mirrored *Diablo II*, was too punishing. Legendary loot dropped infrequently and didn't seem to be as powerful as lower-tier items, while useless gray armor appeared all the time. Blizzard had failed to test *Diablo III*'s endgame at a large enough scale, and Wilson's team was now learning about some of these problems for the first time. "It's easy now if you play the game—you play it and you can see what's wrong," said Jason Bender, a designer. "While building it, it was hard to tell in the long view whether things were coming in at the right rate."

Players then began to realize that they could circumvent this stingy loot system by going to the auction house, which felt like a big, glaring cheat code for *Diablo III*. When the game seemed too hard and loot wasn't dropping quickly enough, all they had to do was click over and charge a few new pieces of gear on their credit card. The intentions behind the system may have been noble, but to players, it now seemed manipulative.

On August 19, a few months after release, David Brevik spoke publicly about *Diablo III*, criticizing its loot system in an interview with a video game website and noting that "some of the decisions they have made are not the decisions I would make." The next day, Chris Haga posted a link to the interview on his Facebook page, writing that he felt like he was "thrown under a bus." Members of the *Diablo III* team expressed their solidarity in response, including Wilson, who chimed in with: "Fuck that loser." Someone took a screenshot and posted it on a gaming forum, and soon enough the internet was full of people screaming that *Diablo III*'s director was a tactless jerk.

Wilson instantly regretted the comment, which he had written while drunk at a party in hopes of standing up for his colleagues. "I felt protective of the team, and posted that hoping it'd make them feel better," he said. But it was too late to do anything about it. The Facebook post had gone viral.

■　■　■

The first death threat was rattling enough. After a week, Wilson had received so many that he had to contact his local police department and even the Federal Bureau of Investigation, which marked several of the threats as credible and dangerous. "There were several people put on the no-fly list," Wilson said. He paid a digital security firm to purge his personal address from the internet and asked police to send extra patrols to his house. "My family was frightened whenever I wasn't home," he said. "If we had anyone come to the door at night, my wife would dial 9-1-1 and wait."

The messages had started arriving shortly after *Diablo III*'s release, when players began complaining about the state of the game. Some of the feedback was easy to ignore, like gripes that *Diablo III* was too short (it was roughly as long as the last game), but other issues, like the flawed item system, were already on Blizzard's list to fix. Wilson figured there would be plenty of time to address feedback and implement new systems in the months following release—after all, it took dozens of patches and a major expansion before *Diablo II* became the game that people remembered as an all-time classic. "I knew we were going to get some things wrong, but I thought the audience was going to stand by us to fix it," said Wilson. "We were told in no uncertain terms: 'You've destroyed *Diablo*. You're horrible people. You deserve to die. You should kill yourself, and if you don't, I will.'"

Wilson felt like a failure—like he had ruined a beloved video game series for millions of people—and by insulting Brevik, he turned himself into an even bigger target. Even the incredible financial success of *Diablo III*, which quickly outsold its predecessors, couldn't stop him from spiraling, and he began suffering from a mental breakdown whose effects wouldn't come to fruition until much later. For now, he decided he would leave the *Diablo* team and do something else at Blizzard, much to the dismay of many of his colleagues. "I was so sad when Jay left," said Travis Day, a designer. "He's a sincerely very good human being. He got a raw deal." Even the former Blizzard North staff who had battled endlessly with Wilson respected the work he had done. "Jay may be within the top ten best designers in the industry," said artist Julian Love.

Wilson moved over to Blizzard's secret *Titan* project for a few months, then began chatting with a colleague, Mike Booth, who was best known for leading design on the popular game *Left 4 Dead* and was now looking to join Blizzard full-time. Both had coincidentally come up with a similar idea for a new *Warcraft* game based on *Minecraft*, the popular survival game that allowed players to chop down trees and build elaborate structures. Wilson and Booth thought that maybe they could do to *Minecraft* what *World of Warcraft* had done to *EverQuest*: take the core idea, fix everything they didn't like about it, and give it the Blizzard polish.

The two of them pitched the game, which they called *Avalon*, and got the thumbs-up to start developing prototypes. But Wilson had been suppressing his depression and anxiety, and even the excitement of a new project couldn't stop it from bubbling back up. The internet threats and insults had never really stopped, and he'd been experimenting with alcohol and hard drugs to try to ease the pain. Contemplating suicide, Wilson took a sabbatical from Blizzard. "I realized I needed to lower the pressure I had on my life or I was going to lose my marriage and possibly lose my life," he said. He checked into a mental hospital and was later diagnosed as bipolar.

When he returned to the office, Wilson decided not to go back to *Avalon*—the project had evolved in ways he didn't love, and it would later be canceled. Instead, he joined the *World of Warcraft* team, where he worked on refining the decade-old combat to feel more energetic and satisfying. Wilson enjoyed his time on Team 2, although it was hard to envision staying there for the rest of his career. "It wasn't challenging enough in the long run," he said.

In 2016, four years after *Diablo III*, Wilson decided to leave Blizzard. His family no longer wanted to live in California, and he was feeling burnt out after everything he'd been through. Years later, gamers on Reddit and Twitter would still occasionally bring up his name as a symbol of *Diablo*'s flaws. He and his family moved to Portland, Oregon, where he took a long hiatus from the video game industry. Much later, he would team up with his former *Diablo* teammate Julian Love to start a new game company, but for now, he was done. *Diablo III* had taken its toll.

SIXTEEN

REDEMPTION

Years before Wilson left the *Diablo III* team, his boss Rob Pardo offered some words of wisdom. "You're going to get really good at making *Diablo*," Pardo told him, "right around the time you ship *Diablo*."

Pardo's advice proved prescient. Once *Diablo III* was out in the world, Wilson and his team could look at the game and understand exactly what it was. Experienced computer programmers often said the hardest part of writing code wasn't figuring out solutions—it was identifying the problems. Now, Blizzard's developers could clearly see the game's strengths, like the snappiness of combat, and pinpoint its weaknesses, like the unbalanced difficulty. By the summer of 2012, more than ten million people had bought *Diablo III*, which allowed the development team to lean on Blizzard's increasingly advanced analytics teams to collect player feedback and keep track of how they played, when they stopped, and where they ran into walls.

Most fans agreed that if you played the whole game just once, *Diablo III* made for a good time. It was what happened after you finished and kept playing—referred to as the endgame—that led to some issues. The difficulty ramped up quickly, the best gear only dropped sporadically, and it was too tempting to buy weapons at the auction house, which led cynics to wonder if Blizzard was trying to exploit them. Now, the *Diablo III* team had to decide how to move forward.

Morhaime offered a clear directive: stick with the game. Over the previous two decades, Adham's old vision had come to fruition— Blizzard had cultivated a brand so powerful that people probably would buy a box of rocks if the logo was attached. But Morhaime knew that reputation was a fragile thing. Every perceived failure would chip away at Blizzard's status as one of the world's top game developers, and despite *Diablo III*'s commercial and critical success, it had soured fans unlike any of the company's previous games. To win them back, Blizzard would dedicate all of Team 3's resources to making the game better.

Throughout 2012 they fixed bugs, adjusted character balance, and tried to address as many complaints as they could. They divvied the work into two categories: short-term fixes, which would be implemented through patches; and long-term fixes that would be part of *Diablo III*'s first expansion, *Reaper of Souls*. The more they assessed, the more they realized that *Reaper of Souls* would essentially make *Diablo III* feel like a new game. "By a year we were fully into changing everything," said lead designer Kevin Martens. *Reaper of Souls* would include a new class, a new area, and a host of features that they hoped would change the rhythm of *Diablo III*'s endgame.

Wilson was replaced by Josh Mosqueira, a veteran designer who had been leading an effort to bring *Diablo III* to consoles. Like Wilson, Mosqueira had come from Relic Entertainment and had been reluctant to take charge of a *Diablo* game. But he applied for the director job nonetheless, and by the end of 2012, with *Reaper of Souls* in production,

Mosqueira began overseeing Team 3. They had a plan, a new leader, and the resources to overhaul *Diablo III* in whatever way they saw fit. Now they just had to execute.

■ ■ ■

Morale on Team 3 was surprisingly high when Skye Chandler joined as a producer in the spring of 2013. It had been a year since Error 37 and the launch debacle, and *Reaper of Souls* was moving ahead at full speed. As a *Diablo* devotee who had started in QA and climbed through Blizzard's ranks, Chandler was relieved to find a group of developers who saw *Diablo III*'s flaws not as a catastrophe but as an opportunity for redemption. "The mood was: 'Chill, we're in this together,'" she said. "Let's make cool stuff."

Diablo III's new production director, John Hight, pushed the team to play the game regularly to understand how players might feel. They revised the difficulty system and devised features that spiced up the endgame, like Adventure Mode, which brought in new types of quests and dungeons. They brought in Travis Day, a designer from *World of Warcraft*, to lead what they were calling Loot 2.0: an item overhaul that would give players better, more relevant gear. "Working on *Reaper* was amazing," said Day. "It was an all-star MVP team." For game designers like John Yang, who joined the team to make *Diablo III*'s legendary weapons feel more powerful, it was a rewarding experience. "We knew we were making so many great improvements," Yang said.

But there was one lingering obstacle: the auction house. If the purpose of *Diablo III* was to hunt for the best gear to make your character as strong as possible, then having that gear available on a marketplace was always going to be at odds with that experience. Day and the other designers experimented with ways to circumvent the auction house, like a special tier for items that would prevent them from being sold, but they just kept running into the same problems. "It was fundamentally eroding the experience of *Diablo*," Day said.

During one monthly strategy meeting, *Diablo III*'s top developers met with Blizzard executives and began debating the pros and cons of the auction house. "Mike just let them all talk," said Jeremy Masker, the producer. "Eventually he said, 'We're going to do what's right for the players—shut it off.'" In the leadup to *Reaper of Souls*, Blizzard announced, to much fanfare, that it was removing the auction house from *Diablo III*. "*Diablo* is best experienced when, as a result of slaying monsters, you get better items that allow you to make your character more powerful," said systems designer Wyatt Cheng in the book *Blood, Sweat, and Pixels*.[13] "And if the activity that I do to make my character more powerful does not include killing monsters…then that's not a good place to be."

As they grew closer to finishing *Reaper of Souls*, Team 3 began talking about what was next. They had been operating under the belief that *Diablo III* would follow the *StarCraft II* model—one base game followed by two robust expansions—and they had even started brainstorming what the next expansion might look like. "We were looking at really big ideas, but nothing definitive yet," said writer Brian Kindregan. Then, during an all-hands meeting shortly before *Reaper of Souls* came out, they got news that vacuumed the energy out of the team: *Diablo III* would not get a second expansion. No matter what happened with *Reaper of Souls*, they were done. "Getting your next project canceled is scary," said Yang. There was no clear explanation as to why this was happening—Blizzard's executives were complimentary of their work on *Reaper of Souls* and said the decision was

---

13 Insert your own meme here—the Spider-Men pointing at each other, or maybe the one where Leonardo DiCaprio points at a TV.

not made because of any sort of failure on their part. "None of the answers met the sniff test," said Masker.

What they didn't know was that a host of factors was working against the *Diablo* team. Morhaime and the rest of Blizzard's C-suite saw *Diablo III* as a failure—a game that had damaged the brand—and several of the executives didn't think *Reaper of Souls* would be good enough to turn it around. Morhaime was also feeling pressure from Bobby Kotick and his lieutenants at Activision, who were concerned that the developers in Irvine were trying to work on too many projects at once. And then there was the demonic elephant in the room: Despite its big sales numbers, *Diablo III* wasn't equipped to deliver long-term revenue. People only bought the game once, which made it difficult for Blizzard to justify keeping together a team of one hundred people to work on ongoing support.

Yet it also seemed absurd to view the game as a misstep. *Diablo III* was one of the most popular games ever made, to the point where other companies would gripe that their own games' user counts went down significantly whenever a new *Diablo* patch came out. "Did it make *World of Warcraft* money? No," said Jay Wilson. "But it made more money than most things that Blizzard makes." John Hight begged Morhaime and the other executives to wait until they shipped *Reaper of Souls* to make the call on a second expansion, but it was futile. "The team was devastated," said one executive. "Not just the *Diablo* team, but really the whole of development."

On March 25, 2014, Blizzard released *Diablo III: Reaper of Souls*, and with it came a slew of big changes that fans loved. One reviewer wrote that "with *Reaper of Souls*, and the recent round of content patches, Blizzard has transformed *Diablo III* into something far more akin to what long-time fans like me wanted all along." Versions of the game for Xbox and PlayStation proved that Blizzard had also mastered console development—*Diablo III* felt just as good if not better on a controller—and would help the company transition away from exclusively making PC games in the years that followed.

Now, *Diablo* players wanted to know what was next. Morhaime decided that the best move was to leave *Diablo III* on a high note and start fresh with a fourth game as quickly as possible under Josh Mosqueira, who was now one of the company's golden boys, both internally and to the outside world, where he had cultivated a reputation as the guy who rescued *Diablo III* from failure. "We joked about him having been called the savior of *Diablo*," said artist Jill Harrington. "Because everyone online said he'd rescued us from the clutch of evil Jay Wilson. On the team we knew that wasn't the case."

After years on *Diablo III*, Mosqueira was ready to try something completely new. He gathered a few artists and designers and began conceptualizing the next *Diablo* game, which was code-named *Hades* and would diverge from the series in several important ways: The camera would be over-the-shoulder rather than isometric; the combat would be punchier, akin to the *Batman: Arkham* series; and the game would have permadeath—every time your character died, they'd disappear for good, giving you perks for the next run. It was a drastic departure from what people were expecting from *Diablo IV*, but Mosqueira had earned the executive team's trust to experiment.

The problems with *Hades* began to pop up right away. Like other *Diablo* games, *Hades* would support cooperative multiplayer, but in the *Arkham* games, groups of thugs would circle around the Dark Knight, comic-book style, waiting to be punched in the face. It was impossible to envision how that could work with two or more players, especially because so much of *Arkham*'s combat relied upon time dilation—if your buddy was beating up monsters and time slowed down, what would you see? Designers on the team began to wonder: Was this really still *Diablo*? "The controls are different, the rewards are different, the monsters are different, the heroes are different," said Julian Love. "But it's dark, so it's the same."

Hades only required a small subset of Team 3, so the remaining developers found themselves with little else to do. A few of them began calling themselves Team Summer Camp in an echo of what had happened at Blizzard North many years earlier. "People would come in at 11:00 a.m., play *Diablo III*, do a two-hour lunch," said Masker. "They might do a meeting or an hour of work and then go home at 4:00 p.m." Then, as some of those people moved over to the *Hades* team, the pressure grew on Mosqueira to make decisions so they'd all have work to do. He became harder to track down, coming in to the office only two or three days a week, which hampered some of the designers' progress as they waited for feedback.

In July 2016, Mosqueira announced that he was leaving Blizzard. Shortly afterward, he launched a new game studio with some other former employees. When a group of Blizzard executives and lead designers came to evaluate the progress of *Hades*, they left unimpressed. Believing that the project wouldn't be feasible without Mosqueira, they decided to cancel it. *Diablo IV* would have to start from scratch.

■　■　■

As Blizzard scrambled to find a new director, the rest of Team 3 began working on a new content pack for *Diablo III*. During the development of *Hades*, the developers had held a game jam where they all spent a few days hacking together quick prototypes based on wild ideas. One group had prototyped a new version of the scythe-wielding, skeleton-conjuring, corpse-exploding Necromancer from *Diablo II*, which the team then decided to flesh out and turn into a proper release. "It was one of the best development times ever," said Julian Love, who helmed the project. "Everybody was so busy trying to get *Diablo IV* running, they left us alone."

It was called *Rise of the Necromancer*, which suggested some sort of grandiose expansion, but all players received was a new class, which made the price tag sting. "For $15, you're right to expect more," wrote a *GameSpot* reviewer. And that was the end for significant new content in *Diablo III*. One of the rationales behind canceling the second expansion had been to release a new game more quickly—now, they had neither an expansion nor a quick sequel. The game remained the black sheep of Blizzard's lineup, part of a franchise that had been created by another studio—Blizzard North—and one that some Blizzard veterans scoffed at. "I was directly told by one of the top people in the company that *Diablo* wasn't a 'real game,'" said Jay Wilson.

Morhaime and other Blizzard executives would later privately admit that canceling *Diablo III*'s second expansion before *Reaper of Souls* even came out had been a tactical error. *Reaper of Souls* was a win for the company, and to leadership, it had helped make up for the original game's failures, but they lost momentum shortly afterward. Later, the lack of new content for *Diablo* would have other repercussions—and it would be many years before the release of another *Diablo* game. Since *Hades* was never publicly announced, fans spent years wondering why the franchise was dormant.

But the *Diablo III* story was ultimately a triumph for Blizzard—a sign, both to players and to employees, that the company wasn't going to just accept failure. Other game makers might have given up after the polarizing launch of *Diablo III* and immediately moved on to their next product. But to Morhaime and his inner circle, "commit to quality" wasn't just about a game's development—it was also about what happened afterward. As video games moved away from one-time releases and began transforming into living products, other companies across the industry would look to *Reaper of Souls* as proof that what appeared to be the conclusion of a video game's development was sometimes just the beginning.

SEVENTEEN

CARD GAMES

The first thing people always noticed about Ben Brode was his laugh, a resounding guffaw that would spread like a virus to anyone in its vicinity. Brode was tall, with a closet full of plaid shirts and facial hair that didn't quite connect. His mouth and eyebrows were so expressive that they sometimes appeared to move across his face, like a cartoon character falling in love. "I call him the Mayor of Ben Town," said a longtime colleague, Glenn Rane. "We go into Starbucks and he's acting like he owns the place, knows everybody in there. His charisma is infectious."

One day, Brode would become the gregarious public face of one of Blizzard's most successful games, but in the early 2000s, he was just a college student at UC Irvine who was working two jobs to pay the bills. One was at a pizza place, and the other was at a small video game startup that had promised him and a handful of other students equity if they worked for free. There he befriended another student, Omar Gonzalez, who scored a job working as a tester at Blizzard Entertainment, which Brode was stunned to learn was located on his very own college campus.

Gonzalez asked Brode if he wanted to join him at Blizzard, which he of course did. But Gonzalez was just a tester with no sway or power, so the two of them devised a scheme: Gonzalez, who worked the night shift, would order pizzas from Brode's joint late in the evening. Brode would take the deliveries and use them as an excuse to schmooze with the testing crew. "I went over there a couple times," he said. "When they opened a position, I applied for it. And I'd already met the hiring manager." In March 2003, Brode started working as a tester at Blizzard Entertainment. He helped hunt for bugs in *Warcraft III* and then in *World of Warcraft*, where he became a lead on the QA environment team and immediately began playing by his own rules. "I was still working night crew, and eventually if you wanted a leadership position you had to move to day crew, but I really loved the crew I was with," he said. "So I got them to agree to put me on the Brode shift. I was the only person on the Brode shift: 1:00 p.m.–10:00 p.m."

Brode loved testing games, which made him feel like Batman, or Hercule Poirot, digging for clues and trying to figure out how things had been broken, but he had his sights set on a designer job. During his spare time he'd tool around with *Warcraft III*'s level editor, building maps that caught colleagues' attention, like Worm War, a multiplayer twist on the classic game *Snake*. When an entry-level design position opened on the *StarCraft II* team, Brode immediately applied. They told him that there were only two available positions and that unfortunately, he was the third-best applicant. The good news, they said, was that they planned to open another spot and he could have it. "Then a bunch of time went by," Brode said, "and they hired a third person who was not me."

At the same time, Blizzard's burgeoning creative development department was looking for a new assistant. It wasn't game design—the department mostly handled marketing and licensed products—but to a demoralized Brode it felt like one step closer to his ultimate dream, so he took the chance to leave testing behind.

One of his first projects was to snap marketing screenshots for *StarCraft: Ghost*. When that game was canceled, Brode opined that they should release the impressive multiplayer component as a budget title on Microsoft's new online service, Xbox Live. "But at the time," he said, "Blizzard was not very good at jumping on opportunities." A year later he started working on a new project, *World of Warcraft Trading Card Game*, published by a company called Upper Deck that was best known for manufacturing baseball cards but had recently branched out. To compete with giants like *Magic: The Gathering*, Upper Deck director Cory Jones had pitched that they partner with Blizzard to stuff each card pack with codes for outfits and pets that you could then download in the real *World of Warcraft*, incentivizing those millions of players to buy cards.

Jones moved over to Blizzard, where he shepherded the card game for several years and began pushing for the company to develop a digital version to make playing as frictionless as possible. "We had trouble hitting critical mass," said Brode. "The game was never going to become astronomical if we didn't have a digital client."

Some of Blizzard's executives were skeptical about the idea, but Rob Pardo thought it was a worthy experiment. In 2008, Pardo hired Hamilton Chu, an industry veteran best known for his work as the lead producer of *Halo*, the record-breaking console game that had steered Microsoft's Xbox to success. At Blizzard, he became the director of strategic initiatives, the business group responsible for a suite of projects such as employee surveys and, later, the *Diablo III* auction house. Soon Chu was also putting together documents and spreadsheets for what they were calling *WoW: TCG Online* alongside another top developer who Pardo had recruited: Ray Gresko, an industry polymath and one of the founders of Nihilistic Software, the company that had originally helmed *StarCraft: Ghost*.

Gresko paired up with Brode, who played so much of the *World of Warcraft Trading Card Game* that he had memorized every card, to develop a prototype. But before they could produce much, Gresko was pulled over to help lead *Diablo III*, leaving Brode in a panic as he begged his bosses not to cancel the project. Chu and Pardo briefly thought about finding an outside studio to handle the digital trading card game but instead decided to build their own internal team, bringing in a handful of industry veterans including Jason Chayes, a longtime producer from EA, and Derek Sakamoto, who had been a programmer on *World of Warcraft*. They decided to stay small, capping the team at fifteen developers because they didn't want it to be a huge expense.

By the start of 2009, Blizzard had five development units. There was Team 1, working on *StarCraft*. Team 2 was in charge of *World of Warcraft*. Team 3 was on *Diablo*. Team 4 was developing the unannounced *Titan* project, and now Team 5 was forming to work on the digital *Warcraft* card game. To helm the project they recruited Eric Dodds, a designer from *World of Warcraft* who was lauded within Blizzard for his ability to boil down complicated video game mechanics and make them more approachable. "Eric is, I think, a genius," said Shay Pierce, one of the team's first programmers.

When Brode officially joined Team 5, he was peeved to learn that despite his five years of experience at Blizzard he would get the title "associate designer"—an entry-level position. He grew angrier when Dodds began altering some of the rules of the *World of Warcraft Trading Card Game* for the digital version, complaining that they were too obtuse.[14] One day, after Brode shot down a suggestion, a frustrated Dodds said he was going to go elsewhere for design feedback. "I was

---

14 At one point, Dodds took the *World of Warcraft Trading Card Game*'s "judge test"—an exam that gauged whether a player understood the convoluted rules adeptly enough to be a tournament judge—and failed. He immediately declared to his team: "We will never make a game with these rules."

horrified," said Brode. "Here I am with my new boss, and he just told me he's going to stop coming to me with his ideas." Brode apologized and vowed to commit to more of an additive approach. "I deserved the title of associate designer," he said.

Eventually, he began to realize that Dodds was right: The *World of Warcraft* card game had some serious flaws. Brode had recently discovered a game called *Battle Spirits* that eschewed complicated resource systems in favor of automatically giving players gems that could be used to cast spells. *This is genius*, Brode thought, bringing *Battle Spirits* back to the office and pushing his colleagues to play it. Then they tried an experiment, using paper to replace the *World of Warcraft* card game's resources with automatic gems, which they learned was a significant improvement. Soon they'd come up with another way to make the digital version of the game more pleasant: simplifying all the card descriptions and keeping them hidden until a player's mouse hovered over them. "We tried to make it not be about learning a thousand rules," said Brian Schwab, a programmer. "We wanted it to be fast and furious."

This was when Team 5 began to realize that they were no longer making a digital version of the *World of Warcraft* trading card game, they were designing something else entirely. Brode and his team buzzed that they might have something special on their hands— something that captured the Blizzard ethos of taking a popular genre and making it more polished and approachable.

Then came some bad news: In the fall of 2009, right after Blizzard delayed *StarCraft II*, Pardo called Team 5 for a meeting and told them that Battle.net needed extra help, so most of the team would be moving over there for the immediate future. Again it seemed like Team 5 was doomed, and Brode wondered if their little dream of making a digital *Warcraft* card game was over—but the Battle.net hiatus turned out to be the best thing that could have possibly happened to the project.

■ ■ ■

Brian Schwab had joined Blizzard to work on video games, so he was dismayed when he was forced to move from Team 5 to Battle.net. For more than nine months he wrote code for Blizzard's online platform, which might have driven him to quit if not for his old teammates. Four of them, including Brode and Dodds, had stayed behind to keep working on the card game, and every day during lunch, Schwab would go upstairs to play, offering feedback as the game evolved. With their team gone, Brode and Dodds spent the next nine months drawing numbers and pictures on paper cards. Every day, they had a group of willing guinea pigs in Schwab and the others who wanted a break from Battle.net drudgery. Brode was a fountain of experimental new ideas, while Dodds was adept at figuring out what was the most fun. "To me that was some of the magic," said Dodds. "Brode going, 'What about this?' and me trying to stop the flood and get us to a place where we were both excited."

By the summer of 2010, when *StarCraft II* came out and Team 5 returned to their normal jobs, Brode and Dodds had already designed the majority of what would be called *Hearthstone*. Everything about the game felt streamlined, simple, and approachable. Players would assemble decks based on *World of Warcraft* classes, like the priest or the hunter, and they could conjure a menagerie of creatures and spells with the aim of destroying their opponent in one-on-one battles. Every card's ability—like Taunt, which drew all melee attacks to a single minion—was easy to grasp in just a few seconds. Blizzard's decision to relocate all of Team 5 for nearly a year had allowed them to make the best possible version of the game. "We were so frustrated," said Brode, "and it was absolutely a blessing in disguise."

Now reunited, Team 5 began building *Hearthstone*. One of their goals was to make every action in the game feel tactile, as if the player was actually sliding cards across the screen, while another was to design abilities that would only be possible in a computer game. "The natural inclination is to just make it like *Magic: The Gathering*," said Hamilton Chu. "We really wanted to put people in a different frame of mind." Since the team was so small, they were all able to sit and work together—a callback to the older days of Blizzard, even as the company had grown into the thousands. "It was this miraculous moment," said Jay Baxter, a programmer. "Blizzard at the height of its power decided to start up a garage company and let them do what they wanted."

After a couple years of development, they put together a vertical slice, or a sample of the game, to show the rest of Blizzard. It was a mage vs. mage battle, so they called it the "fire and ice" build, and they brought in the company's executives and directors for a playtest. The following week, Pardo joined their team meeting, which was unusual. He stood up and congratulated them, declaring that *Hearthstone* had been greenlit. "I was thinking: I've been working on this game for four years," said Brode. "It wasn't greenlit this whole time?"

As it turned out, many of Blizzard's executives, especially Paul Sams, had been eyeing Team 5 with some skepticism. Activision also wasn't sold on the project, and Bobby Kotick would occasionally ask why they were bothering to make this little *Magic: The Gathering* thing instead of putting those resources into *World of Warcraft*. One of Blizzard's core values was to make "epic" experiences, while this was the opposite—but Pardo had managed to convince Blizzard's executive team to at least play *Hearthstone* and see how it felt. What Team 5 later learned was that if the top staff hadn't liked it, the game would have been doomed. "Rob told me beforehand, 'This is it, man,'" said Hamilton Chu. "'If this demo doesn't go well, it's canceled.'"

The rest of Blizzard had a similar experience—skepticism followed by delight once they had played the game—and so did fans. When Blizzard first announced the game at the PAX East convention in Boston in March 2013, there was a smattering of confused "huh?"s from the audience. Then people began playing the game.[15] Wrote one previewer: "Blizzard's entrance into collectible card games may well be the gateway drug hard-core players have been hoping for." Back home, the *Hearthstone* team kept adding flourishes that they hoped would make the game feel polished. "'Charming' was a word Dodds used constantly," said Mike Schweitzer, a programmer. "People got sick of it, but it was the right thing to do." Dodds also pushed for the game to have what he called "over-the-shoulder appeal," which he thought would make it a magnet for in-person observers but wound up shining on Twitch, where millions of viewers flocked to watch players duel.

Developers at Blizzard weren't quite sure what kind of numbers to expect when *Hearthstone* came out on March 11, 2014. The company's previous games had generated revenue from unit sales or monthly subscriptions, but *Hearthstone* was completely free, only charging players for additional content such as card packs and expansions. "When people asked how successful we'd be, I said, 'I guarantee we'll make dozens of dollars,'" said Dodds.

The results blew everyone away. By the end of the month, the game had ten million registered users. Within the next few years it would reach one hundred million—more players than any game Blizzard had ever made—and would eventually generate hundreds of millions of dollars in revenue per year. This was Blizzard's little

---

15 The *Hearthstone* team was so grassroots that it didn't even book a booth, so in 2013, when I met Brode and a couple of other Blizzard staff in the Boston Convention Center to preview the game, we found a corner and sat on the floor.

skunkworks project, the company's lowest priority, a game that had come close to being canceled several times. Now it was one of the company's top money makers.

In the coming months, Blizzard doubled and then tripled the size of Team 5 so its developers could continue making new cards and expansions for *Hearthstone*. It was a resounding success, but to some members of the original team, the magic was lost. "I think *Hearthstone*'s story is a microcosm of Blizzard's story," said Jay Baxter. "We went from creating to churning." Brian Schwab tried to persuade the company to let the original members of Team 5 go off and do something new, but it was futile. "I left because I wanted to keep doing the little team thing, and I knew Blizzard wasn't going to let me," Schwab said.

In the years that followed, Dodds would depart *Hearthstone* to work on his own project, and Brode would become the director and public face of the game, appearing on stage at BlizzCon and in YouTube videos, wearing his trademark plaid shirts, to geek out about balance changes, record unexpectedly competent raps, and guffaw his way into fans' hearts.

Blizzard had turned into an empire by taking other people's video game ideas, polishing them, and turning them into phenomena like *Hearthstone*. But in the years after *World of Warcraft*, as the company grew rich and bloated, Blizzard would also experience something it had never faced before: someone else taking from one of their games and turning it into a phenomenon.

EIGHTEEN

THIRD PLACE

B ack in 1995, Blizzard decided to stick a map editor into *Warcraft II*, allowing players to use the same tools as the developers to create their own wild scenarios. For *StarCraft*, Blizzard implemented scripts that made it possible to construct levels just as elaborate as the ones in the official campaign. Players concocted all sorts of absurd creations, from epic recreations of *Final Fantasy* scenes to color-coded battle royales with characters named after *The Simpsons*.

Many of these custom maps were silly gags, but some were inventive and genuinely fun. One of the most popular maps, called Aeon of Strife, featured two large armies waging war on a battlefield that was divided into three narrow lanes. Rather than commanding an entire army, each player would control a single, hyper-powerful unit. These matches required less multitasking than a standard game of *StarCraft* but proved just as exciting because an individual player's actions could turn the tide of any battle. When *Warcraft III* came out, players flocked to another map, Defense of the Ancients (DOTA), which took the old formula and made it five-on-five, allowing for more teamwork and competitive strategy.

By 2005, Blizzard had noticed that hundreds of thousands of people were playing DOTA and its spinoffs, and the company's top executives wondered if they should embrace the trend. They discussed creating an official version of DOTA for *Warcraft III* or even developing a sequel in-house, then tracked down the main architect of the popular variant DOTA All-Stars, who went by the handle Icefrog, and flew him to Irvine for a meeting. But Icefrog, a reclusive designer who avoided using his real name, arrived with a list of requests that Blizzard's executives considered unreasonable. "He wanted full creative control," said Richard Khoo, a designer on Team 1. Plus, *World of Warcraft* demanded everybody's attention, so DOTA seemed like a trend they could safely ignore. "My recollection is that Blizzard wasn't in a place to start building the game at the time," said Icefrog in a statement through his agent, "so discussions never really got far at all."

At the same time, two business consultants in California named Marc Merrill and Brandon Beck were playing a whole lot of DOTA and talking about starting their own video game company. By the fall of 2006 they had established Riot Games, with the goal of creating a single game that could be played endlessly. "We'd play thousands of hours of *StarCraft*, *Warcraft III*, you name it," said Merrill. "And so we wanted to build games for players like us who really wanted that sort of incredible depth." The pair teamed up with another top DOTA modder, Steve Feak, to come up with a new game based on the map they'd all spent so much time playing.

The result was *League of Legends*, which came out in October 2009. It played exactly like DOTA, but it was a standalone product with frictionless matchmaking and a huge roster of original heroes. Merrill and Beck also made it free to play, gambling that by opening up the game to everyone, they could build up a huge audience, particularly in countries where players generally had less disposable income than they did in the United States. To generate revenue, the game would sell heroes, outfits, and other perks for small fees. Rather than moving to *League of Legends 2*, Riot would continue updating the game with new characters, outfits, and balance tweaks, ensuring that people played for decades to come.

By the end of the year, *League of Legends* had more than 100,000 concurrent players, and two years later Riot Games would sell a majority stake to the Chinese conglomerate Tencent for a whopping $400 million. Riot became a titan of the video game industry, with a sprawling campus in Santa Monica and an army of recruiters who began calling Blizzard employees and offering to double their salaries if they came to work on *League of Legends*.

Blizzard's executives were livid about the rise of Riot. In the past, they had outlasted direct competitors like Westwood and Sony Online Entertainment by making the most polished games on the market. *StarCraft* and *Warcraft* had surpassed *Command & Conquer*, while *World of Warcraft* blew away *EverQuest*. But now there was a new player in Southern California that had beaten Blizzard at its own game.

In the summer of 2010, as *League of Legends* took off, Blizzard was juggling too many projects to compete in this burgeoning genre. But Team 1 saw an opportunity to experiment when their designers were tasked with preparing BlizzCon demos for *StarCraft II's* upcoming marketplace, which would allow players, for the first time, to sell their own custom maps for real money. To demonstrate the power and flexibility of their map editor, *StarCraft II's* designers would develop levels that fans could play at the convention, like a cooking competition called Aiur Chef and a *Left 4 Dead* sendup called Left 2 Die. One of these maps would smash together characters from the *StarCraft* and *Warcraft* universes in what was called Blizzard DOTA. "Who wouldn't love a fight between Kerrigan and Sylvanas?" designer Matt

Gotcher said during a BlizzCon panel. "You actually get to play as the characters you've gotten to know and love over the years."

The timing was interesting. Shortly before BlizzCon, the Seattle-based video game company Valve had announced its own game, *DOTA 2*, that served as a standalone successor to the *Warcraft III* mod. In fact, the real name for Blizzard DOTA was *Blizzard All-Stars*—the company had tacked on "DOTA" at the last minute to prepare for a future trademark battle.[16] To lead development, Valve had brought in an outside designer with experience in the genre who preferred to go by his internet handle: Icefrog.

■ ■ ■

At the end of 2010, Justin Klinchuch was considering a move that had previously seemed unfathomable: leaving Blizzard. He'd started in QA five years earlier, then secured a spot on Team 1 during the development of *StarCraft II*, which had required long hours—an acceptable prospect for Klinchuch when he was single and in his twenties, but less feasible now that he was older and looking to start a family. He was especially disconcerted when he heard Blizzard veterans say that *StarCraft II*'s overtime had been easy compared to what they'd experienced in the past. Plus, his current job as a data specialist on *StarCraft* was getting a little boring, and he was getting the itch to go independent.

Just before Blizzard closed for winter break, Klinchuch went to *StarCraft II* director Dustin Browder's office to ask if he could take on more responsibilities. Near Browder's desk was a big whiteboard full of ideas and plans for the coming year, mostly related to *StarCraft II*'s next expansion, *Heart of the Swarm*. One item on the list piqued Klinchuch's interest: the words "mod map team."

---

16 Valve and Blizzard would wind up in a court battle over the DOTA trademark, ending in a settlement that gave Valve the rights to continue using the name.

After New Year's, Browder called in Klinchuch and two other designers and gave them the scoop: *Blizzard All-Stars* had a lot of potential, and they wanted to make it better. It would be Blizzard's first officially sanctioned version of the genre that now had a proper name: multiplayer online battle arena, or MOBA. Browder figured they could release *Blizzard All-Stars* alongside *Heart of the Swarm* as a bonus, or maybe put it out for free afterward to whet players' appetites before the next expansion, *Legacy of the Void*. Klinchuch became one of the first designers on *Blizzard All-Stars*, which was exciting enough to convince him not to quit. To distinguish the game from competitors, they would take advantage of Blizzard's stable of familiar characters, like *Warcraft*'s fallen knight Arthas, *Diablo*'s witch doctor, and *StarCraft*'s supersoldier ghost Nova.[17] It would essentially be *Smash Bros.* for Blizzard games.

Since they were developing the game in *StarCraft*'s familiar map editor, it was easy to experiment with new ideas for heroes or abilities. "We'd meet in the morning and talk about some changes, then could be playtesting those changes by evening," said Klinchuch. Phill Gonzalez, one of the first artists to join the *Blizzard All-Stars* team, relished figuring out how a character like Kerrigan might scale next to the likes of Diablo. "I really enjoyed it as a fan of those pillar franchises," said Gonzalez. "Oh my gosh, we get to blend them all."

As more people at Blizzard played the map and chimed in with positive feedback, the developers began to wonder if burying *Blizzard All-Stars* within *StarCraft II* would be a mistake—perhaps this deserved to be a standalone product, with its own interface and competitive ladder. Rob Pardo told Browder and his team that he thought

---

17 Nova became a key character in *StarCraft II* after her own game, *StarCraft: Ghost*, was canceled, following the same pattern as the orc shaman Thrall, who joined *Warcraft III* after the cancellation of *Warcraft Adventures*. So much for cancel culture.

the game was good, but that they could push a little further and make it stand out in an increasingly crowded landscape. "That's what sent us into overdrive," said designer John Hodgson.

Team 1 split into two separate development units: one on *StarCraft II*'s continued expansions and the other on this swelling new game, which was soon retitled *Heroes of the Storm*. After *StarCraft II: Heart of the Swarm* released in March 2013, the *Heroes of the Storm* team inherited some of its developers, expanding to nearly one hundred staff. Many of them began to feel confident—perhaps overconfident—that they had something special on their hands. "The rallying cry across the whole company was, 'We're going to do to *League of Legends* what *World of Warcraft* did to *EverQuest*,'" said one designer. "Which was dumb, because *League of Legends* already was *World of Warcraft*." By the end of 2013, *League of Legends* had twenty-seven million active daily users and Valve's *DOTA 2* was the most played game on Steam, while companies like Warner Bros. and Electronic Arts had taken their own stabs at the MOBA genre and failed spectacularly. Blizzard was entering a market so crowded it was a fire hazard.

To stand out, the team behind *Heroes of the Storm* figured they'd do what Blizzard always did: make it as polished and approachable as possible. They looked at *League of Legends* and *DOTA 2*, both of which had steep learning curves, and tried to "get rid of all the sharp edges," said Richard Khoo. But one risk to streamlining game design, as the *Diablo III* team had once discovered, was potentially losing depth along the way. Developers on *Heroes of the Storm* had scoffed at *DOTA 2* because it felt obtuse and punishing, but for many players that friction was part of the appeal.

For longtime Blizzard fans, it was a treat to see what might happen if *Diablo*'s Butcher fought against the heroes of *The Lost Vikings*. But many of the younger gamers who were into MOBAs hadn't grown up with Blizzard games—there had been no new ones released between

2004 and 2010—and they had no interest in the company's version of *Smash Bros.* Matt Schembari, a programmer on *Heroes of the Storm*, started to suspect that something might be amiss when he couldn't convince friends or family to accept free early codes for the game. He recalled growing nervous when his younger brother, a teenager, told him that none of his friends wanted it either.

Yet the expectations were only growing as the *Heroes of the Storm* team expanded to 150 people and became one of the company's top priorities. "It got hooked up to the larger Blizzard machine," said Khoo. "We had to think about: How do we do esports? How do we do monetization?" Like its competitors, *Heroes of the Storm* would be free-to-play, which meant selling heroes and cosmetics for real cash. *League of Legends* and *DOTA 2* had both found so much success with that formula that Blizzard executives—and their bosses at Activision—had high revenue expectations for *Heroes of the Storm*. Blizzard Chief Operating Officer Paul Sams began telling his business teams to prepare for a "bare-knuckle fist fight"—for the first time since the Westwood days, he proclaimed, they had serious competition.

In January 2015, *Heroes of the Storm* entered beta, and Klinchuch decided it was time to leave Blizzard for real—to relocate closer to his girlfriend, to make more money, to go develop indie games, and, most pressingly, because he knew that *Heroes of the Storm* would require a stream of new maps and characters for months if not years after the game's release. "I'd been working on *Heroes* for four years at that point," he said. "You're staring down an endless content treadmill." But there was also something bigger—more existential. For Klinchuch, cracks were beginning to form in the company's once-polished facade. "I had a real sense that this is a very different Blizzard than the Blizzard I initially got hired at," he said, "and the longer I stay, the higher the chances of bad memories."

There were little things, like perks that seemed to be disappearing. In the past, each employee would receive multiple free tickets to BlizzCon—now they were lucky to get one. Where the company had once taken employees to Vegas to celebrate the release of each individual game, now they were combining multiple launches into a single wrap party. "I definitely had a real sense of decline happening around me," Klinchuch said.

■ ■ ■

If you squinted a little, you could kind of figure out how *Heroes of the Storm* was performing. Activision Blizzard's earnings report for the first quarter of the 2015 fiscal year proclaimed that *Hearthstone* and Activision's *Destiny* had a combined 50 million registered players and $1 billion in revenue. The next quarter, they added *Heroes of the Storm* to the number stew, declaring that the three games had now signed up 70 million players and generated $1.25 billion in revenue. In other words, Blizzard's MOBA had somewhere between zero and 20 million players and made anywhere from $0 to $250 million. This sort of financial puppetry wasn't uncommon in the video game industry, but it did have a clear purpose: to obfuscate the numbers.

When members of Team 1 asked about *Heroes of the Storm*'s performance, they received vague answers. Reviews were generally positive, outside of a 6.5 out of 10 from IGN, one of the lowest scores in Blizzard's history.[18] And the team continued to expand so it could keep releasing new characters, maps, and "skins," or outfits, every few weeks. But it was never quite clear to developers on the team if the game was generating enough revenue to support a team that had now grown to nearly two hundred people. "They were never transparent

---

18 Video game review sites typically scored big-budget games on a school-grade scale, so for a Blizzard game, a 6.5/10 was basically like getting a 1.

about what our successes and failures were," said Phill Gonzalez, "even to the point where they didn't want to tell us what skins were popular."

Worse, *Heroes of the Storm* hadn't even come close to beating either Riot or Valve. Blizzard's top decision-makers had quietly accepted that they would never actually surpass *League of Legends*, but they had hoped to at least beat *DOTA 2*. A silver medal would have been acceptable. But bronze? For more than twenty years, Blizzard had cultivated an image as a hit machine, generating blockbuster after blockbuster and leading the market in every genre it decided to explore. Now, the company found itself in a situation it had never faced before: third place.

NINETEEN

TITAN

N early a decade before *Heroes of the Storm* failed to dethrone *League of Legends*, Blizzard's developers had a different target in their sights: *World of Warcraft*. It was 2006, and video game bloggers and analysts crowed daily about the long-awaited *"World of Warcraft* killer"—the game that would draw away its millions of subscribers. Every month, another game failed to pull off the feat, from *The Matrix Online* to *Age of Conan*. To paraphrase a certain beloved HBO character: you come at the Lich King, you best not miss.

Still, Blizzard's executives suspected that a WoW killer would be on the horizon sooner or later—so they figured they should be the ones to make it. The natural next step seemed like a *World of StarCraft*, but they struggled to envision *StarCraft* lore fitting into an MMORPG, so instead they decided to develop a new fictional universe. Rob Pardo began gathering a small team of the company's top developers to incubate this project, with the hope of gradually bringing over the best designers, artists, and programmers from *World of Warcraft*. Leading the way would be people who had been at Blizzard since the

1990s: Chris Metzen would pen the story, Shane Dabiri would head production, and Justin Thavirat would be art director on the new game, which they called *Titan*.

Every day, the group would hold long lunches to bounce around ideas for the look and theme of *Titan*, which would be unlike anything they'd done before—grounded, near-future scifi rather than space or high fantasy. "How do you follow up on the biggest game ever?" Thavirat said. "I couldn't see how we could outdo the same formula." Other video games, like *Half-Life* and *Fallout*, painted a grim, dystopian picture—in contrast, *Titan* would feel bright and optimistic, perhaps attracting people who wouldn't normally play Blizzard games. "We were really excited about appealing to a broad audience," Thavirat said. "Gamers, non-gamers, young, old, men, women, everything in between."

Titan would be set on an alternate version of Earth in the 2070s. The hook was that it was essentially two games in one, with players taking control of superhero-like characters who lived normal lives during the day and secretly battled against evil forces at night. An early presentation showed the player, as a professional chef, popping a dish into the oven before going off on a secret mission. When they returned, the dish was perfectly cooked and ready to serve.

A couple of years into development, *Titan* had a small but growing team of engineers, artists, and designers who would meet for brainstorming sessions every week. Their unit, which they called Team 4, was envisioned as an all-star team, bringing in the best staff that Pardo could find both within Blizzard and from elsewhere in the industry. People on other Blizzard teams would look over in envy, sometimes begging for a spot on what would be the company's first brand-new franchise in more than a decade.

But behind the shiny veneer of this new team was a nasty political battle—a long-running feud between two of the company's top executives that was growing uglier every day.

■ ■ ■

Chris Metzen and Rob Pardo had never seen eye to eye. Metzen was a boisterous, emotional artist and a fountain of story ideas, while Pardo was quieter and more analytical, with a head for game design and an aloof demeanor. The two had first worked together as creative leads on *StarCraft*'s expansion, *Brood War*, then paired up to help steer *Warcraft III* and *World of Warcraft*. Both grew increasingly powerful at the company, becoming vice presidents when Adham retired in 2004. The success of their creative collaboration was hard to deny, although to Blizzard staff who worked with them, it felt like parents about to get a divorce. "We'd just sit there for a full hour and watch Metzen and Pardo argue," recalled one developer on *StarCraft II*. "Metzen would say it should be pink. Pardo would instantly say it should be blue, and only an idiot would make it pink. It was painful to watch."

During *Titan*, their battles were more muted but just as frustrating for observers. At least on *Warcraft* and *StarCraft* they'd had a clear vision and years of established lore—now, they were starting with nothing but a blank piece of paper and a desire to make the next big MMORPG. Metzen would hold brainstorming meetings and fill up whiteboards with ideas, only for Pardo to insist that they weren't good enough. "There was a lot of fishing around and we couldn't really land anything," said one early designer. "We're rocking, doing all this stuff, and then it's just getting erased because Rob's not liking it."

People who worked with the pair quickly learned that they had divergent visions for what *Titan* should become. Metzen wanted to create a superhero universe, like the Marvel and DC comics he loved, with godlike figures duking it out in the skies and streets, while Pardo wanted characters to be more like secret agents—spies with super-powers who worked in the shadows to protect the world from insid-ious threats. As a result of these battles, Metzen left and returned to the project multiple times, which created more chaos and confusion. *Titan* cycled through several writers, each with their own take on the game's lore and story. "The core fantasy of the world was constantly changing," said Jacob Repp, an engineer.

As the *Titan* team expanded, bringing in veteran developers from across the video game industry, they built an endless number of proto-types for the civilian portion of the game: fishing, farming, photogra-phy, gardening, hacking. This non-combat section, which they called Titan Town, was essentially Blizzard's take on *Animal Crossing* or *The Sims*—players would be able to deck out a house with furniture, run a business, and go on quests in their neighborhoods. During playtests, the *Titan* team found that some of these game mechanics were fun in isolation, but nobody could envision what game developers called the "core loop," or the sequence of actions that players would spend the bulk of their time doing. "It always felt like it was right around the cor-ner," said Thavirat. "Right around this milestone, this is where things will come together."

The combat side felt more coherent but was facing its own issues. Each player would be able to select from one of a handful of superhero classes, like the speedy Jumper, who could teleport short distances, or the sharpshooting Ranger, who wielded a powerful sniper rifle. Play-ers could group up with friends to battle through dungeons or fight one another in team-based competitive battles. These matches could be fun in bursts, but the *Titan* team struggled to figure out how to keep players engaged over a long period of time.

During interviews and financial earnings calls, Blizzard execu-tives hinted to the public that they were working on a "next-generation

MMO." A leaked slideshow even revealed the name *Titan* to the outside world, which led reporters to probe Morhaime and Pardo for more information on the project. Bobby Kotick touted the game during investor presentations and Hollywood parties, occasionally bringing Blizzard developers to meet celebrities like Tom Brady. *These guys made* World of Warcraft, he'd say—*and now they're making something even bigger.*

Every mention of the game only increased the pressure for the *Titan* team, which was encountering obstacle after obstacle. Riot Games was using all that *League of Legends* cash to poach Blizzard's staff—including, at one point, nearly the entire animation team. And the underlying technology behind *Titan*—all designed from scratch for this project—was hampering their progress, whether it was laggy, incomplete tools or a faulty "version control" software that would sometimes prevent the team from working for hours at a time.

The industry had evolved since the days of *Warcraft* and *Diablo*, when video games had simple 2D art and could be programmed by a dozen people over the course of a year or two. Technological advancements made video games look more beautiful every year, but they also ramped up the complexity of development. By the 2000s, teams were swelling to more than one hundred and their games might take three years or longer to produce. The larger a game team grew, the harder it became to coordinate tech, develop a consistent art style, and execute on a single coherent vision.

Team 4's artists drew concepts for *Titan's* colorful classes and futuristic cities—bright, idyllic versions of regions like Eastern Europe and the western United States—but many of the designs kept changing as the game evolved in different directions. An internal repository called TitanArt grew so bloated, with thousands of images, that artists would sometimes draw characters or cities only to later learn that someone else had already done the same years earlier. "The amount of art we did was enough for five games," said artist Vadim Bakhlychev.

One artist described working on the project as an interminable state of déjà vu—like they were living in *Groundhog Day*. They'd draw costumes and furniture, take long lunches, and then fine-tune what they'd already made. There were no seasons in Irvine—it was always dry, sunny, and 60–80 degrees—which made it hard to tell the weeks apart. "Was that yesterday?" the artist said. "Was it last year? What day was this?" They were proud of the art they were making, but it was hard not to wonder if one day, someone was going to come down from high and realize that they weren't making much progress. "There was a feeling that Blizzard had essentially written a blank check to fund this game and that bred a sense of complacency within the team," the artist said. "We were not working with any kind of urgency."

Making games was always hard. Making new franchises was even harder. And making a new franchise at a company full of perfectionists, with the pressure of surpassing *World of Warcraft*, with a team that was growing larger than any project in Blizzard's history—well, that was proving to be impossible.

Later, several developers on the team would blame many of *Titan's* struggles on Rob Pardo. As Blizzard's vice president of game design, Pardo was also overseeing *StarCraft II*, *Diablo III*, and the rest of the company's projects, which limited the time he had for *Titan*. "He at times seemed like an absentee game director," said one developer. To mitigate this problem, Pardo had brought in two lead designers: Jeff Kaplan, who had designed quests on *World of Warcraft*, and Matt Brown, who had worked on *The Sims* and *SimCity* at EA's Maxis. But Pardo remained director of the project and would occasionally jump in with feedback, forcing the team to change course and potentially throw out months of work. "I think when you want to lead some-thing, you have a responsibility to lead," said Connie Griffith, who worked as an assistant to Pardo. "And if you are not able to give it your full attention, you need to relinquish control."

■　■　■

Rob Pardo first discovered the joys of game design while playing *Dungeons & Dragons* with his friends, who always wanted him to be the Dungeon Master, allowing him to create his own rules and build his own campaigns. When he wasn't crafting fictional universes, he was gravitating toward anything competitive: ice hockey, Risk, video games. He took pride in being the best at anything he played—a trait inherited from his father. "He's probably competitive to a fault, and instilled that in me," Pardo later said on a podcast. "He'd never, ever let me win. So if I beat him, it was legit, and if I started winning at some activity we're doing, then mysteriously we would stop doing that activity."

Growing up an only child in Southern California, Pardo had first wanted to be a film director but decided it was unrealistic, so he went to UC Irvine intending to become a lawyer. Then, while working at an electronics store, he saw a colleague apply for a game-testing job at Interplay and followed suit. After bouncing around departments for a couple of years, he left Interplay for a startup, where he and his team pitched a new game to Allen Adham. Adham wasn't inter-ested in the game but was impressed by Pardo's multiplayer skills and design chops, and soon the two started talking about Pardo coming to Blizzard.

Adham hired Pardo in 1997, although there wasn't a formal job for him just yet. Instead, Pardo sat with the QA department, played early builds of *StarCraft*, and wrote up his thoughts on balance between the three races. Some of his new colleagues looked over and wondered: Who was this kid sitting with the testers and telling them what to do? It was soon clear, as Pardo was promoted to become the top designer on *StarCraft*'s expansion, *Brood War*, that he was being positioned as Adham's successor, and when Adham left the company in 2004, Pardo took his role as lead designer of *World of Warcraft*. After that, Pardo would oversee every game Blizzard made.

In May 2006, a *TIME* magazine spread declared Pardo to be one of the one hundred most influential people of the year, alongside George Clooney and Stephen Colbert. In a gushing article that referred to him as a "minor deity," the magazine treated him as the sole creator of *World of Warcraft*, a game that had been developed by more than sixty people. Pardo was credited as lead designer, and he had certainly played a key role, but Adham had led the game for the bulk of development. Yet the accolades were breathless. "Pardo didn't invent this kind of game, he merely perfected it," the magazine gushed.

Although the *Time* article wasn't Pardo's doing, Blizzard staff groused about how he had been portrayed. This was a company that tried hard to avoid glamorizing their developers—that would stamp "Design by Blizzard Entertainment" atop the credits of every game as a way of showing that everyone at the company had contributed. Adham and Morhaime had always preached that Blizzard had no rock stars, yet Pardo was becoming an industry celebrity. He bought a red Lamborghini and began wearing more fashionable clothes as Griffith, his assistant, recalled watching him "become this different person"—a smart, thoughtful leader who also "used that power to indulge himself." He wasn't the only one at Blizzard who was changed by fame and fortune, but he was one of the most powerful.

As Pardo rose through the company's ranks, he became a polarizing figure at Blizzard. Employees griped that he would take credit for other people's ideas, and in one interview he even claimed responsibility for Adham's old donut theory, which had been one of Blizzard's core principles since long before he had joined. He also cultivated a reputation for passing the buck when things went wrong. During the development of *Diablo III*, Pardo asked the team to build a new interface for the chat system, according to two people who worked on it. After a few months of development, the team had a check-in meeting with Morhaime, who was shocked that they had wasted their time and asked why they weren't just using *World of Warcraft*'s system. "Pardo said: 'Yeah, why would you guys do this?'" recalled one person on the team. "He threw the team under the bus. We had to scramble to redo it." A charitable explanation would be that Pardo simply forgot he had made the request, but the incident—and several others like it—left Blizzard staff complaining that he tended to use first-person pronouns when things went well and second-person pronouns when they went awry.

As Pardo's responsibilities grew and his time became stretched between projects, he became known for what many of his subordinates called seagull management: He would swoop down, poop on ideas, and then fly away. "He's a brilliant designer; he was just a terrible manager," said Greg Street, a lead on *World of Warcraft*. "Which was common at Blizzard." His negativity could grate colleagues and sometimes blurred the lines between criticism and bullying. Later, Pardo would say on a podcast that he believed in being honest and direct—and that people's most influential teachers were often their harshest critics. "I think the game industry is filled with a lot of really nice people," he said. "I think that makes for really good work environments but it's not always good for teaching. You think about teaching; you need to be willing to tell people they're doing things wrong a lot."

Grumblings about Pardo's management style would sometimes make their way to Morhaime, but his talent—and status as a Blizzard old-timer—appeared to outweigh the problems. Pardo had played a pivotal role in developing hit after hit for Blizzard and had even helped protect *Hearthstone* from getting canceled. As vice president, he had preached about the power of "opportunity hires"—finding and recruiting the industry's most talented people, even if Blizzard didn't have a specific role for them yet—and he had brought aboard some of Blizzard's most important contributors, like Ray Gresko, Hamilton Chu, and Jay Wilson. By 2013, he had joined Blizzard's C-suite as Chief Creative Officer.

At this point, *Titan* had gone from a dream project to demoralizing for many members of Team 4. Designers would spend weeks getting excited about an idea, then set up a meeting with Pardo to review it only for him to shoot it down without offering an explanation or alternative direction. On previous games, not everyone had always agreed with Pardo's decisions, but at least he had made them. On *Titan*, he appeared to be unwilling or unable to commit to a vision——perhaps because of the pressure. "There was this fear of the sophomore album," said Griffith. "What can we do that's as good as *World of Warcraft?*"

With years of development behind them and very little to show, the *Titan* team began building a vertical slice set in the game's near-future version of California, complete with a suite of mechanics like driving and combat. Parts of the demo were excellent, but it became clear that their cohesion problem wasn't going away. It felt as if they had made a dozen different games but had no way to unify them—like a jigsaw puzzle where the pieces wouldn't fit together—and they continued to struggle with both technical and artistic challenges.

But this was Blizzard. Surely Team 4 would get more time to nail down *Titan*. "The work was super inefficient, and the scope constantly grew," said one artist, "but everyone trudged along calmly, assuming Blizzard would continue funding this endeavor indefinitely."

■   ■   ■

One morning in the spring of 2013, as developers on the *Titan* team trickled into the office, they noticed that rows of folding chairs had been set up in the common area for an impromptu all-hands meeting. When it started, Pardo stood up and dropped the big news: *Titan* wasn't working out, so he and the other Blizzard executives had decided to reboot it.

For Justin Thavirat, the art director, this was bittersweet news. On one hand, they were throwing away countless hours' worth of work from his nearly seven years on the project that would never be seen. On the other, he recognized that *Titan* couldn't keep going the way it was headed. "It was tough," Thavirat said, "but there was also a little bit of relief."

At the end of the day, *Titan* cost Blizzard around $80 million, according to people with knowledge of the financials. Many of its staff moved to Blizzard's other teams, while a few were laid off. Jeff Kaplan, Chris Metzen, and a handful of other artists and engineers stayed behind to try to figure out whether *Titan*'s remains could be salvaged.

Later, Pardo stood up in front of the company, tears in his eyes, as he gave a presentation about why *Titan* had failed. He noted that he should have done more about the game's technical and artistic problems, which Team 4 members saw as a backhanded way of blaming other people for the game's issues—the last straw for some. The longtime Blizzard designer had stewarded a lot of great games and was Morhaime's heir apparent, but now he had lost the trust of Blizzard's other leaders. Several executives and directors, including Metzen, demanded that he be removed from a position of leadership. They didn't want to report to him anymore; didn't want him overseeing their new projects.

But Morhaime may have still been haunted by his decision to remove Mike O'Brien as lead of *Warcraft III* back in 1999, which had led to the departure of three top Blizzard programmers and the creation of ArenaNet, a significant competitor. In retrospect, Morhaime would tell confidants, he felt like he should have taken a more diplomatic approach back then. Now he didn't want to repeat the same mistake and drive away one of the people who he believed was most integral to Blizzard's success.

Problem was, by doing nothing, Morhaime might drive away a group of other people who were integral to Blizzard's success, as Paul Sams and other executives tried to make clear during a series of lengthy conversations in the weeks that followed.

Pardo took a sabbatical as Morhaime and his team tried to determine his future at Blizzard. At first they talked about potentially shifting his responsibilities, but after a few months, Morhaime met with Pardo and told him it would be best if he resigned. In the summer of 2014, Pardo announced that he was leaving Blizzard, saying publicly that he had made the "difficult and bittersweet but ultimately exciting decision to pursue the next chapter in my life and career."

The failure of *Titan* would have ripple effects for years to come.

TWENTY

TO THE MOON

A s *Titan* was falling apart, Bobby Kotick was fighting a battle for his corporate future.

Back in 2008, when Activision and Vivendi merged to form Activision Blizzard, Kotick relinquished control of the company he'd led out of bankruptcy. He retained the CEO job and oversaw Activision Blizzard's day-to-day operations, but Vivendi owned the majority of shares. A few years later, the French conglomerate was again struggling, facing an overwhelming amount of debt and market confusion over its long-term strategy as both a telecommunications and entertainment company. With its stock tanking, Vivendi ousted its CEO and began hunting for liquidity, telling press that it planned to sell off its $8.1-billion stake in Activision.

Kotick and his longtime business partner, Brian Kelly, saw an opportunity and began canvassing potential investors for a deal that would allow them to regain control of the company. At the beginning of 2013, Kotick and Kelly made a formal proposal: Activision Blizzard itself would take on debt to buy two-thirds of Vivendi's shares, while their investment group would snag the rest. To evaluate the deal, the board hired an outside banking firm that subsequently opposed Kotick's offer, according to court documents filed later, suggesting that it would give him and Kelly "disproportionate influence" on Activision Blizzard's future. The committee began exploring other options, including selling the rest of Vivendi's shares through a secondary offering or restricting Kotick and Kelly's voting power to less than 10 percent.

This was unacceptable to Kotick, who said he would only agree to the deal on his terms. The bank J.P. Morgan, which was underwriting the loan that would allow Activision Blizzard to buy two-thirds of Vivendi's shares, backed up Kotick's position by threatening to walk if he resigned. Wall Street bankers loved the audacious CEO, who had led Activision Blizzard to generate more than $4 billion in revenue per year.

In the tense weeks and months that followed, both Vivendi and the board made other counterproposals, but Kotick refused to budge. Vivendi executives mulled over firing Kotick, suggesting in emails that they'd have support from at least one other board member if they did, but the French company was desperate for cash and saw risks in hanging on to Activision Blizzard, like the *Titan* implosion and an upcoming console transition, which was making investors skittish. There were no other buyers; Kotick had all the leverage.

On July 9, 2013, Kotick won the staring contest, and Vivendi accepted the terms as originally proposed. Vivendi agreed to sell at $13.60, about 10 percent less than Activision's share price at the time. The deal was announced on July 25, and just four days later, Activision closed at $18.27, generating an instant profit for Kotick's investment group. Kotick and Kelly personally netted a total of $178 million, according to court documents.

More importantly for the future of the company, the deal meant that Activision was now free to operate without Vivendi's influence. On paper, the voting power of Kotick and Kelly was capped at around 25 percent—later reduced to around 20 percent by a legal settlement—but in practice they were now in control. Vivendi retained a small stake in the company (that it would sell off over the next few years) but gave up all six of its seats on the board of directors. In a press release announcing the news, Kotick vowed to "emerge even stronger" with "a best-in-class franchise portfolio and the focus and flexibility to drive long-term shareholder value and expand our leadership position as one of the world's most important entertainment companies."

Down in Irvine, people who were paying attention to this boardroom drama could only wonder: What did a newly empowered Bobby Kotick mean for the future of Blizzard?

■　　■　　■

When Greg Street first started at Blizzard in February 2008, it seemed like *World of Warcraft* would never stop growing. Street, a veteran designer who became popular among fans for his frequent posts about game balance on the company's message boards, had joined to work on the second expansion, *Wrath of the Lich King*. As they prepared to release the third expansion, *Cataclysm*, which would overhaul the entire world of Azeroth through a series of apocalyptic events, Blizzard announced that the game had reached 12 million subscribers. There were more people paying monthly for *World of Warcraft* than there were buying just about any other game on the market.

But then the inevitable happened: *World of Warcraft* began to decline—first to 11 million subscribers, then to 10 million. Players were upset with some of the changes in *Cataclysm*—the world felt too empty; the dungeons were too hard—and loudly voiced their discontent. Suddenly, Kotick and other executives were showing up at Team 2 meetings to talk about retention and engagement, while Morhaime promised on investor calls that they would work to produce content more quickly. The solution, they decided, was to add new areas, quests, and characters to the game on a more rapid cadence. "It was obvious for everyone to look at," said Street. "When did we get money, subscriptions? It was when we shipped an expansion."

But developing an expansion for *World of Warcraft* was a slow, inefficient process hampered by clunky tools, content bottlenecks, and a chaotic culture inherited from the old days. "In my head I thought it'd be a really organized structure, but it wasn't," said designer Chris Kaleiki. "It was completely based on tribal knowledge: if you want to know how to do something, go to someone and ask them." For each new expansion, the design leads needed to figure out a setting and theme—be it an invasion of demonic hordes or a sojourn to an Asia-inspired continent full of sentient panda bears—and work from there. "I felt like a lot of the holdups were on the design side," said engineer Kyle Radue.

Even with numbers slumping, *World of Warcraft* still drove the bulk of Blizzard's business, giving the other teams extended timelines to work on *Diablo* and *StarCraft*. During company meals and parties, members of Team 2 would end arguments with colleagues on other teams by sniping, *We're paying for your game.* Back in the office, the pressure only kept increasing, not just to produce expansions more quickly but to release a regular stream of dungeons, raids, and updates. Whenever they realized they were behind schedule, they'd switch to crunch mode, in which the producers would order dinner and most staff would work from 10:00 a.m. until 10:00 p.m. for weeks or even months. "It was kind of a battlefield mentality," said Street.

One day, *World of Warcraft* production director J. Allen Brack took the senior staff to a nearby steakhouse, where he'd rented a private room. As they scarfed down T-bones and filet mignons, Brack began paraphrasing a famous speech from John F. Kennedy—"We choose to go to the moon in this decade and do the other things, not because they are easy but because they are hard"—and revealed that Blizzard would be embarking upon its own ambitious moonshot plan to release a new *World of Warcraft* expansion every year. Their expansions typically took about two years to make, so they hoped to double the size of the *World of Warcraft* team and divide it into two units, each alternating so they could stagger new expansions every year.

But as the old saying goes, nine women can't make a baby in a month. More people couldn't solve their efficiency problems, and hiring new designers and programmers just inflated their ambitions for each new expansion. "A lot of people got really excited about all the content they can do now that we have so many people," said Eric Braddock, an artist. "So the work ballooned." Then they would face the same problem they'd been facing for many years: whatever was next on the schedule needed as much help as possible to get out the door. When the release of the next expansion, *Mists of Pandaria*, was imminent, anyone who might have been working on the following expansion, *Warlords of Draenor*, had to drop everything and help. "It wasn't a bad strategy; it was an ambitious strategy," said Street. "But it totally failed. We never were able to hire enough leaders to get the second team up and running."

Bobby Kotick couldn't understand Blizzard's inability to release *World of Warcraft* expansions at a faster pace, grumbling that the company was failing to serve its players. Since the early years of Activision, he had filled his corporate suite with executives from consumer packaged-goods companies like Procter & Gamble in hopes of driving more efficient production. "Wall Street predictability was something Bobby was looking for," said Dusty Welch, who worked for Nestlé and Dole before joining Activision.

During the early days, Kotick often used an acronym called SPEED: Stability, Predictability, Efficiency, Equity Building, Development of Organization. He wanted his games to be good, but he also wanted them to be predictable—to fit neatly into Activision Blizzard's fiscal calendar so the company could show growth from year to year. One of Kotick's favorite stats was the comparison between Activision and the stock market at large. In a 2013 annual report, he wrote that since 1993, his company had "delivered 1,608 percent in total shareholder return compared to 484 percent for the S&P 500."

It was a stark contrast to Blizzard, whose leaders saw schedules as malleable and were always willing to delay games, although Activision executives liked to joke that Blizzard actually shared that desire for predictability: if they agreed to a deadline, you could rest assured they'd miss it.

■　■　■

Kotick was once asked by a journalist what made Activision so successful. He responded by describing his company as "ruthless prioritizers of opportunity"—a mantra that concisely summed up how Activision had done business for the previous twenty-five years. Kotick had spent decades betting on video games that had, in his words, the "potential to be exploited every year across every platform," and the floors of his company were littered with the corpses of franchises that had been sucked completely dry. Whenever Activision released a hit game, Kotick would greenlight sequels and spinoffs to be released as quickly as possible—no matter what it meant for the game's long-term health.

Back in 1999, Activision had found unexpected success with *Tony*

Hawk's Pro Skater, a skateboarding game that let players ollie and kickflip to a killer pop-punk soundtrack. Kotick acquired the game's developer, Neversoft, and they began producing new sequels every fall. Sales tapered off after a few years, and by the late 2000s fans were wondering why Tony Hawk's name was attached to so many duds. In 2010, the critic Keza MacDonald wrote that "Activision's original mistake was probably in making the *Hawk* series annual," noting that fans grew exhausted of the formula by the fourth game. "It's been faltering since then, making ill-advised forays into novelty without doing anything creatively brave, declining consistently in quality," she wrote. Mick West, a cofounder of Neversoft, said the company never questioned or even regretted the decision to go annual—until much later, after the fifth or sixth games, when he departed. "There were concerns that it was getting harder to be more creative in a limited time frame," West said.

But Kotick's demand for annual franchises wouldn't be abated. In 2005, the Boston-based company Harmonix released a game called *Guitar Hero* that allowed players to pretend to be rock stars by tapping buttons on plastic guitars. Kotick thought the idea was absurd—until he saw the game generate $45 million and decided to acquire the publisher. Activision released a barrage of new sequels and spinoffs (*DJ Hero! Band Hero!*) through 2010, and just as with *Tony Hawk,* both sales and review scores fell gradually every year until the series was eventually killed. Dusty Welch, who was head of publishing, recalled one memorable planning meeting in which Kotick stopped him in the middle of a discussion about yearly releases. "He said, 'Dusty, I like this, but this is not aggressive enough,'" Welch recalled. "'I want to get to a launch every quarter, and then I want to get to a *Guitar Hero* launch every month.' My mouth must have dropped open."

Kotick believed that players had an insatiable desire for new content, but even if that was true, the downside of this strategy was that it didn't allow for much time to innovate. Paul Reiche, whose studio created the lucrative toy-based game series *Skylanders*, watched his franchise find massive success and then die off a few years later. "I think annualization made money," Reiche said. "I think annualization sort of hurt the creative capabilities."

The only Activision franchise that had successfully been annualized without collapsing was the military shooter series *Call of Duty*, which hadn't skipped a fall release since 2004 thanks to a dependable formula and a stringent, factory-like schedule that saw different development studios passing the baton every year. *Call of Duty* had topped sales charts every year since 2009 due to its photorealistic graphics and addictive multiplayer modes. Fans often complained about the games feeling stale, and there would be some misses, like the later release *Call of Duty Infinite Warfare*, which would fail to meet Activision's expectations. Still, *Infinite Warfare* became the year's bestselling video game.

■ ■ ■

Gio Hunt started working at Blizzard just a few months after Kotick took the company independent. He'd never worked in the video game industry—he'd been a lawyer and an executive at tech companies like AOL—but he'd played enough *World of Warcraft* to strain his marriage, so he thought he might be a good fit at Blizzard. Morhaime was looking for a new chief of staff, and a mutual colleague recommended Hunt. The two of them clicked, and in December 2013, he began serving as Morhaime's right-hand man.

When he arrived, *World of Warcraft* was on the decline and the company was still reeling from the implosion of *Titan*. Kotick had bragged about the project to colleagues, shareholders, and celebrity friends, touting that the teams who had made *World of Warcraft* were now working on something bigger and better. Now, he and his Chief Operating Officer, Thomas Tippl, were pointing fingers and applying pressure, asking Morhaime and the other executives just how the debacle had happened. Whose fault was it? Why did nobody step in?

Since the Davidson days, Blizzard had always enjoyed an unusual amount of autonomy from its corporate owners. Whether it was a mail-order catalog company or a French utility provider, Morhaime and Sams had always been able to assure executives above them that Blizzard had things covered, and in return for that trust, Blizzard delivered nonstop hits. Morhaime's company may have had its own unique, often sluggish process, but that process had proven to be successful—until now. *Titan* was Blizzard's first high-profile failure, a black mark on the company's record, and, in a newly independent Kotick's eyes, a reason to start getting more involved.

To mollify Kotick and Tippl, Blizzard began expanding a process called long-range planning. Each development team was asked to assemble a presentation deck that mapped out the next three to five years for their franchise, including content, features, and potential monetization plans. "There was a tremendous amount of resistance to that," said Hunt. Some teams, preoccupied with their short-term needs, simply made things up, stuffing their presentations with imaginary goals to release new expansions or launch on consoles.

This kind of planning had been done at Blizzard in finance before, but now it was more elaborate and all-encompassing—and for the first time, it would be owned by the game teams. "Part of the messaging was that planning isn't supposed to be a prison, it's supposed to be an enabler," said Hunt. "I think that was an improvement, not just because it kept Activision at bay. It also makes sense."

Blizzard's fortunes turned around in 2014 thanks to the *Reaper of*

Souls redemption story, *Hearthstone* becoming a smash hit, and most importantly, a new *World of Warcraft* expansion. Blizzard's revenue grew from $1.12 billion in 2013 to $1.72 billion in 2014, while operating income (profit) doubled. Still, despite the adoption of long-range planning, the pressure from Activision continued. Kotick and Tippl preached that Blizzard was neglecting players by not releasing *World of Warcraft* expansions on a more consistent cadence and encouraged the company to keep expanding the development team. "It was just Bobby's continued sense that we were not 'extracting enough value' out of the IP," said Hunt. "Even the way he'd say something like that would just make everyone at Blizzard upset."

At the end of 2015, Activision Blizzard announced that *World of Warcraft* had fallen to 5.5 million subscribers—less than half of its count five years earlier. The company also declared it would stop reporting subscriptions "as there are other metrics that are better indicators of the overall Blizzard business performance." *World of Warcraft* was still enormously profitable, but it was clear that the game had peaked, and attempts to speed up the development of expansions weren't working.

StarCraft II's two expansions, *Heart of the Swarm* (2013) and *Legacy of the Void* (2015), met Blizzard's modest expectations but weren't breakout hits, leaving many of the company's leaders regretful that they had committed to releasing three games. *Heroes of the Storm* was a commercial disappointment, and the next *Diablo* game was many years away.

But Blizzard still had an ace up its sleeve—a game planned for 2016 that was set to be one of the company's biggest successes. The *Titan* story wasn't over yet.

TWENTY-ONE

CAVALRY'S HERE

One morning shortly after *Titan* collapsed, Bobby Kotick and a contingent of top Activision executives headed down to Irvine to look at a new project. The previous months had been a reckoning for Blizzard's top staff. They had canceled plenty of games before—*Shattered Nations*, *Nomad*, *Warcraft Adventures*—but none had been this consequential. *Titan* was the company's biggest failure to date, at $80 million and nearly seven years of development time, and it had come with a large opportunity cost, taking some of Blizzard's most experienced staff away from other projects. Some of the company's higher-ups began to feel, for the first time in Blizzard history, like they had failed.

For a publicly traded company like Activision Blizzard, the *Titan* cancellation was damaging less because of the money they had already spent and more because of the potential future growth that was lost. For Kotick, one of the appeals of the Activision-Vivendi merger had been the promise of a next-generation MMORPG from Blizzard—a new cash-printing machine that could rival *World of Warcraft* on the balance sheets—and now, he undoubtedly felt betrayed.

After the cancellation, Blizzard shrunk down Team 4 to a small group of developers and gave them six weeks to pitch a new idea. Led by Jeff Kaplan, one of *Titan's* top designers, the team briefly played around with making another MMORPG or perhaps a *StarCraft* shooter. Then, as they pored over old *Titan* art, they came up with a new pitch—a small-scale multiplayer game based on *Titan's* super-hero portion, where players could battle in first-person combat. They would transform each of the old classes into a unique hero, with their own personality and suite of powers. Kaplan and his colleagues had long been obsessed with *Team Fortress 2*, a player-vs.-player shooter from Valve that allowed players to control mercenaries with distinct abilities, and this could be a Blizzard twist on that concept.

The team put together a presentation for the project, which was code-named *Prometheus* but would ultimately be called *Overwatch*. It was a lengthy slideshow with financial forecasts and concept art, both new and inherited. *Titan's* Jumper became Tracer, a teleporting sol-dier with a pistol in each hand, while the Juggernaut class morphed into a bruising tank named Reinhardt. Metzen led the creation of a Marvel-inspired version of near-Earth in which a squad of superheroes called Overwatch had convened to defend humanity from rogue AI but were now dismantled. It was the story of a group of talented peo-ple who had once failed but now had a shot at redemption.

Now, Kaplan and the *Overwatch* team had to pitch their game to a room full of executives that Blizzard staff called "sweater vests"—a pejorative reference to one of Kotick's favorite outfits. The meeting was scheduled spontaneously, which felt ominous—was Kotick com-ing down to cancel the game? Did he plan to insist that Blizzard move everyone to *World of Warcraft*?

Things seemed dire for Kaplan and his team as the presenta-tion began. Activision's executives seemed disengaged and were skeptical of Blizzard's lack of experience developing shooter games. Did Blizzard even know how to design controls for first-person shooters? Up at Activision, they had been making *Call of Duty* games for a decade—why would Blizzard try to do it too? And did *Overwatch* really fit into their portfolio when they had made a massive bet on another sci-fi shooter, called *Destiny*, that was due to come out in 2014?

As the tension grew, Kotick began staring at a key piece of art that *Overwatch* artist Arnold Tsang had drawn: a team "photograph" of more than a dozen heroes. There was the angel-like Mercy, with her staff and big gold wings; the armored ape Winston, whose furrowed brow hinted at unexpected intelligence; and many more, from hulking titans to nimble snipers. Kotick looked. And looked.

Everyone in the room was quiet, waiting for their charismatic, intimidating boss to say something. Finally he spoke up: *These are the most unique characters I've ever seen. I love these guys.*

Meeting the confused glances of his executives, Kotick explained that he believed these heroes were distinct enough to bring the shooter genre to a broader audience. "It became about the art at that point," Kaplan said later in a Blizzard artbook. Kotick was especially charmed by Torbjörn, a diminutive engineer with a mechanized weapon suit and a bushy yellow beard that split into two braided ends. Blizzard staff would later share sneering stories about this revelation—Torbjörn? Unique? The guy who looked just like a *Warcraft* dwarf?—but for now, they just needed to nod and agree.

The entire tenor of the meeting changed as the other Activision executives followed their boss's lead, and the *Overwatch* team went back to work with a newfound optimism. But behind the scenes, Kotick still wasn't entirely convinced, complaining to Morhaime and Sams that Blizzard's best people should instead be working on releasing *World of Warcraft* expansions every year. As one Activision executive would later frame it: "If a kid really wants to go to Disneyland, then first they have to do their homework."

Morhaime convened with his inner circle and decided it was worth the battle, then told Kaplan and the *Overwatch* team to keep working. They had two years to make it happen.

■ ■ ■

The most impressive thing about the *Overwatch* team, thought Rachel Day during her first few months there, was that they were willing to say no. "The ability to confidently say 'no' to something is so powerful," Day said. On *Titan*, the answer to just about every question had been affirmative. Paralyzed by unparalleled ambition, overwhelming pressure, and unlimited resources, the team was willing to explore any idea that seemed worthwhile, from house customization to joyrides around the streets of San Francisco, *Grand Theft Auto*–style. Now they had a clear vision, a constrained timeline, and the ability to turn down anything that seemed superfluous for a hero shooter. "The added pressure of, 'You guys have to prove yourselves now,' definitely made that team say no to a lot of things," Day said.

Day had started at Blizzard a few years earlier as an intern in QA, where she was the only woman in a group of ten. She received her first taste of sexist workplace treatment when a manager had to bring his kids to the office and asked Day to spend the day babysitting them. *Oh, you found the one woman,* she recalled thinking. Still, she stuck with the company, eventually scoring a job as a visual effects artist on *Diablo III*, where she stayed through *Reaper of Souls*, sprucing up the graphics of runes and fireballs.

When she learned that *Diablo III* wasn't going to get a second expansion, she followed a friend to *Overwatch*, where she was immediately hooked. "The *Overwatch* team is the kind of development experience that you only get once," said Day. "That alignment, that cooperation, that true magic." Early in development, Kaplan sat down Day and the other few women on the team and told them to come to him if they ever felt uncomfortable. "He made it a very welcome, open space," she said. In the beginning of 2014, when Day started, *Overwatch* was just a few basic prototypes and half-finished characters. By the end of the year, as they prepared to reveal the game at BlizzCon, they'd built a full demo, with a dozen heroes that players would be able to take into six-on-six combat. No game at Blizzard had coalesced that quickly since the 1990s.

On November 7, 2014, Chris Metzen took the stage at the crowded BlizzCon theater in Anaheim, California, to announce the game. In jeans and a black-and-red hoodie, he paced back and forth while working the crowd, asking how many had played each of Blizzard's franchises: *Warcraft*, *StarCraft*, *Diablo*, *Hearthstone*. "In a moment like this it strikes me," he said to the audience. "It has been something like seventeen years, if my math holds up, since Blizzard opened the door to a new adventure." Metzen choked up as the moment appeared to hit him: the weight of *Titan's* development, his battles with Pardo, and the failure that had haunted Blizzard. "Seventeen years is too long to wait," he said, to raucous applause. "And my friends, the wait ends now."

Then came a short film: an introduction to the fallen group of elite superheroes called Overwatch, followed by a set of scenes, fashioned after a Pixar movie, featuring two brothers in a museum—one, younger, excited to see his favorite heroes; the second, older, more cynical about the now-shuttered Overwatch taskforce. Then the heroes popped out—Winston the brilliant ape scientist, Tracer the good-natured, teleporting prankster, Widowmaker the single-minded sniper—and brawled over a magical artifact. The older brother, stunned, picked up the artifact and accidentally activated it, saving the day. As he handed it to Tracer, she offered what would become one of *Overwatch*'s most memorable slogans: "You know, the world could always use more heroes."

Fans were exhilarated, taking to message boards and comment sections to express their excitement for Blizzard's first new franchise in nearly two decades. BlizzCon attendees loved what they played, while the video trailer racked up millions of views online. Whereas *Heroes of the Storm* had struggled to catch up to its competitors, *Overwatch* already seemed like such a dominant force that it was making the rest of the market nervous. Veteran designer Cliff Bleszinski, who was leading a game called *Lawbreakers* that was similar in several ways, wrote in his memoir that when the *Overwatch* trailer went live, one of his artists offered a pithy declaration: "We are so fucked."

Over the next year, director Jeff Kaplan became an internet celebrity, winning fans over with his nasal cadence and palpable love for the game. Every few weeks he would promise upcoming features and address fan feedback on the *Overwatch* YouTube channel, where audiences were hooked by his nerdy charisma. "He was an absolute natural in front of the camera," said social media manager Griffin Bennett. One player, who went by the handle dinoflask, racked up millions of views on YouTube by mashing together clips of Kaplan to create absurd declarations. (*"I just want to… let you know… that… if I… go down… I'm… taking… Blizzard… down… with me."*)

It was clear that they had a hit on their hands. Even people who didn't normally take to first-person shooters seemed interested in *Overwatch* because of the game's diverse cast and vibrant universe, just as Justin Thavirat and the *Titan* team had hoped all those years ago. The game itself wouldn't feature much story—there was only so much time for characters to chat between shooting matches—but

Metzen still wrote pages and pages of lore, retaining the old *Titan* themes of optimism and superhero grandeur. James Waugh, a writer in Blizzard's creative development department, pitched that they make comics and short films for each character, using the company's powerhouse cinematics team to tell stories that couldn't fit into the game. "It was this beautiful harmonic moment," said Waugh. "Different disciplines coming together, trusting each other."

Internally, Kaplan liked to use the expression "crawl, walk, run" to refer to their plans for *Overwatch* as a franchise. They'd start with this first game, which was limited to player-vs.-player multiplayer, then add a story and computer-controlled enemies for the sequel before culminating in an *Overwatch* MMORPG that would finally execute on the vision of *Titan*. But for now, they would stay focused. Thanks to the coherent direction, team chemistry, and the work they'd inherited from *Titan*, the process was smoother than just about any game Blizzard had made before. "It was a strangely easy development cycle," said animator Michael Biancalana. "Having been at numerous companies, seen different projects, this was the least drama filled."

At the beginning of 2016, Kotick met with Morhaime and some other Blizzard executives and told them he had concerns about *Overwatch*'s marketing. This was the first time Blizzard had ever released a game for both PC and consoles on the same day, and the data showed that despite all the BlizzCon hype, many customers weren't aware that *Overwatch* existed. Retailers had told Activision Blizzard that there was little demand for the game and that they didn't plan to stock many copies. "We knew it was really good," said executive Gio Hunt, "but we did not have the brand awareness around it."

Kotick encouraged Blizzard to bump *Overwatch* back from its planned May release to November to hit the all-important holiday season release window, but the development team was resistant, saying they didn't want to sit on a finished game for an extra six months. Morhaime said he would stand by his developers and keep the May release date, even if it meant scrambling to get the game in front of more eyeballs.

The *Overwatch* marketing team, led by veteran John Heinecke, began an unorthodox blitz that included events at conventions, TV spots, and a heavy focus on the upcoming beta. Waugh and the cinematics team crafted a series of videos that felt like Pixar short films, pulling at viewers' heartstrings by telling poignant origin stories about the game's reluctant soldiers, fallen heroes, and sibling rivals. The videos aired during hit shows like *Better Call Saul* and went viral across the internet, reaching both longtime Blizzard fans and curious newcomers—a success far beyond what Duane Stinnett could have envisioned back in the 1990s, when he started Blizzard's cinematics department. One short, showing the gorilla Winston as he reassembled the Overwatch task force, offered another key slogan: "Never accept the world as it appears to be. Dare to see it for what it could be."

In early May, just a few weeks before *Overwatch* released, Blizzard allowed anyone to join the beta for free, banking that word of mouth would do wonders for a game they couldn't stop playing at the office. Television advertisements for the game pointed players to the beta rather than the final release date and helped bring in nearly 10 million players, making it one of the largest betas of all time. Blizzard ended the free period just two weeks before launch, confident that fans would be desperate to play more when the game came out.

The strategy worked: *Overwatch* launched on May 24, 2016, and became the fastest-selling game of the month. In December, it won Game of the Year at the industry's biggest award show, The Game Awards, and after a year it had become a billion-dollar franchise. It was such a smash hit that during one Activision Blizzard board meeting,

Kotick stood up and led a round of applause for Morhaime. From the failure of *Titan* had emerged one of the most successful games in Blizzard's history.

But the win wasn't enough to keep Activision from getting more involved with Blizzard. If anything, the success of *Overwatch* just made the Blizzard cow seem ripe for more milking.

■ ■ ■

Way back in 1998, when Mike Morhaime first took the reins as president of Blizzard, he was a programmer who didn't know much about how to run a business, so he leaned on Paul Sams as his partner. As Blizzard grew, Sams oversaw business operations, eventually becoming the company's Chief Operating Officer, but no matter how much power he accrued, he demanded that his division stay in its lane. Marketing, community, finance, legal—any departments that weren't making video games existed to serve the ones that were. Executive producers of the game teams had all the power, and developers were explicitly told by peers not to discuss money or business during meetings. *This is Blizzard*, people would say. *We only talk about what's fun for players.*

This was diametrically opposed to the Activision approach, which concentrated power in commercial organizations such as marketing and finance. After the merger, Sams told subordinates in colorful language that if anyone from those departments at Activision reached out and tried to offer feedback or interfere with Blizzard's operations, they should contact him instead.

But as the years went by, Bobby Kotick and Thomas Tippl began to believe that Sams was doing a subpar job. They said Blizzard needed to hire more people with what they called "best-in-class" experience, like the consumer packaged-goods executives who made up Activision. After *Titan's* collapse, Kotick demanded that Blizzard bring in an experienced Chief Financial Officer—someone who could wrangle the company's spreadsheets and squeeze more revenue out of franchises like *Warcraft* and *Diablo*.

Blizzard spent more than a year trying to fill this CFO role. They enlisted a recruiting firm and came close with a few candidates, but one pulled out at the last minute and nobody else seemed worthy. The perfect person had been all but impossible to find—someone with the experience and MBA gravitas to impress Activision but also the gaming background and sensibilities that would allow them to fit into Blizzard's culture. Blizzard's old finance boss, Mark Almeida, was well-respected and played *World of Warcraft* with his team every week, but Activision didn't think he had the chops, telling Blizzard they wanted someone who had worked in the C-suite of a public company.

As the search continued, Tippl suggested that Morhaime talk to an old colleague of his named Armin Zerza. Like Tippl, Zerza was Austrian and had spent many years working for Procter & Gamble, where he'd marketed and distributed products like detergent, shampoo, and diapers. Over the course of a few hours, Zerza interviewed with several of Blizzard's top executives and game team leaders, who convened the following week and agreed: *No way*. They all had a similar takeaway: Zerza didn't express much interest in gaming or Blizzard's player-first culture—he just kept talking about how to make as much money as possible. He was clearly a sharp businessman, but his values seemed at odds with Blizzard's.

Tippl asked Morhaime to give him another shot, so Zerza came back for another round of interviews. His performance improved, and it started to feel to Blizzard's executives like this was a losing battle. Morhaime could only push back against so many of Activision's requests, especially when the CFO position had gone unfilled for so long. Morhaime also thought it might be beneficial to have someone in Blizzard's C-suite who spoke Activision's language and could see firsthand what made people love the place. Perhaps Zerza could be an intermediary between the two companies, helping Kotick and Tippl understand why Blizzard had spent so many years trying to maintain its autonomy.

In the summer of 2015, Zerza joined Blizzard as the company's first CFO. From the get-go, it was clear that he didn't fit in with the game-developer crowd. At various points, he introduced himself to staff with a slideshow that showcased his interests and hobbies, such as sports cars and helicopter skiing. Workers in attendance looked at each other, puzzled. Some of them were living with roommates and struggling to pay their bills—why was this guy telling them how much he enjoyed Ferraris? Zerza said he loved competition and that his business philosophy was all about winning. He didn't mention video games, video game development, or anything that had much to do with Blizzard.

Back in the 1990s, Blizzard had maintained an ironclad rule: from the CEO to the receptionist, only gamers were allowed at the company. This rule had been relaxed over the years as the company aimed to diversify beyond traditional video game fans, but the idea was to ensure that everyone cared about the mission to prioritize players. Now, one of Blizzard's most powerful employees seemed to embody another approach. "This guy doesn't care if he's selling *StarCraft*, or tires, or cereal, or diapers," one former Blizzard executive recalled thinking. "That really made me profoundly sad."

Around the same time, Sams quit Blizzard to move closer to his wife's family in Texas. His domain was mostly split between two people: Jean-Philippe Agati, the head of Blizzard's Europe operation, and Gio Hunt, who had been Morhaime's chief of staff; but soon a messy corporate power struggle unfolded in which Zerza wiped the floor with them both. "He was willing to go behind people's backs, talk shit about us with Bobby all day long," said Hunt. "He out-politicked all of us." Blizzard staff would joke that Zerza, with his thick Austrian accent and direct way of speaking, seemed like a James Bond villain, but his actions as a savvy operator more closely resembled *Game of Thrones*.

Zerza said he wanted to build Blizzard a world-class finance department and began bringing in new employees with ivy-league MBAs and backgrounds at firms like McKinsey. Suddenly, finance people who had otherwise been relegated to the background were pivotal parts of Blizzard strategy meetings, asking why *Hearthstone* wasn't pushing players to buy card packs more often and why they weren't selling maps and heroes for real money in *Overwatch*. "He would never speak on behalf of the franchise or the player," said Ryan Ward, a product director. "It was all about revenue, engagement, KPIs, performance."

Each game team received dedicated finance directors who would eventually become known as commercial leads, responsible for every franchise's monetization strategy. The change rubbed some old-timers the wrong way, but in theory, it wasn't a bad idea. At Blizzard, the classic box-product model had been usurped by live-service games that would be updated for years and needed to keep generating revenue to justify ongoing support. Some of these new commercial leads were big gamers and had clout within Blizzard, like Paul Della Bitta, who had helped start BlizzCon back in 2005. But the responsibilities of the role were always a little fuzzy, and eventually, commercial leads reported directly to Zerza, leaving teams unsure who had the final say.

At first, Zerza tried to learn as much as possible about Blizzard's culture, regularly asking Morhaime and other top staff about the industry. With some assistance from colleagues, he started a *World of Warcraft* character and tried to learn how the game functioned.

Although he wasn't as organically charming as Kotick, he was willing to hear people out and would work as hard as anyone. But when he didn't care for someone or their performance, he made that clear. Blizzard employees grew frustrated over his blunt speech and his tendency to express completely different opinions to different groups of people, telling staff in a meeting that he agreed with an idea only to later eviscerate it in private.

Matt Weiss, an analyst, said he was once reprimanded by his boss for approaching Zerza at someone else's desk with a project update rather than going through formal channels. "Armin would put on a nice front, nod and smile," Weiss said, "but then he'd go, 'Remove this man from my sight.'" Members of the business intelligence department, which handled analytics for many of Blizzard's games, were soon told that they reported to Zerza and that they were expected to have business school degrees. "He said, 'Well you can't be in a finance org without an MBA, so you guys should start looking for work,'" said Nicki Broderick, a project manager.

Zerza questioned why the company was putting any resources into the games that weren't performing as well—such as *StarCraft II* and *Heroes of the Storm*—and why they weren't finding more ways to monetize them. He seemed perplexed by any team or department at Blizzard with low profit margins, such as BlizzCon, which cost tens of millions of dollars but didn't make much money. Blizzard managers tried to explain that having their own convention was a unique opportunity to serve their community. Even if it wasn't a profit center, it was a massive gain for their brand, a marketing opportunity for their products, and a morale boost for both employees and players. Zerza suggested that they kill it.

Because of his corporate history, Zerza arrived with a completely different mindset from anyone else in Blizzard's boardroom. He frequently made analogies to shipping commodities at Procter & Gamble, asking why, say, Blizzard couldn't just speed up development of a game by opening a new office, as he had done to ship soap more quickly in Brazil or Argentina. Across two decades working on brands like Crest and Huggies, Zerza had never needed to think about the strengths of a company like Blizzard. It was hard to imagine people flying thousands of miles to attend shampoo conventions or meeting lifelong friends through a shared love for their favorite toothpaste bottles. In the coming years, as Zerza consolidated more power, staff began to grumble that he was just an avatar for Kotick, there to serve the CEO's will—a reasonable if not 100 percent accurate characterization. (Occasionally, Zerza would disagree with Kotick and push back against budget cuts, according to people who were in meetings with them both.)

Back in 1994, Allen Adham and Mike Morhaime had agreed to sell to Davidson & Associates only because Bob and Jan Davidson had assured them that they would be able to make games in whatever fashion they saw fit. In the decades that followed, as Blizzard bounced between corporate parents, Morhaime became revered for his ability to protect Blizzard's developers. Guided by trusted lieutenants such as Paul Sams and Mark Almeida, Morhaime always made the same promise: Blizzard's games might be late, but they would always be critical and commercial hits. Now, after the *Titan* debacle, Activision's executives felt like they could no longer trust that promise.

World of Warcraft had completely transformed Blizzard, evolving it from a simple video game studio into one of the industry's biggest corporations. Years later, Kotick's ongoing interest in Blizzard's operations and the rise of Armin Zerza were about to have a very different kind of impact.

A new era of Blizzard Entertainment was about to begin.

PART

3

. . .

FUTURE

TWENTY-TWO

INCUBATION

I n the summer of 2016, Allen Adham walked onto the sunny Irvine campus of a company that was much different from the one he'd founded. Decades earlier, Blizzard had been a handful of guys in a cramped office. Now it was part of Activision Blizzard, which *Fortune* named one of the five hundred most lucrative companies and one of the one hundred most desirable workplaces. If you polled a random group of enthusiasts and asked their favorite video game company, the most common answer would be Nintendo—but Blizzard would be second or third.

It had been twelve years since Adham resigned. During this lengthy hiatus, he had played a lot of *World of Warcraft* and he had started a hedge fund—an unusual move for a video game designer, but Adham had long been interested in the inner workings of the stock market, which he saw as its own sort of video game. By 2015, he was managing $50 million from nearly one hundred people, but the fund was struggling and Adham decided it was time for another pivot. He and Morhaime began talking: Blizzard was failing to get new games off the ground, and Adham had always considered himself particularly good at starting projects—what if he came back to help Blizzard cultivate new ideas?

While Adham often told colleagues he wasn't motivated by money, everyone knew that by leaving Blizzard before the release of *World of Warcraft* and the Activision merger, he'd missed out on a huge payday. He had made millions by selling Blizzard to Davidson, but it wasn't the kind of "eff you" money that some of his former colleagues later saw. Leaving Blizzard, Adham would later say, had been the biggest mistake of his life—because he missed making games, for sure, but also because of the cash.

So Adham wound down his hedge firm and returned to the video game company he had started. Morhaime sent out an email to reintroduce him as head of Blizzard's new incubation department, encouraging employees to send him ideas for new games. Adham would then help turn those ideas into pitch presentations for Blizzard's "product strat" group, which consisted of the company's C-suite and top developers. Fresh off the unexpected success of *Hearthstone* and *Overwatch*—billion-dollar franchises that had come from small, focused teams—Blizzard wanted to see if it could capture yet another bolt of lightning in yet another bottle.

Colleagues warned Adham to move slowly—advice he ignored. He was accustomed to a Blizzard that had operated quickly and chaotically, and, perhaps most importantly, where he was in charge. As he emphatically offered his opinions on the company's direction, Blizzard's executive producers began to squirm. Those who had never worked with Adham before started to wonder: Who was this guy telling them what to do and trying to poach their people? Blizzard's newer power players, like *World of Warcraft* executive producer J. Allen Brack, weren't familiar with Adham's style and didn't react well to the idea of losing their top developers. When Adham tried to move people from Team 2 to his own projects, he was told he'd have to wait a few months or even a year before they would be ready.

In the months that followed, Adham helped kick off two games. One, code-named *Orbis*, was a *Warcraft*-themed twist on the massively popular *Pokémon Go*, which allowed players to catch fantasy critters in "augmented reality" using a phone's camera. The *Orbis* pitch had been circulating before Adham joined, but he took over and helped shape it. The other was *Odyssey*, a Blizzard spin on survival games such as *Rust*.

But many of the other ideas Adham shepherded never made it out of product strat, frustrating some developers who were told that they needed to prove that there was a potential billion-dollar market for their projects—logic that seemed backward if they wanted to do something innovative. Some Blizzard employees wondered if Rob Pardo's departure had zapped the company's creativity, despite his struggles as a manager. "So many of the things that were making Blizzard special and dynamic and interesting disappeared with him," said Jonathan Bankard, a business director.

The return of Blizzard's founder seemed to be a broadly positive development for the company as it grappled with identity questions and increasing pressure from Activision, but Adham's colleagues began to suspect that he was in the wrong role. This sort of middle management position was an awkward fit; instead, he should be either higher (in the C-suite) or lower (the director of a game). Seeing how many Blizzard employees didn't even recognize his name proved to be an uncomfortable new reality for Adham. In many ways, Blizzard had moved on without him.

At the same time, the *Diablo* franchise was floundering. A few years earlier, Morhaime had nixed a second expansion for *Diablo III* in favor of quickly moving to the next game under Josh Mosqueira, but when Mosqueira quit Blizzard and his project, *Hades*, was canceled, Team 3 was left leaderless. Morhaime called up a couple of old friends to see if they might be interested in taking the reins: Bill Roper and Dave Brevik, who had resigned from Blizzard North all those years ago. They talked for several months about the possibility, but Brevik sniffed out some of the same politics that were hounding Adham and the conversations fizzled. "That's not why I make video games," Brevik said.

Adham, who had been involved with the series since it was just a pitch on Brevik's computer, sat next to the *Diablo* team and thought he might be able to help, perhaps as the franchise's executive producer. The other executives agreed, but in this new era of Blizzard, everything moved slowly. During one product strat meeting, Adham grew frustrated and barked at Frank Pearce, asking why it was taking so long for him to take over the *Diablo* team. Pearce, who had once been Adham's first employee but was now Chief Development Officer and his boss, shot back in his gruff tone: Adham wasn't in charge of the company anymore. He needed to chill out.

Adham apologized, relented, and waited, until a few months later he was named executive producer of the *Diablo* team, where he helmed several new projects. Later, he would regret moving so quickly rather than trying to build trust with the other Blizzard leaders. By necessity and design, Blizzard's culture had morphed as the company expanded, transforming each team into its own fiefdom, with its own relationships and power struggles. Management by chaos was no longer an option.

■　■　■

The hope was that Adham's incubation initiative would lead to more Blizzard games for mobile, which was now the biggest gaming platform in the world. Tens of millions of people might play games on PCs, where Blizzard had always reigned, and consoles, where Blizzard had more recently engaged, but *hundreds* of millions were playing on their smartphones. People who would never think of themselves as gamers spent hours on their phones on the subway flinging birds at pigs or mindlessly sliding tiles as they waited for the dentist. Blizzard's own *Hearthstone*, which had come out on phones shortly after it was released on PC, had reached huge audiences that wouldn't have previously considered picking up one of the company's games.

Although Bobby Kotick had originally dismissed mobile gaming as a fad, the eye-popping numbers on Apple and Android phones changed his mind. Mobile games could feature aggressive monetization models that wouldn't be tolerated by gamers who played on PCs or consoles. The colorful, addictive puzzle game *Candy Crush*, for example, was free to play but accosted players with in-app purchases—a model that brought in more than a billion dollars in revenue per year for King, the Swedish company behind the game. In 2015, Activision spent nearly $6 billion to purchase King and began pushing for other mobile investments across the company.

For Blizzard, there was another compelling reason to invest in the world of mobile games: They were typically smaller and less ambitious than their PC and console counterparts, and they were often developed in less than a year. Perhaps these smaller projects, free from the tortured production cycles of major sequels like *StarCraft II* and *Diablo III*, could help fill the gaps looming in Blizzard's release schedule.

But, as Adham had learned, Blizzard had an efficiency problem. Developers who had been at the company for decades were set in their ways, even if that meant working more slowly than their competitors. Weekly stand-up meetings that were ten minutes at other companies might take an hour at Blizzard. Sprints, or periods of time dedicated to completing a set amount of work, typically unfolded over a few weeks—at Blizzard, they could take three months.

Even the most rudimentary company functions took extra time. Prospective employees would face months of silence after job interviews and then give up, assuming they hadn't been hired, only to receive offers in the mail a year later. "I've joked before that Blizzard is aptly named," said Glenn Rane, a longtime artist. "It's glacial."

Blizzard had tried to smooth out its game production process over the years, but few attempts had stuck. Veteran developers were resistant to change and didn't want to veer away from what had worked in the past. The bigger the company grew, the more slowly it moved, and the Blizzard brand was too revered, pressuring everyone at the company to embrace perfectionism. "I think the Blizzard process keeps them from advancing too quickly," said one developer. "They have layers and layers of cultural due diligence, so every single decision winds up recalculated multiple times."

One driver of Blizzard's success had always been ensuring that the games were as polished and bug-free as possible, which also slowed everything down. Dan Johnson, a QA analyst, found what appeared to be an insignificant graphical glitch in *StarCraft II* during his first few weeks at the company. At previous companies, he might have been instructed to skip it for more important bug reports, but Blizzard was different. "They said, 'No, write that up,'" Johnson said. "There was not a bug that was too small."

The bulk of Blizzard's staff were now working on games that were already live, churning out new content for *World of Warcraft*, *Hearthstone*, and *Heroes of the Storm* every month, which also made new projects take longer. The other big factor was crunch, which was still present but had been reduced significantly since Adham's first stint at

Blizzard, when developers had sacrificed their personal lives and slept on couches in the office for weeks at a time. Better work-life balance kept employees happier and healthier—a win in the long run—but it meant that games took longer to make.

Most people who worked at Blizzard, especially those who had been there for decades, felt like there was something special about the place, and it was impossible to know which Jenga pieces they could remove without destroying the whole tower. Developers on most of the company's recent projects—*StarCraft II*, *Diablo III*, and even *Titan*—had struggled with this same dilemma. Blizzard's executives and developers were terrified to alter the company's processes because they didn't want to inadvertently kill the magic that made Blizzard such a success in the first place.

■　■　■

Bobby Kotick also said he didn't want to kill the magic, but his actions made Blizzard loyalists believe otherwise. While Adham tried to navigate the new internal politics of Blizzard, Morhaime was facing increasing external pressure from his corporate overlords. Kotick and Thomas Tippl asked why Blizzard had so many people in non-development departments—particularly cinematics and customer service—and why the company wasn't improving its efficiency. During long-range planning meetings, Activision executives would point out that they had more than one thousand people on *Call of Duty* while *World of Warcraft* only had a few hundred. Tippl offered "man-month" calculations to prove to Morhaime and his team that the only way to release new expansions more quickly—a goal that both companies shared—would be to add hundreds more people to Team 2.

Activision's messaging was always the same: Blizzard was letting its players down by not putting out more *World of Warcraft* content on a regular cadence. To Morhaime and his circle, these demands seemed to be contradictory and unreasonable. Kotick celebrated when Blizzard incubated smash hits like *Hearthstone* and now *Overwatch*, but at the same time, he expected Blizzard's best people to work on its most lucrative games rather than experiment with those new franchises. And there was skepticism among the veterans—who felt like they understood players better than Kotick did—as to whether people wanted *more* content if it wasn't going to feel fun and innovative.

One of the most significant fights between Blizzard and Activision was over how to reward staff. Kotick believed in giving the biggest bonuses to teams that delivered the largest profits, which would encourage more people to move to *World of Warcraft*, while Morhaime thought that the entire company should benefit from profit-sharing—otherwise, there'd be no incentive for people to go experiment with new ideas. They struck a few compromises over time, as Morhaime agreed to shift a greater portion of profit-sharing to the *World of Warcraft* team without eliminating bonuses for other divisions, but the argument was always simmering.

Activision Blizzard's board of directors wanted to convert the top staff's equity into "performance shares" that would only vest on certain conditions, like if yearly operating income (profit) hit a predetermined goal. Morhaime was livid about this change, arguing that the system incentivized short-term thinking and would punish his teams if, say, they delayed a game. Kotick and Tippl fired back that the whole point of a bonus was to reward teams for shipping on time—it shouldn't be guaranteed even if teams failed to deliver. Morhaime said that when things went awry, that was when they wanted their top executives and directors working the hardest, not hunting for new jobs because their equity vanished. And on and on the two companies battled.

Blizzard's leaders couldn't understand why Activision felt compelled to interfere with their operations. They had five franchises—*Warcraft, Diablo, StarCraft, Hearthstone,* and now *Overwatch*—that other big video game publishers would kill to get their hands on. The company had generated a whopping $2.4 billion of revenue in 2016 thanks to *World of Warcraft* and the runaway success of *Overwatch.*

But Activision was looking for consistent growth, which Blizzard, with its spotty release schedule, wasn't delivering. Blizzard's profit output was like a pendulum, swinging back and forth between good and bad years:

> **2010:** $850 million
> **2011:** $496 million
> **2012:** $716 million
> **2013:** $376 million
> **2014:** $756 million
> **2015:** $561 million
> **2016:** $1 billion

Now it was set to plummet again in 2017, and at this point, Blizzard had no other significant games on the horizon. Massive hits like *Overwatch* were great, and the fact that Blizzard was able to generate nine or ten figures of profit every year was itself something of a marvel in what had become a volatile, hit-driven industry. But shareholders weren't holding onto Activision Blizzard stock because of its current success; they were holding on to the expectation of success to come. Kotick and his team didn't demand linear increases from year to year, but they did want Blizzard to show steady growth over longer horizons, and during long-range planning meetings, Tippl would ask how the company planned to reorganize so it could achieve that goal.

If they couldn't release a new *World of Warcraft* expansion every fall, maybe they could alternate with new *Diablo* or *Overwatch* sequels?

Most Blizzard employees weren't aware of the battles their CEO was fighting with Kotick and his lieutenants. But many—especially those outside of the development teams—did start to notice Activision influencing Blizzard in ways they'd never witnessed before. "Everybody was seeing it," said one staffer. "Oh, this Blizzard person left; they were replaced by an Activision employee." Morhaime had hoped that Armin Zerza could help explain Blizzard's values to Activision, but instead he appeared to be bringing Activision's values to Blizzard.

In the past, even the finance people had channeled Blizzard's player-first ethos. Back in 2011, when discussing how much of a cut Blizzard would take from transactions on the *Diablo III* auction house, Blizzard's accountants told the team to lower the numbers, saying they were creating the system only for the benefit of players. "It was one of the most incredible things I've ever seen in the video game industry," said designer Jason Bender. Even when Morhaime pushed his game teams to add more recurring revenue models to their games, like character boosts in *World of Warcraft* or the map marketplace in *StarCraft II*, they were supplemental. When a model didn't work out, like the auction house, the company would kill it. "I think Blizzard's forte was really leaving a bunch of money on the table," said Jonathan Bankard, "and investing in, the term we used was, the 'player sentiment bank account.'"

Now, the landscape was different. Traditionally at Blizzard, the executive producer of each game team had the autonomy to run their franchise however they saw fit. But in this new era, Zerza and his finance department would sit in meetings and offer input, making suggestions that sounded a whole lot like demands. *World of Warcraft* executive producer J. Allen Brack, who had firmly opposed Zerza's hiring, complained to colleagues that their CFO's goals were at odds with the company's values. "Armin wanted to make as much money as we can," said Frederic Dumas, the publishing director for *World of Warcraft* in Europe. "J. wanted to be as right as possible to our players. You need to find the right balance between both."

By the end of 2017, Zerza had been promoted to Chief Operating Officer at Blizzard and was overseeing many more departments, leading some long-time staff to begin accepting a dismal reality: going to work every day was getting less fun.

■ ▧ ▪

With an MBA from Wharton and years of experience leading Blizzard's strategic initiatives group, Hamilton Chu knew how to speak Zerza's language. After steering *Hearthstone* to become one of the company's biggest hits, he had earned enough clout to be able to shield Team 5 from some of the financial pressures that were hitting the rest of the company. But every time *Hearthstone* surpassed revenue expectations, the next year's targets only grew larger, which forced him to spend more time in business meetings. "It made my life unpleasant," Chu said. "I was just spending 80 percent of my emotional energy on that rather than working on the game."

By 2017, *Hearthstone* had drawn significantly more attention from Zerza and his finance team, who were looking to push harder on live games to make up for the lack of big new products. "There were a series of meetings, pressures, and discussions about monetization," said Steve Fowler, the vice president of global publishing. "Why are we not running bundles? Why are we not running more frequent sales? Can we get a fourth expansion pack every year into the game?" People who didn't play a lot of games didn't seem to understand why some of these suggestions might be detrimental. "There is a breaking point, or at least a bending point, where if you continue to extract as much revenue out of players in the short-term, that has an effect on the long-term retention," said Fowler.

Zerza's own incentives were tied to short-term financial results, and he proved to be savvy at finding ways to boost the numbers for a given fiscal quarter, striking big deals across Blizzard and pushing for discounts and promotions inside games like *Hearthstone*. Chu and his team argued that these sales would dilute the value of card packs. "Once you train people to look for price discounts, bundles, they're trapped on that," said Bankard. "It's like K-Mart vs. Costco. You feel good at Costco because it feels like they price everything fairly—they don't need to put specials on."

In December 2017, the *Hearthstone* team released a free single-player mode called Dungeon Run that tasked players with beating a series of increasingly difficult computer-controlled bosses. The mode was popular but didn't bring in any money or encourage players to buy card packs, which led to endless battles for Team 5—not just with Activision-minded executives but even with Blizzard leaders like Morhaime, who now had to grapple with tough questions. The company's philosophy had always been that if you made great games, the money would follow, but was that still true in the world of free to play?

At the same time, Chu was getting calls from an ex-Blizzard employee named Jay Ong, now head of gaming at the comic book giant Marvel, who said that if Chu left Blizzard and started a new company, he could work on a Marvel video game. Chu went to Ben Brode, who was now the director of *Hearthstone* and who had also grown frustrated with the changes at Blizzard, to gauge his interest in a partnership.

Brode was an easy sell, both because he would follow Chu

anywhere and because he had missed spending his days developing games rather than sitting in meetings. "I'd lost touch with the product," Brode said. "The idea that I could get back into making games was really exciting for me." As the two of them began talking about what leaving Blizzard might look like, they decided to coin a code phrase for their secret mission. That way, if someone popped into a room and asked what they were talking about, they had an easy explanation. "The code word," said Brode, "was 'Dungeon Run monetization.'"

In the spring of 2018, Chu and Brode quit Blizzard. The company had seen significant departures in the past—Chris Metzen had resigned shortly after the release of *Overwatch*, citing burnout—but this one felt different. More existential. Rumors were starting to swirl about Kotick's plans and whether Morhaime would even stick around for much longer. "It felt like I was leaving an uncertain thing for an uncertain thing," Brode said.[19]

Brode's departure was especially painful because he had become one of the public faces of Blizzard, regularly appearing on promotional *Hearthstone* streams and recording silly videos for the game. One YouTube compilation featuring nothing but clips of him laughing racked up half a million views. "When he left Blizzard, that's when I knew something was not right," said Brian Schwab, an engineer on the original *Hearthstone* team. "He would have stayed on *Hearthstone* until the sun death of the universe—that's how much he bled Blizzard."

It was now clear to everyone at Blizzard that the company was changing in big ways. New hires were warned: *It's not like it was before.*

---

19 Chu and Brode would go on to start a video game studio called Second Dinner, where they used that Marvel license to create another hit card game: *Marvel Snap*. Suddenly, Brode found himself having to worry about lingo like the CPI (cost per install) and LTV (lifetime value) attached to each player. "At Blizzard, we just never thought about those things," he said.

Sure, they still got to make video games for a living, and they still worked on franchises that were beloved by millions, but Blizzard was starting to feel like other corporations that prioritized profits over players.

At the same time, Blizzard was about to launch one of its most ambitious initiatives yet—an effort that would take one of its biggest games to a new level. The world had never seen anything else like it. For better or for worse.

TWENTY-THREE

THE NFL OF VIDEO GAMES

The first documented video game tournament took place in 1972, when a group of Stanford University students battled in the primitive spaceship fighting simulator *Spacewar!*. First place won a yearlong subscription to *Rolling Stone* magazine. Thirty years later, Koreans were packing stadiums to watch their favorite players duke it out in high-stakes matches over virtual soldiers. By the 2000s, competitive gaming had an official name—"esports"—and the best digital athletes were able to make a living doing nothing but playing games like *Quake* or *League of Legends*.[20]

Blizzard's games were at the center of this esports revolution, largely thanks to *StarCraft*'s ubiquity in South Korea. In the early 2000s, Korea's World Cyber Games became one of the biggest esports tournaments on the planet, with a prize pool in the millions of dollars and prime slots for both *StarCraft* and *Warcraft III*. By the 2010s, grassroots esports communities had sprouted around all of Blizzard's games. Even *World of Warcraft*, not normally associated with

---

20 Some may write "eSports," but we will be having none of that here.

competitive gaming, joined the party with a dedicated mode in which players could swing swords and sling spells at one another.

To video game companies, it wasn't clear what to make of this burgeoning industry, or how to monetize it. Morhaime was a big fan of esports, and he was thrilled to host *Warcraft* and *StarCraft* tournaments at BlizzCon every year, but the company kept its own esports initiatives low-key. In 2012, after resolving the KeSPA dispute, Blizzard launched an event called the *StarCraft II* World Championship Series that would collate various international tournaments into one big organization with a final match at BlizzCon. Still, the goal was to make a cultural impact and serve fans, not to create a viable business. "At no point in time was I ever asked how much money we'd make or what the profitability was," said Ilja Rotelli, an executive who helped launch the series.

Morhaime's wife, Amy, became head of the esports department as it slowly expanded to facilitate events around the world. The pair were compelled to invest more in esports for three big reasons: 1) to protect players from the sketchier elements of the grassroots scene, where careers were volatile and contracts were often violated; 2) because they believed it was a big opportunity to engage with players and bring in new ones; and 3) so Blizzard was positioned as a leader in esports if it ever did become a viable business. Esports might not be lucrative yet, they thought, but they wanted to be at the front of the pack when it was.

Trevor Housten, a professional *StarCraft* player who had gained prominence as one of the few non-Koreans to compete in the big leagues, was one of the first members of this esports department. He helped organize events for *World of Warcraft* and *Hearthstone* and soon began working on ideas for the company's next big game, *Overwatch*. "Whether or not we were going to have a competitive scene was not a

question," said Housten. "It was: 'How are we going to approach it?'"
With its six-person teams and potential for big, match-changing plays,
Overwatch seemed ripe for a flourishing esports scene. As the game
entered its final stretch of development, Housten and a few colleagues
began exploring a new idea: a professional league that was owned and
operated by Blizzard itself.

Nate Nanzer, the director of Blizzard's consumer insights department, was intrigued by this initiative. He'd spent the last few years
studying the metrics behind esports: how much Blizzard players cared
about competition, what they liked to watch, and what the value
might be. "When I played the game, I saw all these interesting paral-
lels to traditional sports," he said. By the end of 2015, he had teamed
up with Housten and a small group of other staff to pitch an *Overwatch* esports league based on the National Basketball Association or
the Premier League. This new league would be divided into teams,
each tied to a major city, like New York or San Francisco, with players
receiving annual salaries and health benefits. They began talking to
the NBA, which was also interested in esports, about a potential partnership. The next step was taking it to Activision.

■　■　■

Bobby Kotick was an esports skeptic, and for years he and his lieutenants had asked Morhaime and other Blizzard executives why they
were even bothering with competitive gaming. But by the fall of 2014,
he was reversing course. Riot Games, his neighbor in Santa Monica,
put together a *League of Legends* tournament that reached twenty-seven
million viewers during the championship round—nearly twice as
many people as the NBA Finals. That same year, Valve's annual *DOTA 2*
International tournament gave out a prize pool of close to $11 million
and brought in twenty million viewers of its own. Companies with

names like Evil Geniuses and Team Liquid were getting hefty valuations to field squads of competitive gamers, but people still hadn't figured out how to monetize all those eyeballs—a challenge that Kotick thought he could take on.

Kotick had always harbored a not-so-secret desire to expand his empire beyond video games, and in 2015, he started making big moves. He launched an Activision Blizzard film and television studio, promising a *Call of Duty* "cinematic universe" and hiring Stacey Sher, the producer of films like *Pulp Fiction* and *Erin Brockovich*, to help run it.[21] Later, during a presentation to investors, he outlined plans for Activision to become more like Disney, with a string of complementary business models including in-game advertising that he declared would lead them to an ambitious 15 percent compound annual growth rate (CAGR) in the near future. Esports, too, would be one of the pillars of Kotick's lofty strategy. He brought in former ESPN CEO Steve Bornstein to launch a new esports division for the whole company and announced that Activision planned to buy the organization Major League Gaming for $46 million "to create the ESPN of esports."

The Morhaimes weren't thrilled that Kotick had suddenly pivoted from questioning their small investments into esports to making his own huge ones. They had pushed back against the Major League Gaming purchase, arguing that the organization's streaming platform wasn't very good—and that it certainly wasn't worth $46 million. Blizzard had explored an investment in Twitch, the more dominant streaming website, but was rebuffed. Now, Twitch had been purchased by Amazon for nearly $1 billion and Activision was buying a seemingly inferior product.

---

21 This was independent from the long-troubled *Warcraft* movie, loosely based on the first game, which was eviscerated upon its release in 2016. "Rarely is so much time, money, and cutting-edge technology expended on a spectacle so devoid of wonder," wrote critic A. A. Dowd for the A.V. Club.

Still, Kotick's esports turnaround could prove beneficial for Blizzard's own initiatives. In the summer of 2016, Nanzer and his team met with Activision's executives to formally pitch what they were calling the Overwatch League. Kotick loved the idea so much that he told Blizzard's staff he didn't want to work with the NBA or any other external partner—he wanted them to do it themselves, using Activision's marketing muscle to create the NFL of video games.

Then Kotick dropped another bombshell. Nanzer had originally planned to sell teams for $250,000 each, which seemed like an unrealistic goal to his colleagues given the lack of substantial money in esports, but he thought a city-based model could generate enough revenue to justify it.

Kotick said they should aim bigger: $20 million per franchise.

Everyone was shocked. They were going to charge potential owners $20 million to buy an Overwatch League team? Most of the world didn't know what *Overwatch* even was. But Kotick wanted to recruit billionaires who already owned traditional sports teams and could bring their expertise to this project, and he knew that they wouldn't care about potentially turning $250,000 into a million or two—that was a pastime for mere millionaires. Kotick's peers would only be interested if they believed they could turn $20 million into, say, $100 million. The downside was that each *Overwatch* team began $20 million in the hole—an inauspicious start for a business with no proven model for generating revenue.

That November at the BlizzCon opening ceremony, Morhaime declared that they were "looking for the top players in the world, and the team owners, who will form the Overwatch League." Upstairs in a private theater, Nanzer gave a pitch to a room full of sports owners and wealthy executives, including New England Patriots owner Robert Kraft and Los Angeles Rams owner Stan Kroenke. Later, Kraft and his son would help Kotick convince a number of other heavy-hitters to buy into the league. "It was pretty surreal," said Nanzer, who became the commissioner.

Over the next year, Activision Blizzard built a new esports division for the Overwatch League, poaching executives from the NFL and NBA rather than leaning on Blizzard's existing esports group—a move that angered Blizzard veterans as their colleagues at Activision began handling marketing and operations. In 2017, Activision also absorbed Blizzard's consumer products division—the group responsible for selling gear and striking deals with outside companies like LEGO—to license and develop merchandise.

Matt Beecher, Blizzard's vice president of consumer products, called it the "tip of the spear"—the first division that was directly transferred from Blizzard to its parent company, hinting at grander consolidation to come. But Kotick didn't want to dismantle consumer products—if anything, the opposite turned out to be true, as he told the division to aim to surpass traditional sports. Expectations for revenue grew higher as the company prepared to develop hats, sweatshirts, and mugs based on the Overwatch League. "We were hiring people left and right," Beecher said. "It was just wild."

In Irvine, the excitement was palpable: *Overwatch* was going to become an international sport. The league sold twelve franchises, each attached to a city either in the United States or Asia. Buyers included both traditional sports owners and large esports organizations, all tantalized by the idea of getting in on the ground floor of the next NFL. For the first two years, Overwatch League matches would unfold at an arena in Burbank, California, until they reached the finals, which would take place in Brooklyn, New York. Along the way, the league would build up an audience and cultivate fan loyalty for teams like the New York Excelsior and San Francisco Shock.

The league's initial revenue would come from sponsorships and a hefty deal they signed with Twitch for the streaming rights. Then, for the league's third year, they'd move to a home-and-away model where teams would play in their respective cities, selling tickets and hot dogs to thousands of fans. At the same time, they'd come out with an *Overwatch* sequel, which would lead to a surge of new interest.

The Overwatch League kicked off its inaugural season in January 2018, reaching an impressive 10 million viewers in the league's first week, and by summer they'd even announced a broadcasting deal with ESPN. But there were problems beginning to emerge. Team owners grumbled about certain rules, like how the league would restrict their ability to sell sponsorships so that they could all be packaged together. In the NFL, the organization and its commissioner existed to help teams make money, while in the Overwatch League, the organization and its commissioner existed to help Activision Blizzard make money.

Then there was the X-factor. Years earlier, the Korean esports organization KeSPA had scoffed that it was FIFA and Blizzard was just the soccer ball—but unlike a soccer ball, video games were constantly changing. And unlike FIFA, the Overwatch League was reliant on a group of game developers who had their own goals and priorities.

■ ■ ■

For the people who had made *Overwatch*, the Overwatch League was a surreal experience. A few years earlier, Jeff Kaplan and his team had been reeling from the cancellation of *Titan*, the biggest failure in Blizzard's history, which Kaplan told one interviewer had impacted him in "a deep, profound way." Now their creation was the center of a massive initiative that could change the way the world thought about esports.

Many of the artists and programmers who had worked on *Overwatch* were happy to work on the Overwatch League. They created brands, designed team logos, and even built tools like an in-game replay viewer that would let *Overwatch* players watch matches from any angle. But soon it became clear that Team 4 had too much work to do. Kaplan's team needed to simultaneously: 1) help out with features and art for the Overwatch League, 2) develop the sequel, and 3) create new heroes and updates for *Overwatch*, which had almost accidentally turned into a live-service game over the previous two years.[22]

Although *Overwatch* was sold in boxes like a traditional product, Team 4 knew they also wanted to keep updating it after release. Kaplan had promised fans they would never sell maps or heroes, so instead they came up with an eclectic collection of cosmetic items such as outfits, voice lines, and victory poses for each character. There were so many types of items—like stickers and sound effects—that it seemed too messy to classify them on a storefront, so the developers decided to put them in randomized packages called "loot boxes" that were inspired by *Hearthstone* card packs. Players could buy loot boxes for real money in the *Overwatch* store (two for $2 or up to fifty for $40). Some pundits took issue with the principle of a game getting microtransactions when players had already paid for it, but *Overwatch* distributed so many loot boxes for free that they didn't seem like they'd be all that profitable. Members of Team 4 were subsequently shocked to learn that loot boxes were leading the game to generate more than $1 billion in revenue.

But developing new heroes and seasonal events required significant resources, and when the Overwatch League popped up, the *Overwatch* team found itself stretched thin. Kotick and his circle proposed

---

22 A fourth task that also took up a significant amount of time for some staff was to look over ancillary products like LEGO and TV shows—which the *Overwatch* leadership wanted to supervise and control themselves.

the same solution they'd been pushing on *World of Warcraft* for years: hire more people. They should create a second development team to work on the sequel, Kotick said—just like *Call of Duty*. Failing that, they should double or even triple the size of their team so they could handle these demands and live up to player expectations.

Kaplan and Ray Gresko, who was now *Overwatch*'s executive producer, believed that expanding too much would ruin the culture, which was one of the main reasons they had been able to develop *Overwatch* so efficiently. Kaplan would personally onboard staff and liked to know every single person on his team. By 2018, they had crossed 150 people, but they refused to grow to the scale Kotick wanted, saying they didn't want to repeat the mistakes they'd made on previous projects like *Titan*. Plus, they argued, it would destroy morale if half of the team got to incubate cool new stuff while the other half had to stay behind and update the first game.

More quietly, the developers scoffed that they didn't want *Overwatch* to transform into a soulless machine like *Call of Duty*.

Later, some members of the *Overwatch* development team would come to resent the Overwatch League, viewing it as an unnecessary distraction that had been forced upon them. For year two, the league would add eight new expansion teams, which meant more logos, branding, and other miscellaneous work for the developers—plus more pressure as team owners asked Team 4 to create unique cosmetics that each team could sell. "The tension between running a live-service game and an esports league—those priorities are not going to be aligned," said Nanzer.

Leaders on the *Overwatch* team weren't the only ones feeling pressure from their corporate overlords. In the spring of 2017, Activision Blizzard Chief Operating Officer Thomas Tippl stepped down (although he stuck around as vice chairman of the board), and tensions began to ramp up even further. Although Morhaime and other Blizzard executives often battled with Tippl, he had also served as a counterweight to Kotick and had been willing to say no to some of the CEO's wilder ideas. Tippl liked to say that Kotick was the "unreasonable man"—it was how Activision had achieved so much success over the years—and that it was his job to channel that vision into a feasible plan.

Blizzard's bosses were initially excited to work with Tippl's successor, Coddy Johnson, who had struck them as cordial and reasonable a few years earlier, when he had been Kotick's chief of staff. But in April 2018, Johnson put together an off-site conference for leaders across all three of Activision Blizzard's divisions: Activision Publishing, Blizzard, and King. The theme was unification: streamlining operations into "One ABK" rather than maintaining three autonomous entities.

Kotick and his team were spelling out what had been apparent to Morhaime for years: He didn't want Blizzard to be independent anymore. There were no conversations about which parts of Blizzard's culture should be preserved, only directives for how to integrate it into the rest of Activision Blizzard.

For Morhaime and the rest of Blizzard leadership, this was alarming. They were already losing key staff, such as *Hearthstone* leaders Hamilton Chu and Ben Brode, and they were worried that more attrition was on the way as other executive producers and directors expressed their frustration with the changes Activision was trying to bring to Blizzard. Gresko, fuming, filed his resignation before the conference was even over. (He was later convinced to take a sabbatical instead.)

After the offsite, Morhaime wrote a lengthy email to Kotick, shared with several other executives, declaring that Blizzard had reached a tipping point. "I believe that preserving Blizzard's culture and magic is a necessity for preserving Activision Blizzard's advantage of having an organization that can attract and retain the best creative talent in the world and that can consistently produce the highest quality games and experiences," he wrote. "With the new direction that ABK is having, as well as its increased involvement in the operations of Blizzard...it has been increasingly hard for me to provide Blizzard leadership and staff confidence that Blizzard has a stable future as a values-driven organization, where both Blizzard culture and brand identity can be protected.

"We need to get clarity and stability around the boundaries between Activision Blizzard and Blizzard," he added.

By the summer of 2018, even ground-level Blizzard employees were accepting a reality that had long been shielded from them: Activision was all over the company. For the first time in Blizzard's history, there was widespread messaging from the top down to be budget conscious and cut as many costs as possible. Public relations people had to coordinate with their counterparts in Santa Monica before sending out statements or conducting interviews.[23] Marketing, legal, HR, and many other departments began dual-reporting to executives at both Blizzard and Activision Blizzard, causing widespread frustration and confusion. "It was always very unclear who should be accountable, making decisions," said Vincent Francoeur, head of Blizzard's web & mobile department.

Philosophically, it wasn't a clean divide—there were Blizzard staff who sympathized with some of Activision's viewpoints, and vice versa. Even some Blizzard diehards believed developers at the company were too precious about keeping business out of conversations,

---

23 In November 2018, as I was preparing to first break the news that Activision Blizzard was taking a larger role in Blizzard's operations, I reached out to Blizzard's PR people for comment, got one answer, and was then contacted by Activision Blizzard's PR people with a conflicting response. "Look," I told them. "What I'm writing about is literally happening in front of me right now."

especially as they started making mobile, free-to-play, and live-service games. "It was liberating in a way because it lets the team focus on making the best product they can possibly build," said Tim Morten, the production director for *StarCraft II*. But refusing to think about, say, the cost of a cinematic would ultimately hurt a game's long-term viability, Morten believed. "I think getting development teams closer to the economics was healthy," he said.

But Armin Zerza's approach was so blunt, and Blizzard's top employees were so headstrong, that there appeared to be no room for compromise. Activision was focused on shareholders and devoted to process, while Blizzard was dedicated to players and allergic to timelines. "It felt like one person was speaking Greek, one was speaking English," said one Activision executive.

In the two decades since he'd taken over as Blizzard's president, Morhaime had developed more of a business sense than any of his early peers would have expected. He was just as competitive as his colleagues in Santa Monica—one of his hobbies was playing poker on a professional level—and he'd spent years trying to find ways to satisfy Kotick without giving up what he thought made Blizzard great. "He was a profit-motivated guy like everybody else," said Gio Hunt. "The difference is, he wasn't a profit-motivated-first guy."

But executives in Santa Monica were baffled by Morhaime's insistence on putting up walls and refusing to listen to their advice. The relationship had deteriorated so badly that even when Kotick made reasonable suggestions, Blizzard staff would resist because they came from Activision. Thomas Tippl snarked that Blizzard should change its company value to "Every Voice *Within Blizzard* Matters."

From Kotick's perspective, Blizzard wasn't as successful as Morhaime and his team believed they were. Each new *World of Warcraft* expansion still took two years, and there were no other big releases to fill the gaps. Blizzard's profits were falling—from $1 billion in 2016 to $719 million in 2017 to $685 million in 2018—and with no big products imminent, they were primed to plummet even more.

It was clear to top Blizzard staff that something was going to give. Few were prepared for what would happen next.

TWENTY-FOUR

CHANGING OF THE GUARD

M ike Morhaime and Bobby Kotick couldn't have been more opposite if they had been grown in a laboratory. Perhaps the only things they had in common were that they both ran video game companies and they were both very rich.

Kotick was the guy who skipped classes and dropped out of school—the boisterous CEO who could charm anyone into being his friend—while Morhaime was the nerdy, introverted student who sat in the front row. Kotick went to celebrity parties in the Hamptons. Morhaime called up developers to ask about changes he'd noticed during late-night sessions of *StarCraft II*.[24] Kotick maintained a private art collection worth millions of dollars. Morhaime's house tiles were inscribed with insignias from *World of Warcraft*.

For several years, the two men were able to put aside their

---

24 Greg Black, a designer on *StarCraft II*, recalled Morhaime sending out an email with some thoughts after holiday break one year. "We looked it up: The dude had played hours of *StarCraft II* on the ladder," Black said. "You have to wonder how many people in his position who run these big Fortune 500 game companies are spending their weekends playing the nerdiest, most hardcore game in their slate for hours."

differences in favor of a fruitful partnership. When they first paired up in 2008, as Activision Blizzard was growing every year, Morhaime and Kotick would regularly dine to talk about their strategy and success. But in 2013, when *Titan* failed and Kotick wrested control of the company from Vivendi, their relationship began to fall apart.

Morhaime wanted to preserve Blizzard's autonomy, while Kotick wanted to integrate the organization into the Activision Blizzard umbrella. In 2018, Blizzard generated less profit than King or Activision Publishing yet employed more people, in part because its leaders believed that they needed to maintain internal support teams to preserve their culture and keep players happy. Kotick wanted to streamline those teams and reorganize the company into divisions based on franchises—*Warcraft, Diablo, Overwatch*, and so on—each devoted to releasing content on a predictable schedule.

Both executives had the same fundamental goal—for Blizzard to make great games that brought in millions of players and made lots of money—but their methods were drastically different. Morhaime wanted to create an environment where developers felt empowered, secure, and willing to take risks for the sake of innovation without having to worry that they'd be punished for failure. "At Blizzard, people put Blizzard and gamers first because there is no financial incentive to stay on or leave any given project," he'd written to Kotick in the email. The downside of this approach, in Activision's view, was that developers could coast on indefinite timelines, collecting profit-sharing checks without releasing any games.

Those who sympathized with Kotick pointed out that his strategies took Activision from bankruptcy into one of the most lucrative game-makers on the planet. While Blizzard staff enjoyed their freedom to experiment, Kotick was accountable to shareholders and the board of directors, who would demand explanations whenever the company delayed a game. At the end of the day, Kotick's top priority was to make his company's stock go up, and he believed that for Blizzard to be successful in that goal, it needed to change.

In 2018, Blizzard's release schedule was looking anemic. *StarCraft* and *Heroes of the Storm* were both struggling to generate much revenue, new *Diablo* and *Overwatch* games were still years away, and the incubation projects were too early to count on—even the mobile games, which left executives at Activision scratching their heads. The company was still making money through new content for *World of Warcraft*, *Hearthstone*, and *Overwatch*, but the latter two were slowing down.

People around Morhaime worried that his fights with Activision were taking a hefty toll. In 2017, he'd even submitted a resignation letter, although Kotick had convinced him to walk it back and those close to him encouraged him to stay. As the public face and cofounder of Blizzard, he was the only one with enough power and clout to keep Activision's pressure away from his teams. Sure, Armin Zerza was making a big impact inside of Blizzard, but Morhaime could at least keep the executives at Santa Monica in check. In *StarCraft* parlance, Morhaime was the lone bunker on the ramp that walled in the Terran base, preventing zerglings from swarming the buildings.

But in the spring of 2018, after the One ABK offsite, Morhaime began to realize that he had lost the war, and he started to quietly talk to other Blizzard executives about a succession plan as he geared up to leave the company he had run for two decades.

On October 3, 2018, Morhaime announced that he was stepping down from Blizzard after twenty-seven years. He didn't offer much of an explanation in public, writing in a blog post that he had "decided it's time for someone else to lead Blizzard Entertainment." But those who worked closely with him knew why he'd left: He was tired of battling with Kotick. "He looked like a second-term president," said one executive.

Blizzard staff were devastated by the news. Morhaime was the rare video game CEO who was worshiped by people who worked under him. He would greet receptionists by name, respond directly to emails from low-level staff, and encourage developers to prioritize players above all else. Many Blizzard employees had their own personal stories about the quiet acts of kindness they'd seen or received from their boss. Hundreds wrote emails and letters to Morhaime to wish him farewell and thank him for everything he'd done.

Critics would point out that he was too trusting and that he had either ignored or been oblivious to the behavior of some problematic Blizzard veterans whose misdeeds would come to light later. Morhaime's inner circle included a few people with less savory reputations—people to whom he was loyal because they had been in the trenches with him for decades. "He's the most inclusive, open, tolerant person I know," said one senior woman at Blizzard. "But for reasons that are quite complicated, he was surrounded by bros."

Yet he was beloved by thousands of employees. A 2018 survey on the website Glassdoor determined that he was one of the year's most popular CEOs, with a 96 percent approval rating from Blizzard staff.

Now he was gone, and the zerglings could move as they pleased.

■　■　■

Morhaime's successor was J. Allen Brack, the company veteran who had cut his teeth in the 1990s at the legendary game studio Origin Systems, then worked on the online game *Star Wars Galaxies* before joining Blizzard in 2006. He worked his way up the ranks to production director and then executive producer on *World of Warcraft*, making him the top developer on the company's most important game. Some colleagues saw him as cold or cliquish, but he was well-respected within the company and widely perceived as someone who would stand up for Blizzard's culture.

Yet questions lingered about how much power he would have compared to his predecessor. Morhaime's tenure and reputation had afforded him a significant amount of leverage that Brack didn't have. Sharp-eyed observers noticed that the announcement came with a title downgrade—while Morhaime had been CEO and president, Brack was just president. The press materials announcing Brack's appointment also noted that Allen Adham and longtime producer Ray Gresko (back from his rage-quit-turned-sabbatical) were joining Blizzard's executive team. Left unacknowledged was that Blizzard no longer had its own CEO.

Blizzard staff whispered that at least Armin Zerza hadn't gotten the top job—Kotick undoubtedly knew that would have led to open rebellion—but the changes from Activision were coming in fast and furious. The biggest move was a push for cost-cutting that had started earlier that year, as the company began encouraging employees to do more with less. There were continuations of the moves that Zerza had already made, giving more power to the commercial organization. Other shifts were more subtle. "There was a little more red tape to get things approved," said Kelli O'Leary, a project manager in events. "It was no longer: 'Yes, push the button.' It was: 'Let's take it up to Activision Blizzard.'"

To the outside world, there were small hints as to what was happening. Back in 2017, Blizzard had begun selling and distributing Activision's *Destiny 2* on Battle.net—the first non-Blizzard game on their PC platform. Morhaime reluctantly agreed to allow it but privately vowed to colleagues that he would never put *Call of Duty*, with its bloody military combat, on Blizzard's store. Despite those assurances, Activision announced months later that the next *Call of Duty* was coming to Battle.net—a strange and unwelcome development for some Blizzard fans, who didn't want to see big army ads when they logged in to *World of Warcraft*.

As part of this ongoing collaboration, Activision wanted Blizzard to promote *Destiny 2* at BlizzCon 2018. It wasn't the first time that Santa Monica's executives had asked Blizzard to market their games at the annual fan event, but Blizzard had always refused. Under the current climate, the BlizzCon team didn't think they could turn down the request entirely, but they also didn't want it to happen during the official opening ceremony, where Morhaime would address Blizzard fans for the final time before introducing Brack as his successor. So instead they came to a compromise: Someone from the *Destiny 2* development team would come on the preshow to promote the game. It was a minor but noticeable moment—an Activision game had invaded Blizzard's conference.

The end of the ceremony, which would feature the next *Diablo* game, was a much bigger dilemma—one that many Blizzard employees had been debating for months. Back in 2016, after *Hades* was canceled, a small team of designers had started work on a project code-named *Fenris* that would later be called *Diablo IV*. While *Hades* had been experimental, this was planned as a proper sequel, with the same camera angle and combat style as previous games. It had now been six years since *Diablo III*, and fans were eager to hear about the next entry in the long-running series. For all of *Diablo III*'s faults, it had still sold 30 million copies.

But Blizzard also had another *Diablo* game to show off. The company had partnered with NetEase, its distributor and publisher in China, to develop a mobile game called *Diablo Immortal*. It had been seamless to translate *Diablo*'s gameplay, which centered on mindless clicking, to a phone's touchscreen, and everyone figured the game could be a huge hit in China, where free-to-play action games that could fairly be called *"Diablo* clones" regularly generated billions of dollars in revenue. BlizzCon 2018 needed a big new announcement, and *Diablo Immortal* fit the bill—it was an unexpected entry in a series that had been quiet for years.

Some members of Blizzard's PR and marketing teams feared that the news might be poorly received, and warned their bosses that fans looking for the next *Diablo* game might not react well to the announcement of a game for phones. Mobile gaming remained as lucrative as ever, but many video game enthusiasts, including fans who were flying out to Anaheim, derided phone games for repetitive gameplay and exploitative microtransactions.

To mitigate any potential rage, several Blizzard staffers proposed that they couple the *Diablo Immortal* announcement with a teaser for *Diablo IV*. That way, the messaging would be clear: yes, they were making a phone game, but they were also making a proper sequel. But *Diablo IV* was still years away and the new director, Luis Barriga, was against the idea. Other Blizzard executives agreed with Barriga that they should save their announcement of *Diablo IV* for the following year, when they could have a demo ready for fans to play at the show, not fire it off now just to give cover to a mobile game.

For months, teams across Blizzard debated over how to move forward, weighing their options during weekly BlizzCon check-in meetings. Any suggestion that they push back *Diablo Immortal's* announcement was quickly squashed because Activision executives were frothing at the mouth to see how shareholders would react to a new mobile game from Blizzard. At the same time, the idea that they so much as tease *Diablo IV* was shut down by Barriga and Team 3. Instead they tried to come up with other solutions that would convey to fans that *Diablo IV* was in the works—they just couldn't announce it yet.

Besides, some Blizzard developers and executives thought that once people saw how cool it was to have *Diablo* on a phone, they'd be hooked. "There was this absolute belief that *Diablo Immortal* was going to be the *Overwatch* of 2018," said Sarah Borger, a project manager on the events team. "That it would blow everyone out of the water."

The BlizzCon team put together a series of contingency plans, such as a video where Adham, now executive producer for both *Diablo* games, told fans that *Diablo IV* was on the way, but instead they put up a blog post on Blizzard's website, aiming to obliquely convey to fans what was going on. "We currently have multiple teams working on different *Diablo* projects and we can't wait to tell you all about them...when the time is right," they wrote. "We know what many of you are hoping for, and we can only say that 'good things come to those who wait,' but evil things often take longer." The blog post also teased that "we do intend to share some *Diablo*-related news with you at the show," which sent fan speculation into overdrive. Blizzard had intended to tamp down the hype, but if anything, this messaging had the opposite effect.

On November 2, 2018, fans gathered at the Anaheim Convention Center for BlizzCon's introductory ceremony. It opened with Morhaime, taking the stage for the last time in a loose bowling shirt, reminiscing about the company's history and then passing the microphone to Brack, a foot taller than him, with a long ponytail and a teal Blizzard button-down. "Thank you for all you've done," Brack said. "We wouldn't be here without you." The show closed with Wyatt Cheng, the longtime *Diablo* veteran who was now helming *Diablo Immortal*, announcing that "we are making a full-fledged action RPG you can play everywhere with everyone" before showing off trailers for the game. With a wisp of a goatee and a nervous energy, Cheng ended his presentation with an awkward pause, as if about to tease something else. Instead, the show came to an end.

There was a smattering of polite applause and a whole lot of consternation both from fans online and at the convention center. Blizzard's vague messaging about *Diablo IV* hadn't quite hit the mark, and people wondered if this mobile game was arriving in lieu of a sequel. Had Blizzard abandoned their core audience? During a panel presentation later, one fan asked if *Diablo Immortal* would be playable on computers as well. "We don't have any plans at the moment to do PC," Cheng said.[25] When the crowd booed in response, he jokingly retorted: "Do you guys not have phones?" The clip hit the internet by storm, symbolizing what fans saw as Blizzard's distaste for their core customers. Later, another fan went viral after asking if the game's announcement was a delayed April Fool's joke.

At the convention center, a team of Blizzard staff huddled in a makeshift war room, trying to figure out how to change the narrative. They tried to push journalists and fans to play the *Diablo Immortal* demo, knowing it was a solid adaptation of the beloved franchise. Before the show they'd already assembled talking points, knowing that reporters would ask about *Diablo IV*, so they doubled down. "We continue to have multiple teams work on multiple unannounced *Diablo* projects," Adham would tell reporters, trying to announce the game without officially announcing it.

The widespread outrage represented video game culture at its worst—fans of the medium expressing anger at individual game developers for the truly unforgivable sin of announcing a game for phones. Cheng, who had been working on *Diablo* since the Blizzard North days and who was beloved by teammates for his design skills

---

25 This changed later, and the game would ultimately launch for both PC and mobile.

and genial demeanor, became an internet meme and the perceived face of Blizzard's greed, much to the horror of his colleagues.

But the *Diablo Immortal* snafu was also the beginning of what would become a much bigger problem for Blizzard—a fan base that was starting to turn on the company. The outside world wasn't aware of Armin Zerza or Activision's growing level of influence on Blizzard's operations, but to the loudest players, mobile games often represented industry greed due to their rampant microtransactions. Blizzard had always towered above the other video game companies that were known for chasing short-term profits. Now, with Morhaime gone and *Diablo Immortal* as the first big announcement after his departure, fans feared that might change.

■　■　■

There was perhaps no better example of the old Blizzard approach than *Heroes of the Storm*. Unlike its free-to-play peers, *Heroes of the Storm* avoided using virtual currency. When players went to the in-game store, they'd see the prices listed in dollars (or their local equivalent) rather than jewels, gems, or casino chips. To Blizzard veterans like executive producer Chris Sigaty, being clear and direct about their prices rather than obfuscating the real costs was an obvious part of taking a player-first approach to game design. But when business-minded people looked at the *Heroes of the Storm* shop, they were stupefied. Virtual money was a standard component of free-to-play games, both because it increased spending and because it allowed the developers to offer in-game promotions and new account bonuses. "This was a given," said one newcomer. "If you're doing free to play, you use a virtual currency. They were hardcore against this."

Following the underwhelming release of *Heroes of the Storm*, the team began working on a new update called *Heroes 2.0* that would reverse this decision in a push for profitability. Although the update was marketed as a gameplay overhaul and it did offer some significant changes, it also brought in loot boxes and overhauled the store, replacing all those real prices with virtual currency. The message was clear: *Heroes of the Storm* needed to generate more revenue, and with Blizzard's overall culture changing, business needs became a regular part of conversations that might have otherwise focused on the game. "It became less about, 'How can we do this in the coolest way?' and more about, 'How can we make more money than X or Y?'" said one designer.

Heroes of the Storm remained an important pillar of esports, where Blizzard supported a collegiate league called Heroes of the Dorm (televised on ESPN) and a high-stakes tournament known as the Heroes Global Championship. At BlizzCon 2018, professional *Heroes of the Storm* players battled over a $1 million prize pool and were told that Blizzard planned to support the program for at least another year. A trailer teasing new *Heroes of the Storm* content for 2019 included "HGC" as part of a large montage of upcoming features, and behind the scenes, Sigaty and the rest of the leadership team had developed an esports plan for the coming year that was approved by J. Allen Brack, Ray Gresko, and Armin Zerza.

But now the entire Activision Blizzard organization was gearing up for significant cost cutting, and the *Heroes* 2.0 update hadn't been as lucrative as they'd hoped. In the middle of the night on December 13, 2018, Blizzard put up a blog post declaring that the company had "made the difficult decision to shift some developers from *Heroes of the Storm* to other teams." The struggling MOBA would still receive new content updates, Blizzard said, but "the cadence will change" as the company pivoted to "long-term stability." Many members of the team wound up getting jobs elsewhere within Blizzard, while others were laid off.

Supporting esports for another year would require them to cut even more jobs at Blizzard, so Brack and his team decided to reverse course on their previous plans, announcing in the blog post that both Heroes of the Dorm and the Heroes Global Championship were canceled. This came as a shock to the *Heroes of the Storm* players, team managers, and announcers who had been told just a month earlier that the programs would continue, with some taking to Twitter to share their outrage. "We are troubled by the way the announcement was made," wrote one team manager, "namely the impolitic choice to use social media to share such a message that effectively ended the careers of hundreds of players, content creators, casters, production crews overnight."

Chris Ivermee, a British announcer who went by the handle Tetcher, said at the time that he was making around $4,000 a month during the season, upon which he relied to pay rent and bills. Like other announcers and players, he was disappointed to learn that he was losing his livelihood on Twitter. Later, they received emails from Blizzard offering severance payments, but the damage had been done. Years earlier, Blizzard had started its own esports division in part to thwart behavior like this, which had been common among grassroots organizations and tournaments, and now, they were part of the problem they had been trying to solve.

As Blizzard employees headed off for their holiday vacations, it was clear that their company was going to look much different in the post-Morhaime era. And there were more costs still to be cut.

TWENTY-FIVE

COST REDUCTION

O n February 12, 2019, Bobby Kotick declared to investors during the company's quarterly earnings call that they had "once again achieved record results in 2018" by hitting an all-time high for revenue. But, he cautioned, the year "didn't quite live up to our expectations" and the company would be making big changes "to enable our development teams to create better content for our biggest franchises more quickly." As a result, Activision Blizzard would slash nearly 8 percent of its staff, or around eight hundred people.

Rumors of layoffs had been swirling for months, culminating in a *Bloomberg* report the previous week indicating that they were about to hit. As Blizzard employees arrived at work, they began seeing mysterious meetings pop up on their calendars. Some were ten or fifteen minutes; some were an hour. "We were all sitting in a room: 'When's your meeting? What does that mean?'" said Kelli O'Leary, a project manager on the events team. "We all started to overanalyze the situation."

When her fifteen-minute slot arrived, O'Leary was called into a room with a small group of other Blizzard employees who were told their positions were being eliminated. They were presented with papers to sign and informed that they'd be receiving severance packages based on how long they'd worked at the company, then asked if there was anything they needed on their desks before they left. O'Leary was hurt and infuriated, but at the same time, she had been growing frustrated with the cultural changes. "It was probably for the best," she said. "Who knows how long I would have lasted and how much more I would have had to deal with."

It was a bloodbath at Blizzard, particularly in the publishing department, where years of political battles and reorganizations had led to a bloated head count.[26] Employees shared whiskey and donuts, exchanged hugs, and waited to see who would survive. In an email to staff, J. Allen Brack explained that "staffing levels on some teams are out of proportion with our current release slate" and said the layoffs were taking place primarily within non-development teams. "There's no way to make this transition easy for impacted employees," he wrote, "but we are doing what we can to support our colleagues."

Cory Larson, a manager in the esports division, went through what he described as the five stages of grief: denial, anger, bargaining, depression, and then acceptance. After thirteen years at the company, the hardest part of getting laid off was having to rethink his routines. "All my clothes were Blizzard clothes," he said. For Larson, the company had been safe. Comfortable. Now, it felt like something had been shattered. Every hoodie with the company logo; every meeting implying that they were all part of something bigger than themselves; every comment about how they were one big family—it all felt irrevocably broken.

---

26 One particularly messy reorg, helmed by Gio Hunt, had divided Blizzard's publishing department into "global" and "regional" divisions, leading to a significant number of redundant roles that were eliminated during this layoff.

Blizzard had enacted a mass layoff seven years earlier, but back then, the company had been much less profitable. Activision Blizzard had grown from a market cap of around $12 billion in 2012 to more than $45 billion in 2018, while the entire company's operating income (profit) had leaped from $1.7 billion in 2012 to $2.4 billion in 2018. Kotick's compensation had swelled to $30.8 million, or about 319 times more than the median employee salary at Activision Blizzard, according to SEC filings. He was mostly paid in stock, but the disparity was still striking.

"I was really angry," said Sarah Borger. Laid-off employees were told to say their good-byes in the parking lot, where they convened for tearful hugs. But not all were sad to be leaving this new incarnation of Blizzard. "I kind of feel like they gave me a parachute filled with money," one colleague told Borger, "and kicked me out of a burning building." She couldn't help but agree.

■　■　■

The layoffs arrived during a busy time for Blizzard. That fall, they would finally announce the two games that fans (and investors) had been eagerly awaiting: *Overwatch 2* and *Diablo IV*. As they tried to put aside survivor's guilt and get back to work, the company's staff began preparing for a big BlizzCon, where both games would be playable on the show floor.

As the company doubled down on those sequels, two other projects were on the chopping block. One was *Orion*, an experimental mobile RPG with asynchronous turns helmed by former *Hearthstone* director Eric Dodds and a few of his old Team 5 colleagues. During playtests, they found that it was a blast to play in a room together, but it was much less fun when people were on the go and it could take hours between each turn.

The stakes were much higher for the second project, which had a bigger team and higher expectations. Dustin Browder, who had been director of *StarCraft II* and then *Heroes of the Storm*, had stepped down from that gig at the end of 2016 to pitch something new: a first-person shooter set in the *StarCraft* universe, code-named *Ares* and heavily inspired by EA's *Battlefield* series. Vast teams of players would wage war while controlling iconic *StarCraft* units like Terran marines or Zerg hydralisks. Over the next three years, the *Ares* team expanded to more than fifty people as the game progressed, but there were headwinds coming. Executives at Activision were skeptical of *Ares*, in part because of their distaste for *Battlefield*, a series that once had been *Call of Duty*'s chief rival but had dwindled over time. They didn't care much for *StarCraft*. And there was a lingering sense that it was a waste of time to have Blizzard staff working on a second shooter when they could all instead be helping make *Overwatch 2*, which was behind schedule and remained, in Kotick's view, severely understaffed.

Blizzard's developers had a history of defeating corporate skepticism. Jason Chayes, the producer of *Ares*, had also worked on *Hearthstone*, a game that executives at both Blizzard and Activision had wanted to cancel until the team had proven itself with a killer demo. After three years of development, they thought that surely *Ares* would get the same chance—but this was a different Blizzard. In the spring of 2019, word arrived from above that there were too many projects in development and that Blizzard needed to refocus. Both *Orion* and *Ares* were canceled, with each team's staff moving to either *Diablo IV* or *Overwatch 2*.

Leadership of the *Ares* team was livid—not just because the game had been axed, but because the news came out of nowhere. A small portion of the company's product strat group called "product strat core"—J. Allen Brack, Ray Gresko, and Allen Adham—had made the decision before even talking to *Ares*'s leadership, and some observers wryly noted that Adham's own projects had somehow survived this culling. Under Morhaime, company-defining decisions had happened with more communication, ensuring that each team's leaders felt like they had agency. "Projects get killed all the time," said one person close to the group. "They'd be able to handle it if they were treated like adults. The problem was, they weren't treated like adults."

Brack may have been trying to avoid triggering anxiety by telling the team that their project was at risk, but the move torched relationships among people who had been friends and colleagues for years. Browder and Chayes resigned from Blizzard, as did Dodds and several others. An exodus was underway.

■ ■ ■

Another Blizzard game was also coming out that fall, although it seemed more like a novelty than the next big thing. *World of Warcraft* was about to turn fifteen—old enough to have been a significant part of many players' lives. Some longtime players felt nostalgic for the early days, back before a decade and a half worth of updates and expansions had transformed Azeroth. Since *World of Warcraft* was a living game, with quests and zones that could change every time the developers put out an update, there was no way to simply play an older iteration. When you logged in, you'd join whatever version of the game currently existed.

Over the years, players had wondered if Blizzard could let them access those older incarnations. During one BlizzCon panel with the *World of Warcraft* team, a fan asked if the developers had thought about "adding servers for previous expansions as they were then." Brack, who was the executive producer of *World of Warcraft*, offered a quick no. "And by the way, you don't want to do that either," he added.

"You think you do, but you don't." He went on to talk about bug fixes and other significant improvements that they had made to the game, like the automated dungeon group finder.

In 2015, a group of fans launched an unofficial, private *World of Warcraft* server called Nostalrius that allowed players to access a version of the game from 2006—a snapshot in time from when Molten Core raids and accidental pandemics felt new. Other fan servers had popped up with similar goals, but Nostalrius became the most popular, bringing in hundreds of thousands of players who did, in fact, want to do that. A year later, Blizzard filed a copyright complaint, forcing Nostalrius to shutter. Brack wrote on the company's internet forums that they had to make the claim because "failure to protect against intellectual property infringement would damage Blizzard's rights," a move reminiscent of the company's moves against KeSPA years earlier.

There were protests and petitions as fans raged that if Blizzard wasn't going to support old versions of *World of Warcraft*, they should be able to do it themselves. A year and a half later, Blizzard quelled the complaints as Brack took the stage at BlizzCon to announce *World of Warcraft Classic*, an official version of the game just the way people remembered it. For the next two years, a small team led by an engineer named Brian Birmingham worked on a separate branch of *World of Warcraft* designed to re-create the good old days, which even some of the game's developers missed playing. "Over time, it felt less and less like the type of game I wanted to play," said Birmingham, who had been at Blizzard since 2006. "Playing the game like it used to be, that sounded amazing."

World of Warcraft Classic came out on August 26, 2019, allowing subscribers to play either version of the game. Some fans discovered that reality was uglier than nostalgia, but others found that a *World of*

Warcraft without modern conveniences had its own distinct pleasures. Without the group finder that Brack had touted, players needed to find one another manually, which transformed strangers into friends and guildmates. Players found that they had actually missed some of the rough edges that had been smoothed out over time.

What shocked Team 2 most was how many people stuck with *World of Warcraft Classic*. "There was this belief in leadership that a huge amount of people would be tourists—log off and never play again," said Birmingham. Instead, those people just kept playing, and in the years that followed, Blizzard would release servers for early expansions like *The Burning Crusade* and even design new features solely for *Classic*. It was as if they had branched the timeline and created an alternate universe where the game evolved in different ways. *World of Warcraft* executive producer John Hight later told a reporter that the game's community was just as large as the modern version's and that they "probably now hold the record for the two biggest MMOs on the planet Earth."

The successful release helped soothe some of the simmering tension between Blizzard and its fans. The *Diablo Immortal* debacle, the abrupt sunsetting of *Heroes of the Storm*, and the mass layoffs had been gradually eroding Blizzard's reputation, transforming one of the most beloved companies in gaming into a magnet for controversy. But there were few better remedies for player rage than an injection of pure nostalgia.

This relief would prove short-lived. Just two months later, Blizzard would be engulfed in yet another public relations disaster—the biggest it had faced in twenty-eight years.

■　■　■

Ng Wai Chung was always the best gamer in his class. Growing up in Hong Kong, he'd started playing competitive games before he even entered kindergarten, eventually convincing his parents to give him unlimited screen time, so long as he took care of his responsibilities. "When I finished my homework, I just played video games until I slept," Chung said. Like many Asian kids growing up in the 2000s, as esports exploded across the continent, Chung dreamed about playing video games for a living. He had better gaming skills and instincts than anyone else he knew, and he spent every day playing *League of Legends*, but despite years of practice, it seemed unlikely that he'd ever be good enough to compete with entrenched pros.

In high school he discovered another hobby: *Hearthstone*, which took the old *Warcraft* characters he loved and inserted them into an addictive digital card game. He reached high ranks on the competitive ladder and qualified for various small tournaments. "I didn't play the game intending to be a professional," Chung said, "but as you get better at it, you get more opportunities." By the time he'd entered university, he was regularly competing in big *Hearthstone* tournaments, where he went by the handle Blitzchung.

By 2019, Chung had earned thousands of dollars from his burgeoning *Hearthstone* career, but he was growing distracted by world events. A series of protests had erupted across Hong Kong following a proposed bill that would allow extradition of criminals to mainland China. Protesters said the bill was just the latest symbol of encroachment from China, which had maintained control over Hong Kong since 1997 as a "special administrative region" with its own laws and government. Having come to a political awakening during the Umbrella Movement, a 2014 protest of opaque election laws, Chung found his attention divided. "I played in my matches and thought about what was happening outside, what I'm doing here right now," he said.

On October 6, 2019, during a *Hearthstone* tournament in Taiwan called Grandmasters, Chung was slated to be interviewed on the official Blizzard video stream and decided to speak out. Wearing a gas mask—protective garb often worn by Hong Kong protesters—Chung shouted one of the protest's most popular slogans in Mandarin, "Liberate Hong Kong, the revolution of our times." The two interviewers, giggling, ducked under their desks as if to avoid being implicated.

In Irvine, Blizzard took quick action. Chris Sigaty, the company veteran who had stepped in as executive producer of *Hearthstone* when Hamilton Chu departed, huddled with a few esports team members and decided that Chung had violated the tournament rule against "engaging in any act that, in Blizzard's sole discretion, brings you into public disrepute, offends a portion or group of the public, or otherwise damages Blizzard image." The next day, Blizzard announced that Chung would be banned for a year and forfeit his prize money and that the company would no longer work with the two announcers. "I didn't know it was against Blizzard's rules," said Chung, "but I knew it was very controversial."

The public erupted. Political sentiment in the United States was generally in favor of Hong Kong and many players criticized the punishment as overly harsh. On campus, a few dozen Blizzard employees protested with umbrellas and even covered up the plaque saying Every Voice Matters.

The reactions only escalated from there. Ron Wyden, the Democratic Oregon senator, wrote on Twitter that "Blizzard shows it is willing to humiliate itself to please the Chinese Communist Party. No American company should censor calls for freedom to make a quick buck." Shortly afterward, he joined forces with a bipartisan group of politicians including Republican senator Marco Rubio and Democratic representative Alexandria Ocasio-Cortez—an unlikely team—to write a letter to Bobby Kotick. "Because your company is such a pillar of the gaming industry," they wrote, "your disappointing decision could have a chilling effect on gamers who seek to use their platform to promote human rights and basic freedoms."

It was easy to see why the harsh punishment made it seem like they were choosing business interests over free speech—Blizzard had millions of players in China as well as lucrative relationships with the Chinese entertainment conglomerate Tencent, which owned a minority stake in Activision Blizzard, and NetEase, which published their games in China. That same week, the NBA lost hundreds of millions of dollars when Daryl Morey, general manager of the Houston Rockets, tweeted in support of Hong Kong, and China responded by pulling games off the air and canceling sponsorship deals.

But Blizzard's confounded executives also felt like the company would have reacted the same way no matter what kind of political message had been broadcasted—whether a player told people to vote for Joe Biden or declared their love for offshore oil pipelines. "It was perfectly logical to me that we could be sympathetic to whatever cause he's representing," said one executive, "but also not be pleased with the fact that he took our control away from our own platform."

The next few days were the most stressful of Chung's life. He received a barrage of messages—mostly positive, but overwhelming—and more attention than he'd ever imagined receiving. Despite the adulation, he felt unmoored. He'd spent most of his hours either playing in *Hearthstone* tournaments or practicing *Hearthstone*, and now he was banned from the competitive circuit for the next year. "Suddenly it feels like I lost the purpose of my life," he said.

Many observers agreed that Chung should have been punished for using Blizzard's platform to convey a political message, but took issue with the severity. "I could understand a fine, or even a short suspension," blogged Brian Kibler, a game designer and professional

Hearthstone commentator, "but removal from Grandmasters, clawing back the prizes he already earned, and banning him for a full year seems completely overboard." Meanwhile, Blizzard received a barrage of aggressive emails, calls, and even death threats to their public phone lines. Blizzard's top staff and comms teams met for hours every day, trying to figure out how to handle the crisis. Executives at Activision Blizzard also jumped in, slowing down the process as every potential statement was rewritten by rooms full of lawyers and businesspeople.

On October 12, five days after the incident, Blizzard put out a new blog post from J. Allen Brack with their decision: They were not apologizing, nor were they backtracking on the punishment, but they would allow that "our process wasn't adequate, and we reacted too quickly." As a result, they were cutting the suspension from a year to six months and returning Chung's prize money. "I want to be clear: our relationships in China had no influence on our decision," Brack wrote. "We have these rules to keep the focus on the game and on the tournament to the benefit of a global audience, and that was the only consideration in the actions we took."

■ ■ ■

The next BlizzCon was just a few weeks away, and with it, Blizzard would finally announce the long-awaited new *Diablo* and *Overwatch* games. First, they decided to address the Blitzchung debacle. On November 1, 2019, Brack took the stage in Anaheim for the BlizzCon opening ceremony and offered the company's first apology for the incident, avoiding any mention of Chung, China, or Hong Kong. "We didn't live up to the high standards that we set for ourselves," Brack said. "We failed in our purpose. And for that, I am sorry, and I accept accountability." Fans cheered and applauded, content with the apology.

Then came the big announcements. The show opened with a cinematic for *Diablo IV* that introduced Lilith, the game's fiery antagonist. "We are going back to the franchise's darker roots," declared director Luis Barriga in what seemed like a repudiation of the previous game. Later, Jeff Kaplan took the stage to announce *Overwatch 2*, promising that it would feature story missions across the world, from Toronto to Paris, which would allow players to level up and customize their heroes. The big focus, as Kaplan had always envisioned with his "crawl, walk, run" mantra, would be "player vs. environment," or PvE, in which players would be able to fight computer-controlled enemies. Fans had grown obsessed with the characters and world of *Overwatch*, with its bright aesthetics and unabashed optimism, but most of that story had been told outside of the game, in supplemental materials like comics and those stellar short films—now, that would change.

Players knew that they might be waiting awhile for both new games—this was Blizzard, after all—but internally, the pressure was ramping up. Both *Diablo IV* and *Overwatch 2* missed multiple deadlines, frustrating Kotick and the board of directors, who felt like Brack was frequently promising them new release windows and then failing to hit them. The lack of mobile games—which had once been envisioned on shorter timelines than their console counterparts—made things worse. "Blizzard was not delivering," said one Activision executive. "We weren't trying to get in Blizzard's hair too much, but at the end of the day we are a public company, and that comes with a certain level of growth expectation."

Blizzard wasn't the only video game company butting heads with Kotick. A decade earlier, Activision had signed a whopping $500 million deal with Bungie, the storied maker of the *Halo* series, to create a new science fiction franchise called *Destiny*. The contract called for an annualized schedule that was in line with Kotick's usual cadence: new releases every fall, alternating between full games and expansions. The first game, released in 2014, had a rocky start but sold millions of copies. Then came a sequel, *Destiny 2*, that was delayed a year and landed below Activision's revenue expectations. Along the way, Bungie's decision-makers began to realize that *Destiny* was best positioned as a single ongoing live-service game, with continued expansions and seasons. Rather than stick to the contract and develop a *Destiny 3*, Bungie negotiated with Activision to end their relationship, and in early 2019 it was over.

That meant one fewer source of revenue and one fewer distraction for Kotick, but at the end of the day, there was only so much that he could do with his Irvine subsidiary. Blizzard had maintained its stature in the video game industry by refusing to ship video games until they were ready. Even with Morhaime gone, there were plenty of people left at the company who were trying to retain that ethos—although there was one game that was about to throw it all out the window.

TWENTY-SIX

REFORGED

At the start of 2020, Blizzard was mired in turmoil. The company had been through one disaster after another: *Diablo Immortal*, the *Heroes of the Storm* debacle, the mass layoff, the Blitzchung incident. The culture was changing more and more every day, and so many veteran staff were stepping down that the company stopped sending out emails to announce their departures.

Those who loved Blizzard could at least still take comfort in the quality of their products. To players, seeing that blue logo pop up at the beginning of a game still meant that they were about to get a polished, satisfying experience. When Blizzard's leadership felt like a game might need more time to turn into a hit, they would still delay it, no matter how much pressure was coming down from above.

But in January 2020, as the world entered a new decade and Blizzard prepared for its twenty-ninth birthday, the people who worked on one of the company's smallest teams knew that was about to change. And the man in charge wasn't an Activision plant—he was one of Blizzard's longest-tenured veterans.

■ ■ ■

Even Rob Bridenbecker's entry to Blizzard was audacious. It was 1995, and he was giving a ride to one of his best friends from high school, Adam Maxwell. They were both Orange County nerds who played *Magic: The Gathering* and loved computer games, and after a chance encounter with Allen Adham, Maxwell had applied to be a QA tester on *Warcraft II*. Maxwell asked Bridenbecker for a ride to the interview, which turned out to be a formality—Adham offered him the job and said he could start that same day. Maxwell said he'd be thrilled, but that Bridenbecker was waiting for him in the lobby. "Don't worry about it," responded Adham, per Maxwell's recollection. "He's filling out an application as we speak."

Bridenbecker was charismatic, with a sharp jaw and confidence that stood out among his peers. His father was a vice president at a large California power company, which offered him a comfortable childhood. "He had never known a day of hardship in his life," said Maxwell. "And he had a certain amount of swagger and arrogance that came with that." In the early days, Bridenbecker became infamous for dating and flirting with women who worked for Blizzard. "He was a good guy, unless you were maybe a member of the opposite sex, in which case, maybe not so much a good guy," said Maxwell. When Bridenbecker first started, he hit on Blizzard's receptionist, shocking some of his colleagues. "We were taking bets when he first came in how long it'd be until he got fired," said artist Stu Rose. "He eventually became a vice president."

Maxwell left Blizzard after a few years, but Bridenbecker stuck around, developing a close friendship with Mike Morhaime and making his way up the corporate ladder, first on the customer service team and then Battle.net, where he eventually ran the entire division.

He earned credibility among Blizzard's top staff for delivering on tasks that others didn't want to do, like handling the billing system for *World of Warcraft*.

After a reorganization of Blizzard's technology departments led Bridenbecker to leave Battle.net, he floated around for a while before spotting a new opportunity: a small department called the Mac division, which was charged with bringing Blizzard games to Apple computers but, in 2016, had very little to do. Blizzard didn't plan to release *Overwatch* on Mac and had no other games planned for the near future. To stay productive, members of the team had pitched a modernized version of the original *StarCraft*, which was ripe for a graphical overhaul. They figured a remaster of Morhaime's favorite game would be easy to greenlight at Blizzard because production wouldn't be too expensive and it could sell well in Asian countries.

Bridenbecker was intrigued and positioned himself as the head of this department, which would later become known as Classic Games. Remasters were a popular trend in the video game industry because they were relatively cheap, low-risk propositions. It wasn't exactly a simple process to engineer an old game to look and feel good on modern platforms, but it was more predictable than standard game production.

After a year and a half of development, Blizzard released *StarCraft: Remastered* on August 14, 2017, to modest success. It was a slick remaster, letting players swap between new, high-definition art and the original graphics, preserved in all their 1998 glory. The game was a win for the burgeoning Classic team, although internally, some developers voiced complaints about how the project was handled. They had been short-staffed and working on a tight schedule, which led to tough hours. When the team headed to South Korea for a party to celebrate the game's launch, the bleary-eyed programmers were on their laptops, fixing bugs on the airplane and in their hotel rooms. Later, the development team would grouse that Bridenbecker had given them a release date before figuring out how long each task would take. "I think when you succeed by doing the wrong thing," said one person on the project, "that can be even more dangerous than when you fail."

For their next project, Bridenbecker chose *Warcraft III*, a game that was massively popular in China but had never actually been approved for release by Chinese government regulators, so had been pirated by millions of people. Although the business case for a new version was tremendous, *Warcraft III*'s three-dimensional graphics presented a heftier challenge than *StarCraft*'s 2D aliens and spaceships. *Warcraft III* was significantly bigger than its predecessor, with four campaigns instead of three, which meant exponentially more work. Their colleagues on Team 1 suggested that they use *StarCraft II*'s engine, which was updated regularly, rather than trying to wrangle code from two decades ago. But Bridenbecker was against it, arguing that it could break the game's massive library of maps, such as the iconic *Defense of the Ancients*.

Pete Stilwell, the lead producer, pitched an ambitious plan to rewrite the game's script and bridge some of the inconsistencies in *Warcraft III*'s lore that had arisen in *World of Warcraft*. They recruited Christie Golden, the author of a dozen *StarCraft* and *Warcraft* novels, to write new cutscenes for the game, and even brought in designers from the original *Warcraft III* to remake the old levels. Throughout 2018, Stilwell and his team crunched hard to create a demo that would showcase this plan, redesigning an iconic *Warcraft III* mission called The Culling, in which the prince Arthas slaughters a city full of civilians to prevent the spread of a dangerous zombie plague. Rebuilding the level, revising the cutscenes, and overhauling it all took several months, which was a little concerning—Bridenbecker wanted the game out within a year—but they were still optimistic enough to announce *Warcraft III: Reforged* at BlizzCon in November 2018. A video presentation promised fully remodeled characters and revamped levels, while the press release touted "hours of updated in-game cinematics." The game would be out in 2019, they said, and players could begin preordering the game right away.

Back home, a few weary Blizzard staff began to wonder if they'd just made a huge mistake. They would now have to release the game within the next year or would risk being forced to refund preorders thanks to various customer protection laws. The sudden time crunch combined with the team's ambitious plans meant that they quickly needed to staff up, but as Bridenbecker submitted his budget requests for the upcoming year, it became clear that Blizzard's new leaders didn't want to put significant money into a remaster. They were preparing for layoffs and cutting costs across the company as they headed into 2019, and the idea of completely overhauling *Warcraft III* didn't seem like a high priority to J. Allen Brack and his circle. Suddenly, the old designers who were contracted for *Reforged*, like Dave Fried, no longer had a role on the project. "I had a bunch of missions, I was starting to lay them out in the editor," said Fried. "And it just starts going silent."

With their deadline less than a year away, the *Warcraft III: Reforged* team suddenly had to reckon with budgets shrinking across the company. They would reach out to support staff in a department like marketing or localization only to subsequently learn that those people had been hit by the February layoffs. Their own team was understaffed, too, which led them to make bad calls. Fairly or not, Classic had developed a stigma for being a team full of outcasts, where Blizzard would send staff that couldn't find homes elsewhere. The *Warcraft III: Reforged* team was young and inexperienced, and had been relying on seasoned designers like Fried to help lead the way. While planning out schedules, they would look past red flags—like, say, needing five people for a given task when they only had four—because they were all so fresh and excited. "Every single person on the team wanted so badly to make the thing work," said one developer. "You kind of lose your objectivity."

As development progressed, even seemingly minor decisions had significant consequences. In the original release of *Warcraft III*, characters' mouths flapped up and down while they spoke, like an old cartoon. For the remaster, the developers wanted to add lip synchronization to make characters seem like they were really speaking, which created a cascade of bugs and technical complications. "Any of the risks that could go wrong, did go wrong," said producer Jason Savopolos.

Zach Johnson, an engineer, joined the *Warcraft III Reforged* team in the summer of 2019. By fall, they were working long hours to try to finish the game by the end of the year. "There was no formal crunch mandate until late October or early November," he said. "But when your coworkers are staying until 10:00 p.m. and there's food in the kitchen, the unspoken assumption is that you are going to be crunching." One night, Johnson felt his heart racing and his chest tightening. Aware that his family had a history of heart disease, he went to the hospital, where he was told that he was having a panic attack. "You feel like an idiot," he said. "But boy, it feels real." Afterward, he went back to the office, expecting to grab his stuff and leave, only to find his teammates still grinding away.

With their preorder-imposed deadline rapidly approaching, the *Warcraft III: Reforged* team saw overtime as their only option to release anything at all, let alone come up with something good. At one point, managers told the team that they were "going to cut down to the bone and then cut into it," according to one developer on the project. They pulled back on all their previous plans and even excised features that had been present in the original *Warcraft III*, like a competitive ladder and an automated tournament system. The outlook was so bleak that other developers from across Blizzard were dragooned to help finish the game.

Stilwell remained relentlessly optimistic—or, from a different point of view, consistently misleading—as he promised colleagues throughout 2019 that things were on track. "I lead with positivity," Stilwell said. "I had faith we would bring the game together as we neared the finish line." Bridenbecker, meanwhile, stayed hands-off as *Warcraft III: Reforged* struggled. "Sometimes we needed him to make decisions and he was on the other side of the planet celebrating a birthday in Hong Kong or ice-fishing in Alaska," recalled one developer. When he was in the office, Bridenbecker's aggressive managerial style led staff to avoid sharing information with him out of fear they might get yelled at. Later, a Blizzard spokesperson told *Bloomberg* that the game's fundamental problem had been "an early, unclear vision and misalignment about whether the game was a remaster or a remake," which "led to other challenges with the scope and features of the game, and communication on the team, with leadership and beyond, which all snowballed closer to launch."

A slight delay didn't solve the problem, and when *Warcraft III: Reforged* came out on January 28, 2020, it felt like a pie that had been removed from the oven twenty minutes too early. Players and critics panned it for feeling buggy and incomplete and slammed Blizzard for removing the original version of *Warcraft III* from Battle.net, forcing people to play this inferior version. Rather than preserving the company's history, the Classic team had scribbled all over it in ugly black marker. "This is not the remaster that *Warcraft III* deserves," wrote a critic for *PC Gamer*. Within a few weeks it had a 59 out of 100 on the review aggregation website Metacritic—the worst score in Blizzard's history. To alleviate the damage, the company said it would offer refunds to any player who requested one, no questions asked.

In the weeks that followed, Blizzard staff began pointing fingers. Top executives said they didn't know the game was in such bad shape until the final months, while Stilwell said he had made clear to his superiors that they needed more time. "In multiple meetings with executive leadership I said, 'In my opinion, we're not delivering the *Reforged* we promised our players, and doing so will tarnish the company,'" Stilwell said. In a postmortem conducted later, the developers insisted that they had made higher-ups like Bridenbecker aware of the problems with *Warcraft III: Reforged*. "Senior voices in the department warned leadership about the impending disaster of *Warcraft* on several occasions over the last year or so, but were ignored," the team said, according to transcribed notes from the postmortem meetings. They added that the game's leaders seemed "totally out of touch with the velocity/scope of the project until extremely late in development."

After *Warcraft III*, the Classic team had planned to remaster *Diablo II* in a joint effort with another game studio under the Activision umbrella called Vicarious Visions, in Albany, New York. (Vicarious Visions would later be absorbed into Blizzard.) But the company had now lost faith in Bridenbecker's team and instead moved *Diablo II* under Rod Fergusson, an executive who Blizzard had recently recruited to oversee *Diablo IV*. Both Bridenbecker and Stilwell left the company. Savopolos, who would also leave Blizzard soon afterward, looked back at the experience sanguinely. "When you're in the trenches with people, you form good bonds," he said. "Especially when the trenches are pretty muddy."

The debacle was yet another sign to the outside world that the once-revered company had changed in a big way. Now, Blizzard wasn't just stepping on PR rakes. For the first time in three decades, it had released a bad game.

■ ■ ■

For the *StarCraft* team, the failure of *Warcraft III Reforged* came with another tangible consequence: if it had been successful, they might have had a better shot at making *Warcraft IV.*

Over the previous few years, *StarCraft* had become one of Blizzard's lowest priorities. *StarCraft II* was beloved by its fans but had never lived up to the company's lofty commercial expectations, perhaps because of cultural changes in Korea and the KeSPA battle, or perhaps because real-time strategy games weren't as popular in the 2010s as they had been in the 1990s. The genre that Blizzard had once dominated now felt twitchy and complicated, requiring a level of multitasking that wasn't amenable to many casual players. They were getting drowned out by the smaller-scale strategy of games like *League of Legends* and *Clash Royale.*

But Tim Morten, *StarCraft II*'s production director, believed that the genre could be revitalized. At the end of 2015, after the release of *StarCraft II*'s final expansion, Morten laid out a plan to release three short mission packs called *Nova Covert Ops*—a spiritual reincarnation of the ill-fated *StarCraft: Ghost.* Players would be able to deck out the Terran spy Nova with high-tech gear for infiltration and combat missions that pushed the limit of *StarCraft II*'s map editor.

The catch was that Morten was only able to get approval for a year's worth of budget to develop them all. "*Nova* was really tough," said Elena Nikora, a producer on the project. "The team was not used to that cadence." Fans enjoyed the mission packs, but they didn't sell well, and some of the team's top developers were ready to move on.

Lead designer Jason Huck, who had now been working on *StarCraft II* for an entire decade, was burnt out and struggling to come up with new ideas for RTS mission mechanics. "I wanted to work on a new type of game," he said.

Without the resources to build more missions for *StarCraft II*, Morten pivoted again. Many of the game's original developers had moved to other projects, so he put together a small group of mostly new employees to transform it into a live-service game. By the end of 2017, they'd made *StarCraft II* free to play, and in the years that followed they fleshed out an innovative multiplayer mode called co-op commanders and added new microtransactions, such as outfits and voice packs.

Morten figured that if *StarCraft II* was lucrative enough, it would allow him to pursue his real goal: making *Warcraft IV*. It had been more than a decade since *Warcraft III*, and while the franchise had continued with the never-ending *World of Warcraft*, Morten believed players wanted to see a new real-time strategy game in Blizzard's iconic fantasy universe. Really, it didn't matter to him whether it was *Warcraft IV*, *StarCraft III*, or even a new franchise—Morten just wanted to lead another real-time strategy game. "I can't say there was one single vision for what the next RTS should be, but there were lots of ideas," he said. At one point, perhaps out of desperation, he'd even floated a strategy game based on *Call of Duty*.

Back when Morhaime was around, Morten had pitched him constantly, going into salesman mode when they bumped into each other in the halls or at holiday parties. "I have a feeling Mike probably anticipated that every time he passed me, I was going to advocate on behalf of making a new RTS," Morten said. Morhaime was noncommittal, saying that maybe there would be room on the slate for another RTS one day, but the company had other priorities. His personal love for *StarCraft* wasn't enough to justify the bandwidth and opportunity cost of a new entry in a waning genre. Even Allen Adham, one of the people most responsible for popularizing the RTS genre back in Blizzard's early days, was no longer interested. He had instead briefly flirted with a turn-based *StarCraft* game in the style of *Civilization*, but that was canceled.

StarCraft II's live-service effort went well but wasn't as successful as Morten had hoped, and the failure of *Warcraft III: Reforged* only soured Blizzard further on the genre. As it gradually became clear to Morten that the company would not be greenlighting a new RTS game, he decided to leave Blizzard and develop his own version at a new company, Frost Giant Studios, bringing a handful of his teammates along for the ride.

In the fall of 2020, Blizzard began winding down Team 1 and announced that it was putting an end to new content development for *StarCraft II*. There was still plenty going on at Blizzard: Team 2 was on *World of Warcraft*, Team 3 was working on *Diablo IV*, Team 4 was developing *Overwatch 2*, Team 5 was updating *Hearthstone*, and a handful of other small squads were working on incubation projects. Still, it was the end of an era in one major way: for the first time since 1994, Blizzard Entertainment was no longer working on a real-time strategy game.

TWENTY-SEVEN

THE BLIZZARD TAX

Around the same time that *Warcraft III Reforged* came out, news reports began to circulate about a mysterious virus that had originated in China. By the end of March 2020, Blizzard's staff were working from home as the world was ravaged by an infectious disease called COVID-19, which spread through close contact in indoor spaces such as offices. Like just about every company in just about every industry, Blizzard struggled to deal with the pandemic. Drained parents tried to patch together solutions for their childcare woes while designers and artists learned how to collaborate on digital whiteboards.

Blizzard's staff, trying to maintain their sanity during an unprecedented crisis, gathered on video calls to play games and hold virtual happy hours. To keep up morale, teams put together monthly Zoom milestone meetings to show off their games' progress. Many of the programmers, artists, and designers were working in disparate silos and had no sense of the full scope of their projects, so this was a helpful way to check in. "They were the main driver of enthusiasm for me," said one developer on *Diablo IV*. "It was helpful to remember that I'm working on a video game."

At the same time, their corporate overlords were exerting more influence every day. Activision Blizzard brought in a new HR boss, Claudine Naughton, who'd previously spent two decades working in insurance. One policy she introduced, called stack ranking, asked managers to give ratings to each of their employees across a five-grade scale: Top, High, Successful, Developing, or Low. Each of those categories had a quota, and managers were expected to place around 5 percent of their teams in the bottom two—a controversial policy that tech giants like Microsoft had once enacted to cull their lowest performers. At Blizzard, getting a low ranking was like being marked with a permanent scar: Developing employees would be passed over for promotions, denied raises, and would even receive lower portions of the profit-sharing bonus pool every year. Blizzard managers looked for loopholes, like giving the bottom grades to employees who were already on their way out, but the policy still led to widespread resentment.

Across the organization, especially outside of the game development teams, what had once been a focus on nebulous but admirable concepts like quality was pivoting to become about numbers and quotas. Christina Mikkonen, who worked in community management for *Hearthstone*, found herself stressing as she tried to maximize the number of published Blizzard blog articles. "We'd meet the numbers—like, 20 percent more blogs, or some useless metric," she said. "Then they'd say, 'Great—the next metric is 20 percent more than that.'" What had once been a creative, fulfilling job began to feel like working on an assembly line.

Stack ranking only exacerbated the problem, forcing developers to eye one another with suspicion and QA testers to battle over who found the most bugs. "It was very damaging internally to the culture," said one executive. "It created a real dog-eat-dog environment." Nobody wanted to be last in the game of corporate musical chairs. Compensation was enough of an issue already.

■ ■ ■

Erika Rodriguez was about to hit her eighth year as a tester at Blizzard when she got a job offer at Riot Games for double her salary. She went to her manager to see if Blizzard was willing to match. Then he came back to her. "'They gave me a number,'" she recalled him saying. "'It's so insulting that I'm not even going to tell you. I think you should go to Riot.'"

Rodriguez, like many people who worked in Blizzard's quality assurance department, had joined the company because she was obsessed with the games. "I lived and breathed *World of Warcraft*," she said. She'd loved the company's annual rhythms, working for months to put together demos for BlizzCon and then riding the highs of that weekend for the following year. She'd even been given a temporary opportunity to design items for *World of Warcraft*. But after more than seven years in QA, she felt like testers were mistreated. They were underpaid, isolated from development teams, and encouraged to battle with one another for the coveted designer and producer jobs. "This is where I wanted to retire," she said. "I put everything in the Blizzard basket, and it just broke me real hard when I left."

People called it the Blizzard Tax: the acceptance that in exchange for working in one of the most beloved and respected video game companies on the planet, you'd have to agree to less money. "Working at Blizzard was the goal," said John Yang, a designer. "You just kind of accepted whatever they were willing to pay you." The promise dangled by executives was that the company's annual profit-sharing bonuses would make up for lower pay, and often, that was true. Members of the *World of Warcraft* team who had been lucky enough to be there during the game's peak years had been able to buy cars and pay off mortgages with their bonus checks. But nothing was guaranteed, and during fallow periods—like the years following *Overwatch*—the bonuses could be underwhelming.

For Blizzard employees who worked in departments such as QA and customer service, it was difficult to live in Irvine, where rents had skyrocketed. In 2017, the United States Department of Housing and Urban Development determined that a single person would qualify as "low income" in Orange County, California, if they earned $58,450 or less per year. At roughly $20/hour, testers at Blizzard were lucky to break $45,000. The issue hit a tipping point toward the end of 2018, as employees began grumbling on internal message boards that they weren't just underpaid—they were struggling to get by. In a series of emotional posts, they shared stories about missing car payments, skipping meals, and cramming into two- or three-bedroom apartments as groups of four or five roommates. "We do not even bring up kids anymore due to finances," wrote one employee. "I see higher-ups posting pictures at Disneyland with their family. Seems like fun." Some testers volunteered for extra overtime because they otherwise couldn't make ends meet.

In other departments, such as marketing and PR, employees knew they were paid better than the lowest rungs but had no clue if their compensation was fair. Several staff said they were told by managers not to share their salaries with colleagues—a request that directly violated US law. When they did speak openly about their wages, they found disparities that they weren't sure how to reconcile, like five-figure differences among people with the same amount of experience. They discovered that company loyalty was punished: Those who worked their way up from QA or customer service were capped from making as much as colleagues who had arrived from other disciplines. Often, the only way to get a significant raise was to leave for another company and then come back—a trend known as the Blizzard Boomerang. One person later tweeted that by moving from Blizzard to Riot, they went from making $74,000 to $134,000 per year.

A company survey backed up the anecdotes that employees had shared, with more than half of Blizzard staff and nearly two-thirds of QA testers saying they were unhappy with their pay. The company promised that it would investigate the issue, and at the beginning of 2020, Claudine Naughton announced a new initiative called the "Compensation Journey" that promised a full review of every employee to ensure their wages reflected their performance. They would bring in outside experts, do market research, and perform a holistic evaluation across Activision Blizzard.

Normally, salary evaluations were handled at the beginning of the year, but this review lasted until the summer, priming employees to expect big increases. When the results came in, many Blizzard staff—especially those outside of development—were shocked to see that they'd received only 1 or 2 percent raises, which in some cases meant a bump of less than one dollar per hour. Stuck quarantining at home with no way to grumble together at the cafeteria, staff began putting their salaries and raises into a Google spreadsheet. As they shared stories and compared numbers in a lively Slack channel dedicated to compensation, they spelled out the significant disparities among positions across the company.

At the director levels, employees would receive robust compensation packages including lucrative equity grants—Brack had continued Morhaime's battle against shares tied to company performance—but many people at Blizzard weren't getting that kind of money. When one high-ranking staffer shared in Slack that they'd recently received a profit-sharing bonus of around $30,000, someone snarked, "when your yearly bonus is about as much as the average [customer service] yearly pay."

Across the video game industry, game companies saw QA and customer service as fungible positions because they didn't require college degrees or specialized skill sets, so it wasn't unusual that art or engineering would pay more. But Blizzard was part of a Fortune 500 company that generated more than $8 billion a year and in 2020 had paid Kotick a compensation package that was worth a staggering $155 million. Could the company really not afford to pay its testers enough to live in Irvine without having to dodge debtors and skip meals?

Throughout August, a group of Blizzard employees decided on their own to run internal surveys and discern the scale of the problem. The data, from around eight hundred respondents, proved what they'd already believed. Of the quality assurance testers who responded, 27 percent said they had trouble meeting their basic needs and 52 percent said they could pay for rent and meals but had little to no money after that. For customer support staff, the numbers were similar: 23 percent and 45 percent. Close to half of respondents, across every department, said they were "not at all" happy with the company's recent compensation changes, while a whopping 65 percent said they felt like they were paid lower at Blizzard than they would be at another company.

The mass layoffs a year earlier were still having an impact, leading many of those who had remained at the company to inherit responsibilities from those whose roles were eliminated. More than half of staff who responded to the survey said the scope of their jobs had increased but they had not received additional pay. Hundreds of people said they found Blizzard's profit-sharing system to be too opaque, and 78 percent of respondents said they would be happier with the system if they could understand how it was calculated, even if the amounts didn't change.

Even developers on Blizzard's most lucrative products sometimes felt like they were being paid unfairly. "I definitely had financial anxiety," said Chris Morris, a designer on *World of Warcraft*. "I'm working a whole bunch and I'm still not having an easy time making ends meet." When Morris started applying for other jobs, in part due to money woes, he was shocked to receive an offer from the nearby game studio Sony Santa Monica that was 40 percent more than his Blizzard salary. "I know many people left because of that," he said. "It was definitely a factor for me."

On September 3, 2020, a group of Blizzard staff sent a letter to J. Allen Brack outlining their issues. "These concerns include but are not limited to low base pay, few promotion opportunities, continued lack of transparency, unclear approaches to profit sharing, increased employee attrition, and ill-defined career opportunities," they wrote. The letter listed several requests, beginning with the goal of giving every Blizzard employee a living wage, and asked for a response by October 2. "You have asked us to come to you with our concerns and we worked with our peers to make every voice matter," they wrote.

Brack did not respond by the deadline. Later, he recorded a video that broadly addressed the letter but did not offer many specifics. Perhaps his power in the matter was limited. After all, Activision Blizzard controlled the budgets.

■　■　■

As some Blizzard employees struggled to pay their rent, the video game industry was breaking all-time records. Although the pandemic created economic uncertainty across the world, it was a boon for video game publishers, who saw revenues skyrocket as people found themselves with nothing to do but stay home and play video games. Activision, especially, benefited from this period thanks to *Call of Duty Warzone*, a free-to-play battle royale game released in March 2020 that sent players parachuting onto a large map and told them to explore, hunt for new gear, and survive to be the last person standing. It was an addictive formula pioneered by a 2017 game called *PlayerUnknown's Battlegrounds* and imitated by many others, including the megasensation *Fortnite* and now *Call of Duty*. By August, some 75 million people had played *Warzone*, helping Activision's revenue leap from $2.2 billion in 2019 to $3.9 billion in 2020.

The success of *Warzone* made it even more glaring that Blizzard wasn't releasing similarly impactful new games. Some Activision Blizzard executives pointed out that while Blizzard employees were lamenting their salaries, the latest *World of Warcraft* expansion, *Shadowlands*, was slipping a month. *Diablo IV* was struggling with story reboots and directional changes. Perhaps the most egregious offender was *Diablo Immortal*, the mobile game, which seemed to Activision like it should have been released years earlier. "I think there were a lot of efforts made to accommodate longer timelines," said Rob Millock, business lead for Kotick. "You knew you had these people who had this magic touch, would come up with something amazing, but you're in the confines of a public company."

Kotick was not looking to force Blizzard to release games that weren't ready—he wanted them to be hits—but he was clearly displeased with the stagnant progress. Daniel Alegre, who Kotick had hired earlier in 2020 as Activision Blizzard's newest president and Chief Operating Officer (replacing Coddy Johnson), was tasked with speaking to Brack on a regular basis—and ramping up the pressure as Blizzard's two biggest games missed their deadlines. Neither *Diablo IV* nor *Overwatch 2* would be ready in 2020 or even 2021, leaving Brack responsible for explaining these constant delays to the board of directors. "J. kept defending the team for years," said a former Blizzard executive. "And *Overwatch 2* kept slipping, and slipping, and slipping. It got to a point where J. lost his privilege of autonomy with Activision."

When *Overwatch 2* was first announced, Kaplan was asked by an interviewer when it would be out. In retrospect, his response almost feels like it was addressed to his corporate overlords. "I have no idea," he said. "Just let us make it great. That's what we care about more than anything. We don't have a date in mind."

There were several reasons that *Overwatch 2* kept slipping, including the business model, which was a constant subject of debate. Since the release of the first game, most other competitive shooters had gone free to play, and *Overwatch 2* would follow suit, which raised questions about how it would be monetized. Selling heroes would violate the promise Kaplan had made years earlier, but cosmetics alone might not make enough money to allow it to surpass the first game. There were hazy plans for a battle pass—a popular monetization system allowing players to pay to acquire perks—but Blizzard's developers and finance people were still building spreadsheets to try to figure out what that meant.

Activision executives expected a high average sale price (ASP)—the amount that customers would spend when they first picked up the game—because that was their key metric for the annual *Call of Duty* games. At the same time, they also wanted high lifetime value (LTV)—the amount that customers would spend across their entire time with the product—which was the standard measure for the success of a free-to-play game. "It's very hard to make both those things be really big at the same time," said one Blizzard executive.

But the main reason *Overwatch 2* was late was that Kaplan's ambitious vision for PvE had failed to coalesce. The underlying technology of *Overwatch* wasn't built for filling maps with hundreds of computer-controlled enemies, as a PvE mode would require, and the game's heroes were designed first and foremost to fight one another. The sniper Widowmaker's ultimate power was to highlight the location of every enemy on the map—an ability that was crucial for battling against other players, but useless against AI opponents with predictable patterns. While the story modes of most games were typically designed to be finished just once, like *StarCraft II*'s lengthy campaign, Kaplan wanted *Overwatch 2*'s PvE to be infinitely replayable, which proved difficult to pull off.

By 2021, the *Overwatch 2* team was starting to find solutions to these creative dilemmas, but the scope only grew larger as development continued, leading team members to fret that they were repeating the mistakes of *Titan*. Activision executives would call *Overwatch 2*'s leadership on a regular basis, which created more tension as Kaplan fumed to colleagues that he wished he could just be left alone to make the game he wanted to make. "I think Bobby wanted to figure out ways to give more resources to the *Overwatch* team," said Millock. "The *Overwatch* team didn't necessarily want more resources. They wanted less interference."

The biggest point of contention was still the size of Team 4, which remained exponentially smaller than the teams behind rival shooters. Kotick still wanted to make it larger or create a second division in the fashion of his massive *Call of Duty* empire, and even within the team, some developers agreed that *Overwatch 2* needed more designers, artists, and engineers to execute on Kaplan's vision. Newcomers were stunned when they learned that a single person might be responsible for a feature that would typically require dozens of people.

Blizzard leadership, already frustrated by Activision policies like stack ranking, argued that bringing on new people came with plenty of its own costs. Senior staff on *Overwatch* spoke with the shorthand of people who had been teammates for a decade, and it would take months if not years for new hires to acclimate. Interviews, onboarding, and training took days away from *Overwatch* leads who would otherwise be contributing to the game. "The more people we added, the more difficult it became," said animator Michael Biancalana. The larger the team, the bigger the budget, which meant that revenue would have to scale up to match, and there was a persistent fear that Kotick's ultimate goal was to annualize the franchise. Nobody at Blizzard wanted to see *Overwatch* go the way of *Guitar Hero*.

In the spring of 2021, Jeff Kaplan resigned from Blizzard, as did production director Julia Humphreys. They were followed a few months later by executive producer Chacko Sonny (who had taken over from Ray Gresko), leaving a huge leadership void on the *Overwatch* team. On his way out, Kaplan urged his staff not to let business realities overwhelm their creativity. To a group of designers, he shared a video from the singer David Bowie about pushing boundaries in art. "I think it's terribly dangerous for an artist to fulfill other people's expectations," Bowie said in the video. "Always go a little further into the water than you feel you're capable of being in. Go a little out of your depth, and when you don't feel that your feet are quite touching the bottom, you're just about in the right place to do something exciting."

Turnover at Blizzard had become a vicious cycle. Many top employees were leaving because of the ways in which Activision's interference had changed the company's culture. Attrition led to game delays, which made Activision's executives feel they needed to step in more, which pushed out even more talent. At the same time, Armin

Zerza was accruing even more power. Ever since he had arrived at Blizzard, Zerza's colleagues had suspected that his ultimate goal was to climb the corporate ladder—a suspicion that was given further credence in the spring of 2021, when he was promoted to Chief Financial Officer for all of Activision Blizzard. The good news for his detractors was that he would no longer be on the Irvine campus every day, but he was now even more integral to company-wide decisions.

In the summer of 2021, Activision closed Blizzard's office in Versailles, France, which had been operating since the Vivendi days and was largely responsible for marketing, localization, and customer service across Europe. As part of a lengthy negotiation process required by French labor laws, the company was forced to send a letter to affected employees justifying why they had just been fired. The letter included a striking stat: Blizzard consisted of around 52 percent game developers, in comparison to rivals Ubisoft (85 percent) and Take-Two (77 percent), which Activision wanted to change.

But that stat could be misleading. A big chunk of those non-developers worked in Battle.net, which allowed the company to distribute and sell its own games on PC without giving a 30 percent cut to Valve's Steam—a significant boost to Blizzard's profit margins. Divisions that other companies largely outsourced in 2021, such as customer service and cinematics, maintained internal teams at Blizzard. As Activision kept looking to consolidate, Brack and his circle pushed back, arguing that Blizzard's customers were primarily on PC, while Activision's were on console and King's were on mobile, so it made no sense for all three companies to rely on the same marketing or support staff.

Since Morhaime's departure three years earlier, Blizzard had been in a constant crisis mode, sending morale plummeting across the company. Departing veterans like Tim Morten and Ben Brode were starting new game studios that convinced even more staff to leave with them. Riot, Bungie, Epic, and other competitors leaped at the opportunity to poach people from Blizzard. The Morhaimes, too, started a new company called Dreamhaven with an all-star roster of former Blizzard leaders including Eric Dodds, Dustin Browder, Chris Sigaty, and many others in hopes that they could re-create the old Blizzard magic.

But, as the world was about to learn, not everybody who worked at Blizzard had found it all that magical.

TWENTY-EIGHT

RECKONING

Blizzard had always been a complicated place for women to work. In the company's thirty-year history there had been no female executive producers or game directors, which made it difficult for women to see a path to long-term success. Tenure was paramount, and most of Blizzard's female staff had joined in the decade after *World of Warcraft*, so they would never be able to catch up to male colleagues. There was a feeling across many departments that if you didn't fit into the boys' club, you'd always be questioned.

But there wasn't much that women could do about this problem—until the late 2010s, when a few began speaking to attorneys as part of investigations led by both the federal and state governments. On July 21, 2021, the news became public as California filed a lawsuit against Activision Blizzard for sexual discrimination and misconduct.[27]

---

27 Two years later, in December 2023, both parties would agree to a $54 million settlement of the CRD's pay equity-related claims, amending the complaint to remove the sexual misconduct claims and stipulating that "no court or any independent investigation has substantiated any allegations that there has been systemic or widespread sexual harassment at Activision Blizzard."

In a harrowing twenty-nine-page complaint, the government's lawyers declared that "sexism has plagued the male-dominated gaming industry for decades" and pointed to Activision Blizzard as a prime example of this epidemic. The most appalling allegation—that a woman had died by suicide "due to a sexual relationship that she had been having with her male supervisor"—occurred in Activision Publishing, but many of the other claims appeared to focus specifically on Blizzard, which was accused of paying women less than men, ignoring HR complaints, and tolerating known harassers.

The lawsuit's complaint was sloppy and often misleading, conflating different parts of Activision Blizzard and drawing no distinction between Blizzard's departments, when each had significantly different cultures. Still, many of the women who had worked for Blizzard over the years felt like it captured a broader truth. In the days and weeks that followed, dozens of men and women shared personal stories on social media, saying they had seen or faced sexual misconduct, gender discrimination, and an HR department that seemed either unwilling to listen to problems or incapable of addressing them. Many were angry. Some felt relieved that they weren't alone—that they had been justified in the rage they'd felt when looking back at their experiences at one of the video game industry's most beloved companies, despite people around them saying that everything was fine; that they'd made it up; that they were exaggerating. Now, perhaps by speaking out, they could find some peace.

■　■　■

Back in the mid-2000s, when Blizzard was growing at a rapid clip, Morhaime and the other executives found that they were spending too much time on menial issues, so they installed a layer of middle management called "councils" for each discipline of game development:

design, art, engineering, and so on. Leaders across the company's teams would convene for these council meetings, where they would discuss hiring and promotions. Connie Griffith, an assistant, was the only woman in many of the meetings, during which she watched some of the company's male leaders make comments that wouldn't be tolerated in most professional environments. "Some men were clearly from the 1990s," she said. "They complained about hiring women, and how you have to be careful around them."

Blizzard had changed a great deal since the days of fistfights and flooded hotels. It had become a different company as it expanded to thousands of employees, moved to the new campus, and merged with Activision to form one of the biggest publishers in gaming. But it was still mostly men, and women like Griffith found that casual sexism was common, especially in younger divisions like the QA department, where she and other women had to fend off disturbing and sexually charged comments from managers. When Griffith worked at Blizzard's reception desk, she jokingly called it the post office because there would be queues of men waiting to talk to her. "On one hand, I'm a twenty-three-year-old—I kind of enjoyed the attention," she said. "But on the other hand, I'm fucking twenty-three. Some of it was uncomfortable."

Even as Blizzard tried to professionalize, there were very few women in leadership roles and none in the company's executive ranks. Women at Blizzard, usually the minority on a team or in a meeting, constantly had to wonder if they were lagging because of their skills or because of their gender. "It was a self-fulfilling prophecy," said one woman who worked there. "The less we could achieve, the more distressed we became. And the more distressed we became, the less eligible or professional we seemed."

In the 2010s, the sexism grew less blatant but the systemic issues lingered, especially surrounding compensation. Women found that in addition to their daily responsibilities, they had to juggle the extra duty of learning whether they were being paid and promoted fairly. Nicki Broderick, who started off as a QA tester before becoming an assistant producer in the business intelligence department, was baffled when her husband, in another division, was promoted to an "associate" role, leapfrogging her "assistant" status by a rank. "I was two or three years behind my husband even though I'd worked at the company significantly longer than him, because he got to skip a bracket, and therefore was paid fairly," Broderick said. "That was so frustrating."

During her seven years at Blizzard, Broderick was forced to put up with alcohol-fueled hazing rituals and unwelcome sexual advances. Male colleagues would randomly message her to start conversations, which she thought was just part of the friendly atmosphere—until they suddenly stopped talking to her when they learned she had a partner. Once, someone said her "ass looks great in those shorts," she recalled. "I never wore shorts to the office again."

After leaving, Broderick spent months trying to reckon with her time there. In many ways the company had treated her poorly, paying her less than she thought she deserved and playing down her HR complaints. But Blizzard's games had helped her get through difficult times, and her wedding party was comprised almost entirely of friends she had met at the company. "Getting to build these really close relationships with everybody was something that I don't know if I'm going to experience at any other company in the industry," Broderick said.

Many of Blizzard's female employees described similarly contradictory feelings. Skye Chandler, who spent eleven years at Blizzard, loved her time working on games like *Diablo III* but was so frustrated that the company kept printing employee T-shirts in men's sizes, she marched to the licensing department to fight for female fits. "They said, 'Nobody cares,'" Chandler recalled. "I said, 'Dude, they do.'"

Another woman described jobs at other companies as a series of days that she might rank on a ten-point scale as perfectly adequate: 5/10s, 7/10s, and so on. Working at Blizzard, on the other hand, was an exercise in extremes. Some days were 10/10s; others were 0/10s. "The highs were high," she said, "and the lows were *low.*"

It was common for departing staff to lament that what they missed most were the lifelong friendships they'd cultivated at Blizzard. But it also sometimes took leaving the company for people to realize that "bleeding Blizzard blue" wasn't making them all that happy. "I still know a lot of people who are Blizzard diehards," said Erica Hebert, who spent two and a half years working in public relations until she was laid off in 2019. Some of those people, she said, were in their thirties or forties and wanted to have families but couldn't afford it. When they weren't at work, they were playing *Overwatch* or hanging out at Blizzard parties. "I think to myself: 'On their deathbed, is Blizzard going to be holding their hand?'" said Hebert. When she was laid off, she was heartbroken, but with distance, she felt otherwise. "I'm kind of glad my life isn't like that anymore."

From the beginning, the boundary between professional and personal lives at Blizzard had been nonexistent. That had started back in the 1990s, when Blizzard was a few dozen men who spent every day and night at the office, making and playing games together, and it had only continued as the company grew more successful and drew in people from across the world. Many of the people who moved to Irvine for Blizzard didn't have friends or family in the area, and the job was all-encompassing, so their social networks and romantic lives became tied to work.

This led to some unorthodox and uncomfortable situations.

Some of Blizzard's highest-ranking developers and executives were open swingers and would invite colleagues to sex parties. Gossip and rumors circulated frequently about this subculture, and some of the stories were so outlandish that it was never clear how much to believe, but sometimes, at a happy hour or work event, a rookie Blizzard employee might find themselves in a conversation full of innuendo. "They'd be very subtle about it," said community manager Christina Mikkonen. "They wouldn't come out and specifically say it, but you would know."

Jason Hutchins, a longtime Blizzard producer, was up-front about his involvement in this world, saying he believed in consent and that he and his wife vetted everybody they invited to their swinger parties. "We were open and honest about everything," he said. "Those conversations would have happened at a very frank level." But even consensual evenings could lead to messy realities when everyone had to see each other at the office the next morning. "There were issues, but I think we tried to handle them publicly, fairly, and aboveboard," said Hutchins. "Did that bleed over to the office? Probably, in some cases, for some people."

These blurred lines could lead to awkward or even harmful situations, especially during parties that were attended almost entirely by Blizzard staff. Women shared stories about noxious, drunken antics such as groups of men cheering for them to kiss or pressuring them into sexual acts. When they went to HR with complaints about these issues, they were told that there was nothing Blizzard could do because the events had happened off campus.

Women at Blizzard cultivated a whisper network to warn one another about specific men who had exhibited creepy behavior. But then they'd inevitably wonder: If they knew who was problematic, shouldn't management? "There are some people who you very quickly understand to avoid," said Mikkonen. "Because their reputation as predators preceded them. You ask: 'Why are they still here?' and get met with shrugs."

Executives would argue that it was unethical and illegal to publicize the results of HR investigations, and that sometimes, accusers would say different things in public than they did when asked to share their stories with the company. Often, HR departments would chase rumors about alleged offenders but couldn't get concrete answers, and when the company did take punitive action—such as demotions or pay docking—the punishments had to stay quiet for legal reasons, so the victims never learned what had happened. The silence just made women feel like Blizzard was ignoring their problems—especially when some of the worst offenders seemingly acted with impunity.

■　■　■

Nothing was more illustrative of Blizzard's cultural changes than BlizzCon, where the alcohol flowed and fans perceived employees as rock stars. Sometimes this was harmless. "It was hard to walk through there without fans hugging you and wanting to take a picture," said designer Greg Street. Other times, it was surreal. "There's a picture of me and Dave Grohl signing boobs together," said artist Joeyray Hall. "If a girl puts boobs in your face and says sign them, you sign them." And every so often, situations would get so out of control that Blizzard would have to tell employees to stop sleeping with fans.

Michele Morrow, an actress and writer, was attending BlizzCon in 2013 when she got a glimpse of the convention's uglier side. The night before the show, Morrow was out to dinner with Dave Kosak, a top designer on *World of Warcraft*, and his wife Crystal when a drunken man stumbled over. "He was super wasted, and he was hitting on me with wild abandon, saying ridiculous, embarrassing things," Morrow recalled. This was particularly uncomfortable because the man was Kosak's boss.

Alex Afrasiabi, who had started as a quest designer during the early days of *World of Warcraft*, had always played a starring role in Blizzard's whisper network. Even though he'd joined the company with no industry experience—Blizzard found him because he led a successful *EverQuest* guild—he proved to be a capable designer and rose through the ranks to become the creative director of several *World of Warcraft* expansions. He was handsome, charismatic, and brilliant at using the game's tools to implement new content. He also had a reputation for drinking heavily, insulting subordinates, and engaging in questionable behavior with female employees. Now he was drunkenly proposing to Morrow and promising her career opportunities. "He told me if I married him, I'd have the keys to Blizzard, whatever the fuck that means," she said. After some back-and-forth, Kosak stood up and guided Afrasiabi away from the table.

The next night, Morrow and the Kosaks were preparing to head to Afrasiabi's hotel room, at which Blizzard staff would convene during BlizzCon evenings to get away from the chaos of the Hilton bar. They called it the "Cosby suite" due to an inside joke that had started some time earlier, when the carpet in one of their hotel rooms looked like legendary comedian Bill Cosby's sweater. On a group chat with several other *World of Warcraft* designers including Afrasiabi, Kosak wrote that he was "gathering the hot chixx for the Coz," referring to his wife and Morrow, who were standing with him. When they arrived at the suite, Morrow again had to fend off unwanted sexual advances from a drunken Afrasiabi, but the night was otherwise uneventful.

A year later, in October 2014, a stand-up routine by comedian Hannibal Burress resurfaced old rape accusations against Bill Cosby that led to widespread press, new allegations, and criminal proceedings.[28] "I guess we won't be calling it the Cosby suite anymore," Kosak recalled joking to his wife.

But the name resurfaced in 2021 when the California lawsuit declared that "Afrasiabi was so known to engage in harassment of females that his suite was nicknamed the Crosby suite after alleged rapist Bill Crosby." This was not true, and the misspelling added to the overall sense of carelessness, but the allegation went viral. A subsequent article on the gaming website *Kotaku* shared a photo from Afrasiabi's Facebook showing a group of eight smiling Blizzard employees on a bed, gathered around a framed picture of Bill Cosby—a photo that had seemed harmless when it was taken that evening in 2013 but was horrifying eight years later. The article, which also published a screenshot of the group texts, reported that Cosby had been accused of rape in the early 2000s but did not mention that the allegations only became widespread knowledge a year after the photo was taken, nor did it specify that the "hot chixx" text was referring to Kosak's wife and friend. "It was just surreal," said Morrow. "Everyone was being unknowingly offended for me as the subject of this text when Dave is the one who protected me and did exactly what any man should do when their boss is being a creep."[29]

Kosak had left Blizzard in the fall of 2020 to become a creative director at a small company called Deviation Games. When the *Kotaku* article hit, several of his colleagues complained to management and said they no longer wanted to work with him, according

---

28 As comic W. Kamau Bell later said in the documentary *We Need to Talk About Cosby* (2022): "Most of us weren't grappling with it back then. Bill Cosby was still America's dad... But something about Hannibal's joke, plus grainy cell phone footage, plus this new era of social media, was explosive."

29 Later, Morrow began working as an on-camera host and interviewer for BlizzCon, where she was responsible for interviewing Afrasiabi about *World of Warcraft*. "I had to make him look smart, funny, whatever," she said. "That sucked for me."

to a person familiar with what happened. The studio hired an attorney to conduct a four-month investigation and although it turned up nothing else, Deviation fired Kosak. In an interview for this book, Kosak declined to comment on the circumstances of his departure but said he had faced professional repercussions due to the *Kotaku* article.[30] "When negotiating for jobs I still hear about how I have 'a PR problem,'" he said. "Nobody actually accused me of any wrongdoing. But my value as a person—at least in the corporate world—has gone down."

Paul Cazarez, who spent fourteen years at Blizzard before leaving in 2019, was also depicted in the *Kotaku* article posing alongside the framed photo of Bill Cosby. He said that his employer, ZeniMax Online Studios, put him on leave in the summer of 2021 after the article went live and then let him go a few weeks later without explanation. He said he had tried to explain that none of them knew about the Cosby allegations at the time but he was told that a teammate felt uncomfortable working with him. Later, when applying for new jobs, he ran into awkward situations—like recruiters canceling interviews an hour before they were scheduled, as if they had just been googling his name. "When I talk to friends and family, it's baffling to them," Cazarez said. "A photo has caused this much disruption in your career—in everybody's career."

The "Cosby suite" became a catchall term representing everything that was wrong with Blizzard, much to the frustration of people who had been there. "I can't speak for everyone else's experiences,

---

30 I spent about eight years working at *Kotaku*, including several with the article's author, Ethan Gach, although that article was published after my tenure there. I asked Gach if he looked back on the piece with any regret or felt like he would have done anything differently in retrospect. He responded with a statement: "This was a story grappling with allegations in a state lawsuit that sought to expand the public record with images and text conversations illustrating parts of the sexist frat boy culture alleged at the time. I stand by my reporting."

but when I was in that room, there was nothing nefarious except for Alex," said Morrow. Yet at the same time, women at Blizzard felt like the lawsuit was correct about one important element of the story: Afrasiabi was allowed to remain in a position of power despite his misconduct.

For years, women warned one another to stay away from Afrasiabi and PR staff were told to keep a close watch on how he interacted with press and fans. Signs would pop up in public, too. At a Blizz-Con panel in 2010, one woman asked a group of top *World of Warcraft* developers if the game would ever get female characters "that don't look like they stepped out of a Victoria's Secret catalog." The panel, all men, laughed at the suggestion. "We want to vary our female characters, absolutely," said Afrasiabi. "So, yeah, we'll pick different catalogs." In interviews for this book, nearly a dozen people shared their own stories of either experiencing, seeing, or hearing about sexual harassment conducted by Afrasiabi, although one woman, offering a defense of him as a leader and mentor, pointed out that his misdeeds weren't reserved for the opposite gender. "He was an asshole to everybody," she said.

Despite his reputation, Afrasiabi ascended Blizzard's ranks and was made creative director of his own Blizzard project, code-named *Andromeda*, that aimed to create a high-fidelity action game, like Sony's *God of War*, in the *Warcraft* universe. In the spring of 2020, a year before the lawsuit hit, Blizzard fired him for what a company spokesperson later called "misconduct in his treatment of other employees." Members of the small team that had been working under him on *Andromeda* were informed that he had been let go, although they were not told why. Blizzard looked for a new director to run the project but came up short, and it was soon canceled, scattering the team members to other games across the company.

■ ■ ■

Afrasiabi wasn't the only Blizzard leader accused of sexually harassing women. An executive in the esports department was publicly alleged to have groped women against their will, and in interviews for this book, several women shared stories involving harassment from men across various divisions. In some cases, the men were fired; in others, the women chose not to report the incidents or ran into complications, such as HR protocols requiring police involvement that made them resistant to move forward. Some said they watched their harassers receive trivial punishments, like an order not to speak to the women who had accused them. Katelyn Lorenzen, who worked in reception, said she reported a coworker to HR for repeatedly making sexually explicit comments to her but was brushed off. "They told me that since I didn't tell him to stop, they couldn't do anything to him and just told him to avoid me," she said.

In the summer of 2018, Mike Morhaime sent out an abrupt email saying that Ben Kilgore, Blizzard's Chief Technology Officer and Chief Development Officer, was no longer with the company. The message left employees baffled and sent rumors flying. Usually, a major exit would involve a farewell party or at least a paragraph or two about the departee's experience and history with the company, but Morhaime's email simply declared that Kilgore was gone.

Derek Ingalls, one of Kilgore's top lieutenants, held a meeting shortly afterward where, by way of explanation, he told a story about a piece of advice he'd received at Xbox that sounded like a joke: *Don't sleep with your assistant. But if you're going to sleep with your assistant, don't stop.* Many attendees were shocked—both that a top executive would make a joke like that in a public meeting and the implications it had for Blizzard's executive assistants, no matter the truth. Some had heard rumors or had even seen Kilgore acting sexually toward subordinates, but the comment from Ingalls was still striking.

Originally staffed by a single programmer, Battle.net had morphed into a massive organization as it became the backbone for all of Blizzard's games. The division merged with various other tech groups within Blizzard and went through so many reorganizations that staff would joke every year that it was time to update their business cards. Pushed by Activision to hire an experienced CTO following the *Titan* debacle, Blizzard hired Kilgore, a slick Xbox veteran with a Midwestern twang, to oversee the division in 2014. Kilgore brought in some of his old Xbox buddies, and suddenly, the Battle.net department was made up of his inner circle. "The top level was hiring their friends, and that tier was hiring their friends," said Andrew Hunt, a producer. "Everybody that worked there was very aware that promotions were now starting to happen based on who they liked."

Alcohol had always played a big role in Blizzard's culture, but in the tech department, it became the centerpiece. Managers set up a massive bar that was meant for after-work functions but was often used during the workday. Members of the tech division would show up hungover, vomit in trash cans, and take shots during meetings. Staff recalled referring to Ingalls and other top tech staff as characters from *Mad Men* because of their tendency to drink Scotch on the job.

Blizzard events called cube crawls, which in most departments were usually themed potlucks, became rowdier and more belligerent affairs in the tech department. (The California lawsuit depicted these cube crawls as harmful across the company—another misleading accusation that many Blizzard employees disputed.) Later, Blizzard would enact a "two-drink maximum" at after-work functions in response to some of these problems—and to cut down on drunk driving. "It wouldn't be weird on a Tuesday for someone to come up holding two fingers of whiskey while talking about the next sprint," said Tom Broderick, a product manager in Battle.net (and Nicki's husband). "Nobody would really question it."

Kilgore remained well-respected among his peers, perhaps because the details of his department's culture had not widely trickled out. As Morhaime considered quitting Blizzard amidst battles with Activision, he even eyed Kilgore as his successor.

The details leading up to Kilgore's abrupt departure remained hazy. But according to multiple people familiar with what happened, he was fired after an investigation into his behavior—not because of what Blizzard found, but because he was caught lying to the investigators.

■ ■ ■

On July 23, 2021, shortly after the lawsuit hit, Activision Blizzard Chief Compliance Officer Fran Townsend sent out an email calling it "a distorted and untrue picture of our company, including factually incorrect, old, and out of context stories." Townsend went on to write that "the Activision companies of today, the Activision companies that I know, are great companies with good values."

In Blizzard's Slack, employees erupted. It was true that the lawsuit contained inaccuracies and referred mostly to incidents that had happened years in the past. Blizzard had already quietly dealt with some of the alleged offenders, like Kilgore and Afrasiabi, as it tried to fix some of its ingrained cultural problems. Those efforts appeared to be making progress—a 2019 study by the career website Comparably ranked J. Allen Brack as one of the top twenty-five CEOs for female employees—but the issues of widespread sexism still resonated with many staff, and for Townsend to talk about "the Activision companies that I know" seemed particularly absurd given that she had started four months earlier.

In contrast, Morhaime, now three years removed from Blizzard, offered a statement apologizing and asking women to share their stories with him. "It is the responsibility of leadership to stamp out toxicity and harassment in any form, across all levels of the company," he wrote. "To the Blizzard women who experienced any of these things, I am extremely sorry that I failed you." He and his wife, Amy, spent the next few days on video calls listening to the experiences of former employees, some of whom insisted that he must have known about their problems.

Back on campus, Blizzard staff acted swiftly. They organized a walkout outside the front gate, where protesters in masks (both for COVID and anonymity) held up signs like "Nerf Male Privilege" and "Play Nice, Play Fair." They started a Discord server called "A Better ABK" so employees could talk about the issues without using company-owned channels. Townsend then held a video call with female employees that became so contentious, as she dodged questions and told cursing staff to watch their tone, that the company backtracked on a promise to send out a recording of it afterward. When it became clear that Activision Blizzard was facing a reckoning, Kotick reversed course, writing an email a few days later to walk back Townsend's comments. "Our initial responses to the issues we face together, and to your concerns, were, quite frankly, tone deaf," he wrote, adding that he had hired the law firm WilmerHale to "conduct a review of our policies and procedures to ensure that we have and maintain best practices to promote a respectful and inclusive workplace."

Although the lawsuit targeted all of Activision Blizzard, Kotick's subsequent actions appeared to focus solely on Blizzard. In early August, J. Allen Brack was replaced by two new bosses: Jen Oneal, the well-respected head of Activision's Vicarious Visions studio, which was now part of Blizzard, and Mike Ybarra, another longtime Xbox executive who had joined Blizzard's tech department in late 2019 to help clean things up. Staff were alarmed when they subsequently learned that Ybarra had been friends with Kilgore and Ingalls at Xbox—he had tweeted about going out to dinner with them—although his reputation was cleaner.

Blizzard veterans, many of whom were trying to reconcile the revelations with their own experiences at the company, weren't sure what to make of the leadership changes. On one hand, it felt like Kotick was using Brack as a scapegoat and trying to take even more control of Blizzard. Yet it was hard to see how Brack could survive when the California government had accused him of failing to deal with these issues.

In the months that followed, Blizzard fired and reprimanded dozens of other staff who had been the subjects of HR reports, including some high-profile leaders like Luis Barriga, the director of *Diablo IV*, and Jesse McCree, the lead designer.[31] Development teams held meetings and encouraged women to speak up about their problems both publicly and privately. Across the company, it felt like momentum was building toward positive change.

Then, at the beginning of November, Oneal abruptly stepped down, leaving Ybarra as Blizzard's new president. And on November 16, 2021, the world exploded again when a *Wall Street Journal* article reported that Kotick had been aware of several issues, including an alleged rape, but did not inform the board. The story accused Kotick of intervening to keep a *Call of Duty* studio head after an internal

---

31 This was particularly awkward because *Overwatch* featured a gunslinging hero named Jesse McCree, whom the team later chose to rename Cassidy. *World of Warcraft* also had several references to staff such as Afrasiabi that the team subsequently removed. A consequence of these events was the adoption of a new Blizzard policy: no more naming characters after employees.

investigation recommended that he be fired for sexual harassment. The *Wall Street Journal* reported that Kotick had threatened to murder an assistant—as a joke, he said—and that Oneal had stepped down because she was paid less than Ybarra. Another wild detail was that Fran Townsend's controversial email to staff had in fact been written by Kotick.

It was as if a second lawsuit had just dropped. Blizzard staff began to revolt, even going so far as to complain about their CEO on social media—not something that often happened in the buttoned-up video game industry. In a rare move, the heads of PlayStation and Xbox both separately emailed their employees to criticize Kotick's leadership and response to the ongoing crisis. During a series of all-hands meetings across the company, Kotick's lieutenants told staff that despite the most recent allegations, their CEO would not be resigning. One Activision executive told staff that Oneal's compensation had not been less than Ybarra's—it was just structured in a different way. (In a Slack message later, Oneal wrote that she had been offered equivalent pay "only after I tendered that resignation.")

Nearly two thousand employees across Activision Blizzard then signed a petition calling for Kotick to step down, using their real names despite the potential consequences. But the decision came down to a group of just ten people: the board of directors, which was largely made up of Kotick's old pals. Two board seats belonged to Kotick and Brian Kelly, his business partner since the Mediagenic days. Other seats were held by Robert Morgado, Robert Corti, and Peter Nolan, who had all been working with Kotick since 2003 or earlier and earned a great deal of money as Activision shares skyrocketed along the way. It didn't come as a huge surprise to see the board declare in a statement that it remained "confident in Bobby Kotick's leadership, commitment and ability" to achieve the company's goals.

Kotick was the Teflon chief. In thirty years at the helm of Activision, he had successfully seized back control of the company from Vivendi, fended off a nasty legal squabble with the creators of *Call of Duty*, and won endless political battles on his quest to grow the company every year. To the outside world it now seemed that even this crisis wouldn't bring him down, despite increasing attrition and plummeting morale.

But on the inside, it was clear that the status quo couldn't hold. Shaken employees would brace for the worst whenever they saw "Blizzard" trending on Twitter, wondering which Activision Blizzard executive had put their foot in their mouth this time. Players began boycotting the company's games and spamming their social media with comments about the Cosby suite. Something was going to have to change at Activision Blizzard. Kotick would just need to figure out how to turn it all into a win.

TWENTY-NINE

XBOX

Shortly after the *Wall Street Journal* article hit, Kotick got a call from Phil Spencer, the president of Microsoft's Xbox division, asking if Activision Blizzard was for sale. Spencer was a Microsoft lifer who had taken charge of the struggling console department in 2014 and helped turn its fortunes around. He had a slight paunch, wavy brown hair, and pronounced dimples that made it seem like he was always smiling. He quickly won over gamers in the same way that Mike Morhaime often did—by showing that he was one of them. In 2020, Spencer tweeted an image showing that he had played more than 420 Xbox games in the previous decade, racking up nearly 2,600 achievements in the process. He came off as an amicable, respectful leader both to the outside world and within his company, where employees appreciated his candor and generosity.

Spencer's strategy centered on a subscription service called Xbox Game Pass that was often described as "Netflix for video games." Customers could pay monthly for access to a shifting lineup of software including day-one releases of Xbox's own titles, like *Halo* and *Forza*.

But it was tough to convince new customers to shell out $10 a month when Microsoft's history of internal development was so spotty, especially in comparison to rival Sony, which had produced a string of Game of the Year candidates for the PlayStation. To compete, Spencer had spent years acquiring video game companies such as Obsidian, the maker of *Pillars of Eternity*, and Bethesda, the publisher behind games like *Skyrim*, *Fallout*, and *Doom*. Now, with Activision Blizzard stock sliding due to the misconduct scandal and Blizzard game delays, Spencer could land his biggest catch yet.

Kotick looked around for a better offer but couldn't find one, and by January 2022, the deal was in place: Microsoft would buy Activision Blizzard for a total of $69 billion, the biggest deal in video game history.

As groggy Blizzard employees woke up to headlines blaring on their phones and laptops, both companies cautioned that it would be a long time before the deal was finalized. The acquisition would have to be assessed by regulators of every country in which the two companies did business, and some of those regulators, such as the US Federal Trade Commission, suspected that it violated antitrust laws. Microsoft and Activision said they expected the process to take around eighteen months and they set a July 2023 deadline to make it happen.

It also became clear that once the deal closed, Kotick would depart the company he'd been overseeing for more than three decades—a move that seemed unfathomable to Blizzard. For years, it had seemed like Kotick was waging a campaign to reshape the company. When Brack left, observers felt like the war was over and that Kotick could now transform Blizzard in whatever way he chose. Under Mike Ybarra, Blizzard had already reorganized into a new structure in which each franchise, such as *Diablo* and *Overwatch*, had its own general manager and teams swelling into the hundreds—kind of like *Call of Duty*.

Kotick's ambitious initiative to transform Activision Blizzard into the Disney of video games had not panned out. The Overwatch League was struggling, a partnership with the retailer Fanatics for Blizzard gear proved to be unpopular, and Activision Blizzard Studios had wound down after striking deals with Netflix for shows based on *Diablo*, *Overwatch*, and *StarCraft* that were subsequently canceled.[32] Still, it was hard to believe that after everything that had happened, Kotick would soon be gone.

For Blizzard veterans who had resented Activision's increased involvement in their company's operations, news of the acquisition inspired cautious optimism. But it also raised some big questions. What was Microsoft's strategy for Blizzard? How would it differ from Activision's approach? What about their cultural issues, which had been caused in part by transplants from the very company that was now buying them?

More pressing: Would the deal ever actually close?

■ ■ ■

Once the shock had subsided, business continued as usual for Blizzard Entertainment. The development teams kept working on *Diablo IV*, *Overwatch 2*, and other new games and expansions with a newfound hope that they would be free of their loathed boss soon. "Everything went from miserable to optimistic," said Jonathan Bankard. "There's a light at the end of the tunnel—we can be Blizzard again."

The company's next release was *Diablo Immortal*, which had caused so much controversy when it was announced back at BlizzCon 2018. It was Blizzard's first dedicated mobile game and the first new *Diablo* since *Reaper of Souls* eight years earlier. It had been in development as

---

32 At the beginning of 2019, Kotick filed a lawsuit against Netflix for poaching his CFO, Spencer Neumann, which may have been a factor.

a joint effort between a team in Irvine and one in China for more than half a decade—exponentially longer than most mobile games, but a time frame that some at Blizzard justified by saying that this was their attempt to put a console-quality game on phones.

From Irvine, Blizzard developers led the direction of *Diablo Immortal*, offering feedback to NetEase's large team in China. The Americans had to work odd hours, staying late to hop on video calls and using English-Mandarin translators to facilitate every conversation. "NetEase definitely was the engine, but Blizzard was in the driver's seat," said Glenn Rane, who led art on the project. "They'd send over concepts, we would do playtests, we'd give them feedback." As Blizzard's team of perfectionists pushed for frequent changes and iterations, then waited for NetEase to execute, the weeks and months began to add up. "They were super smart and passionate about *Diablo*," said designer Julian Love. "But it can be a really long process."

In China, it was common for mobile games to be released in a semi-finished state and then receive updates over time, which ran counter to Blizzard's philosophy. On a call with investors in 2019, NetEase executives hinted that the game was near completion, but Blizzard's developers believed otherwise. "They were very surprised at our attention to detail," said Kris Zierhut, a senior systems designer. "But at the same time, the reason they wanted to partner with us was because of Blizzard's quality and attention to detail."

Diablo Immortal, like most mobile games, would be free to play and generate revenue through microtransactions. To try to make the concept more palatable to Blizzard fans, *Diablo Immortal* director Wyatt Cheng and commercial lead Joshua Lu put together a list of core principles for their approach to in-game payments. One was that they wouldn't sell anything that would let players skip content while another, perhaps inspired by the *Diablo III* auction house debacle, was that players wouldn't be able to buy items directly.

This became a constant point of debate between Blizzard and NetEase. The joint development deal for *Diablo Immortal* divided profits by region—NetEase received the money generated from China; Blizzard from the rest of the world—which ramped up the tension. In China, gamers were accustomed to spending money on just about everything, from stronger skills to faster player movement. American gamers, including many of the ones who worked on *Diablo Immortal*, were much less tolerant of anything that evoked the dreaded term "pay to win"—an implication that those with the deepest pockets would always be victorious. Americans had grown up with consoles in their living rooms, for which you simply had to buy a cartridge or disc and bring it home, whereas Chinese players were more accustomed to paying for time in internet cafes, so they tended to think about games in a different way.

Ultimately *Diablo Immortal* landed on a convoluted, opaque system of currencies that resembled many other mobile games—a stark contrast to what Blizzard had tried to do years earlier with the *Heroes of the Storm* store. It was easy to play the bulk of *Diablo Immortal* without whipping out the credit card, but players who wanted to maximize their chances at getting the best gear would have to invest in Legendary Gems, Legendary Crests, Fading Embers, and other proper nouns.

To players, it all felt very un-Blizzard—a direct contradiction to the company's core mantra of "gameplay first" that seemed to instead prioritize profits. "To see it submit to mobile gaming's worst tendencies, rather than make any effort to be different, to be better, is galling," wrote a critic for the prestigious *Edge* magazine. "Its structure and pacing [are] designed with one goal in mind: to squeeze as much cash out of every player as it can." But internally, Blizzard developers knew that the compromise was necessary—they were just proud to have released a mobile game that they thought was pretty good.

As part of their ongoing partnership, Blizzard and NetEase were working on another mobile game, code-named *Neptune*, that was planned as a spinoff of *World of Warcraft*. Set in a different era from the PC version, it was designed to bring Blizzard's heaviest-hitting game to a new audience. But the two companies were in the thick of tense contract negotiations that weren't going well, and the Chinese government had put a freeze on new releases. In the spring of 2022, *Neptune* was canceled—for reasons entirely unrelated to the quality of the project. "It was the most crushing loss I've had in the industry," said artist Johnny van Zelm. "We were so proud of it."

Later in the year, Activision Blizzard and NetEase announced that they had been unable to reach a deal and that aside from *Diablo Immortal*, which was part of a separate contract, Blizzard games would no longer be playable in China. The biggest sticking point was a request from NetEase to have more control over operations in China so that it could comply with the country's strict regulations. Kotick and Zerza objected, arguing that it would cost them ownership over their data and IP rights, and the negotiations fell apart.

As a result of the dispute, millions of Chinese gamers lost access to *World of Warcraft* and *Diablo*. In protest, NetEase employees streamed themselves dismantling the massive *Warcraft* statue that rested outside their office. Back in 2006, Activision and Blizzard had merged in part because of Blizzard's strength in China—now, the company no longer did business there. [33]

---

33 Two years later, after Kotick and Zerza departed, Blizzard would patch up its relationship with NetEase, announcing in April 2024 that it was bringing its games back to China.

Still, there was one big reason for optimism as they headed into the fall of 2022. The company was on track to finally release a game that had been delayed for years—the sequel to the company's most successful project in a decade.

Overwatch 2 was coming out…sort of.

■   ■   ■

Back in 2021, when *Overwatch* director Jeff Kaplan departed Blizzard, a new leadership team took over. Aaron Keller, who had worked at the company since the early days of *World of Warcraft*, inherited Kaplan's role as director. Walter Kong, a veteran of Blizzard's strategic initiatives team, returned from outside the company to be executive producer, while former Overwatch League executive Jon Spector transferred to Team 4 to become the commercial lead. There was still pressure from above to get *Overwatch 2* out the door quickly, and the new triumvirate didn't necessarily disagree with that notion. In fact, as painful as it might have been for Blizzard veterans to admit it, they kind of agreed with Kotick when he grumbled that they had failed to live up to their commitment to release new *Overwatch* content for players. To make *Overwatch 2* a successful live-service game, they needed to add more developers to their team.

But even with extra resources, they realized it might be years before they could deliver on Kaplan's original vision for *Overwatch 2*. The team had made some progress on the PvP, a continuation of the first game's competitive multiplayer that would rework the heroes, add new game modes, and reduce teams from six to five players. But the ambitious PvE components still weren't coming together and might not be ready for a long time. It was reminiscent of the problems they'd faced on *Titan* a decade earlier, and the solution was similar: Keller and the leadership team decided to decouple the PvP from the PvE. In 2022, they'd release the competitive multiplayer portion of *Overwatch 2*, and the rest would follow down the road. In a video explaining the decision to the public, Keller explained that they were rethinking *Overwatch 2* "with the singular goal of ensuring it is a living game." He went on to lament that they had neglected players by pivoting to focus entirely on the sequel. "Honestly, we've let you down when it comes to delivering *Overwatch* content," he said.

Overwatch 2 came out on October 4, 2022. It was free to play, but in the weeks and months that followed, players were stunned by what appeared to be exorbitant microtransaction prices: skins (costumes) for characters that could cost upward of $20, and pricy bundles like a Halloween-themed pack that charged $40 for four outfits. Most controversially—given what Kaplan had promised for the first *Overwatch* years earlier—some of the game's heroes were unavailable when you started playing. To unlock them, you could either play a ton of matches or pay to speed up the process.

Loot boxes had fallen out of fashion in the years after *Overwatch* thanks to EA's *Star Wars: Battlefront II* (2017), which used digital treasure boxes in such a brazenly exploitative way that politicians in the United States and Europe began talking about regulating them as gambling. By 2022, loot boxes had been demonized in the press and no longer appeared in most video games, but *Overwatch 2*'s microtransactions were making players wonder if maybe they hadn't been all that bad.

The long-awaited *Overwatch* sequel was also glitchy and unstable on release, with lengthy queues and major bugs that forced Blizzard to temporarily remove characters like Bastion because their abilities were breaking the game. "People said it looked unfinished," said one person who worked on *Overwatch 2*. "That's because it was." Fans and critics couldn't understand why the game was pegged as a sequel when the gameplay and visuals felt identical to the first *Overwatch*.

"Everyone said: 'You worked for six years on this?'" said the person. "No, we worked for one year on this. We spent those other years on all the PvE stuff."

Overwatch 2 saw a huge spike of players on release and then a big plummet—as was common with free-to-play games—which compelled the leadership team to mull over the best approach for retaining players. Then they started wondering: How realistic was their approach to PvE? They essentially had two games on their hands. One was the live-service game that would require a team of hundreds to regularly release new cosmetics, new events, and several characters per year. The other, an ambitious PvE portion that they called Hero Mode, might require a team of hundreds to work for years without releasing anything new.

The split focus spoke to a fundamental question that the *Overwatch* team—and Blizzard at large—was now forced to answer. Did they still live in a world where one of their teams could squirrel away for half a decade and then emerge with a new game?

In May 2023, Keller dropped the news that while the team still planned to release PvE story missions, they were canceling Hero Mode. In an interview with the website *GameSpot*, he explained that the scope was too big, the ambitions were too high, and they didn't want to repeat the same mistakes they'd made on the first game. "We couldn't save up all of that content over the course of what was looking to be at least the next several years to finish it," Keller said.

Their logic was sound, but the news was still poorly received. To fans, the promise of something new and different was what justified calling this game *Overwatch 2* in the first place. Otherwise, it just felt like more of the same—the *Call of Duty*-ification of Blizzard's superhero series. Worst of all, *Overwatch 2* had replaced the first game, which could never be played again—just like *Warcraft III*.

Overwatch had been a cultural sensation—a smash hit that came out of nowhere to reach millions of players and generate billions of dollars. But the landscape of video games had changed. The industry was now stuffed full of live-service games, from *Fortnite* to *Genshin Impact* to Activision's own *Warzone,* and each of them battled for players' time in ways that weren't quite as palpable back when games had real endings. In an oversaturated market, *Overwatch 2* had more competition than the first game ever had, and, thanks to its lengthy development cycle, the expectations were even higher.

It would be some time before Blizzard could truly gauge whether *Overwatch 2* was a successful release, but early signs weren't promising. And it certainly wasn't enough to save the lofty venture that had once been hyped as the NFL of video games.

■ ■ ■

Nobody really wanted to talk about the Overwatch League's biggest problem: *Overwatch* wasn't very fun to watch. Sure, the league had brought in hundreds of thousands of viewers for its biggest matches, but with its jittery first-person camera and busy visual effects, *Overwatch* could be impenetrable to people who didn't play it. A third-person viewer was less nauseating but even harder to follow, as teams of characters leaped in the air and shot rows of projectiles at unclear targets. It was one of the fundamental flaws of esports as a whole—competitive video games were impossible to comprehend unless you already knew the ins and outs of those games. The average viewer didn't need much knowledge to understand the marvel of a one-handed touchdown catch or a circus half-court shot, but they'd struggle to perceive what made a pentakill so impressive or how that one Reinhardt player managed to use Earthshatter to take out an entire team.

Overwatch League peaked in its first year and then declined from there, leading team owners to grumble that they had been sold a bag of magic beans. After the first wave of $20 million franchise fees, the league had charged even more for expansions, so the pressure to generate quick revenue was stronger than ever. Team owners complained about the slow cadence of *Overwatch* updates, demanded more team-specific cosmetics that they could sell to fans, and asked over and over, in the years before the sequel, why the first game wasn't going free-to-play—a move that was unfeasible for Blizzard because it lacked monetization options but might have brought the league more relevance. Due to the lack of new content, the game's player count had fallen significantly. "You can almost project the growth of your viewership based on the growth of the audience who's playing the game," said one Overwatch League executive.

A switch in broadcasting partners from Twitch to YouTube was lucrative for Activision Blizzard but caused a drastic decline in viewership. Sponsors then pulled out due to the California lawsuit—and selling advertisements had always been a tough challenge for the Overwatch League's salespeople. "Team 4 resisted commercialization on every turn," said Steve Brauntuch, a marketing director. "We had a deal at one point for BMW to sponsor the game and the league, and BMW wanted to put a car in the game. Team 4 said no."

And then there was the fact that the league's business model revolved around selling tickets and concessions to fans in cities across the world, like traditional sports, which was upended when a global pandemic rendered it dangerous to attend events at crowded stadiums. "Without the players on stage together, with graphics and lights, what you had was people playing video games and streaming," said Brauntuch. "That's not a great experience." As the league limped its way to each new season, infuriated owners complained about losing money to expensive maintenance costs. "Morale stank," Brauntuch said. "We were left with a shell of what it once was." By the end of 2021, high-level executives and developers across the company were suggesting that they kill the Overwatch League, arguing that the business model didn't work and that they had damaged their relationships with team owners.

Heading into 2022, staff hoped that *Overwatch 2* would reinvigorate the struggling esports league with a surge of new players and press attention. "It's a little stormy, but you can see the lighthouse," said Andy Ochiltree, a brand marketing manager. But the sequel didn't deliver the growth that team owners were hoping to see. In the summer of 2023, five years after the Overwatch League's illustrious kickoff, Activision Blizzard declared in an earnings report that the department's operations "continue to face headwinds" and that the owners would vote on a new operating agreement later in the year. If they voted not to continue the league, each team would receive a $6 million kill fee.

By November, it was official: the Overwatch League was dead. Although Blizzard would continue supporting *Overwatch* esports with external partners, the city-based teams were no more. Kotick had set out to create the NFL of video games. What emerged instead was more like the XFL.

THIRTY

A NEW ERA

n the beginning of 2023, Blizzard lead engineer Brian Birmingham got a call from a manager saying that they would have to lower the score on one of their employees' yearly evaluations. Birmingham, the respected veteran who had led *World of Warcraft Classic*, said he wasn't comfortable with that, but the manager said it was necessary—they needed to fill a quota.

Claudine Naughton had departed Activision Blizzard in 2021, and Blizzard's leads had believed that after companywide pushback—including a letter that many of them, including Birmingham, had signed—they'd fended off the stack-ranking policy she had shepherded. For the past two years, they had been able to treat the numbers more as guidelines than quotas, but now, Birmingham was told that each team had to mark a certain percent of employees as "Developing" to reflect that they were on the bottom of the list. Fuming, Birmingham told colleagues he was going to start looking for a new job that evening. "It's unbelievably unethical and inefficient," Birmingham said. "To have this elaborate process we all go through, making carefully chosen ratings, and then change them based on arbitrary quotas."

That night, *World of Warcraft*'s leads held an emergency video call to discuss the policy. A heated Birmingham logged off in the middle of the meeting, saying he planned to resign. Over the next few hours, several coworkers convinced him to rethink quitting, but in the morning he learned that HR had already started to process his resignation. He sent out a lengthy email to his colleagues explaining the situation, writing that "this sort of policy encourages competition between employees, sabotage of one another's work, a desire for people to find low-performing teams that they can be the best-performing worker on, and ultimately erodes trust and destroys creativity." Birmingham, who had spent seventeen years at Blizzard, wrote that he could no longer work for the company if the status quo continued. "If this policy cannot be reversed, then the Blizzard Entertainment I want to work for doesn't exist anymore," he wrote.

Minutes later, Birmingham watched his access to company servers disappear and began feeling conflicting emotions: stress over future finances, pride that he had stood up for his team, regret that he hadn't been able to protect them. "I miss the opportunity to work on such a cool product, but at the same time I still wouldn't go and work for a place that wanted to mandate" stack ranking, Birmingham said. "I guess what I really wish is: I wish that weren't true. So I could work there again."

■ ■ ■

The Birmingham incident was the first red flag for Leslee Sullivant, who had started working on the *World of Warcraft* team just a few weeks earlier. Blizzard had been her dream job since she first became hooked on the online game in high school, but she'd been rejected year after year until a recruiter had reached out. Even Blizzard's recent cultural problems hadn't dissuaded her from pursuing a job at the company behind the game she loved so much. She had done her due diligence, talking to current and former members of the *World of Warcraft* team before she considered the gig. "It sounded like they had really cleaned house, really held themselves accountable after all of the lawsuit stuff," Sullivant said. "Also, because I was coming into a senior position, I felt more comfortable thinking: 'I've seen it all; it's fine.'"

Before she accepted the offer, Sullivant asked the company's HR staff about their policy on remote work as the pandemic subsided. She lived in Los Angeles, and her commute to the Irvine campus was an hour and a half each way, so this was a potential dealbreaker. She was pregnant, about to have her second child, and she knew that pumping breast milk at the office would be a hassle. "The written response I got was: 'It's up to you and your manager,'" she said. It was clear that Blizzard would be asking employees to return to the office at some point later in the year, but the details remained ambiguous. "I took that to mean: 'Great, I can actually work it out with my manager.'"

Then, about a month after Sullivant started, Blizzard told employees they'd be expected to return to the office for at least three days a week. Blizzard wasn't alone in this proclamation—companies across the world, in every industry, were trying to chart similar paths forward after years of allowing staff to work from home. Advocates of remote work argued that it improved productivity by eliminating lengthy commutes and helped protect against industry volatility by ensuring that workers didn't have to uproot their lives for new jobs. Remote work also helped solve an issue that had been prevalent at Blizzard for decades: anyone who wasn't making enough money to afford to live in Irvine could move to a cheaper city.

Blizzard president Mike Ybarra, on the other hand, argued that creative collaboration was easier in person, that newer staff were missing out on mentorship by working from home, and that being together was better for company morale and loyalty. He wanted the bulk of staff back on Blizzard's Irvine campus, where he expected a "hybrid" schedule of two days home, three days in the office. He said that Blizzard's data showed a massive improvement in productivity when employees were on campus, but as a compromise, each team would allow 20 percent—later changed to 30 percent—of its staff to work remotely, based on department heads' discretion.

Employee frustrations only grew worse when they subsequently learned that 1) Blizzard hadn't hit its revenue goals for the previous year, so they would get only 58 percent of their bonus targets, and 2) Blizzard would be weighting profit-sharing bonuses toward the teams that released successful products—the policy that Kotick had been trying to enact for years.

As the issues cascaded, Ybarra called an all-hands meeting in February 2023. He said that switching to a hybrid schedule had itself been a compromise that benefited employees. "The best thing for the business would be for us to be here five days a week like we were before the pandemic," he said. As the meeting continued, employees began to grumble that his answers were unsatisfying and sometimes even offensive. When asked about compensation woes and pay raises failing to keep up with inflation, Ybarra said they were "working on options" to improve the situation. "And we're also looking at disciplines," he said. "Some disciplines aren't just long-term disciplines to be in."

The comment led to instant outrage. Sure, roles like QA and CS were often stepping stones to other departments, but there were plenty of people who had worked in those roles for a decade or more—wasn't it best for the business if their experience was retained and rewarded? Then, responding to a question about whether the highest-paid employees would cut their own salaries to help lower-level staff, Ybarra said that if "someone believes that executives are making a lot of money and the employees aren't, you're living in a myth." (The 2022 compensation packages for Activision Blizzard executives included $7,282,786 for President Daniel Alegre, $11,242,362 for Chief Administration Officer Brian Bulatao, and $12,087,986 for Armin Zerza.)

Employees fumed about the meeting, which several veterans said was the worst they'd ever experienced at Blizzard. "I've been in game-cancellation meetings that left me in a better mood," one said later. Ybarra sent out an email to try to clarify, writing that "I failed to balance my commitment to transparency with a more thoughtful and holistic approach" and "came off as rough and dismissive."

For Sullivant, the meeting was the final sign that Blizzard, once her dream company, wasn't the place for her after all. "That day, I sent my application to Netflix," she said. She'd asked her own boss about working remotely and was told that her team had already hit the permitted percentage because so many people had been granted permanent remote work in the past. In June, six months after she started, Sullivant quit her job, telling Ybarra, "Maybe I would go into an office, but I'm not going to do it for you."

This push for Blizzard to return to campus was baffling to some employees, who wondered if Ybarra genuinely believed that it was worth losing veteran staff for the sake of filling up desks. Was it a soft layoff—an attempt to cut down on costs without the pain of an actual reduction in force? More questions emerged over the summer, when some Blizzard employees arrived on campus only to be told that there were no desks for them, or saw that some of their colleagues weren't actually coming in. Other times, managers would wink and hint that nobody was really tracking whether they were in the office on the requisite Tuesdays, Wednesdays, and Thursdays. And as more and more people quit because of stack ranking and this new policy—their frustration exacerbated by Ybarra's comments—it became clear that Blizzard's reputation wasn't on the upswing just yet.

■ ■ ■

On June 5, 2023, Blizzard released *Diablo IV*. It was a much-needed win for the company, receiving critical acclaim and—presumably—commercial success. In a press release, Blizzard said the game broke records and generated $666 million in revenue but didn't elaborate on profitability. Later, the company said it had reached more than ten million players.

The development of *Diablo IV* had been lengthy and exhausting, hampered by catastrophes: The director and lead designer were fired in the wake of the California lawsuit, the story was rebooted multiple times, and the team was understaffed for its first few years until it suddenly received an influx of new people, which caused its own set of problems. Still, fans were mostly happy with the game, which was beautiful and felt distinct from its predecessors, with a large open world full of side quests and timed events in which players could team up with strangers to battle massive enemies.[34] Like *Overwatch 2* before it, *Diablo IV* also charged big bucks for cosmetic improvements. As one IGN headline declared: "Now *Diablo IV* Is Out in the Wild, the True Horror of Its Costly Microtransactions Has Revealed Itself."

This time, Blizzard was determined to avoid another decade-long hiatus between new *Diablo* releases. Before they'd even finished *Dia-*

---

34 Like its predecessor, *Diablo IV* drew complaints in the months after release, as players grew disappointed with the endgame. Also like its predecessor, *Diablo IV* fixed the problem with a patch, released in May 2024, that overhauled the gear system. But there was one crucial difference: *Diablo III*'s update was called Loot 2.0, while *Diablo IV*'s was Loot Reborn.

blo IV, the team had pieced together a plan for releasing new content, starting with an expansion called *Vessel of Hatred*, as part of a new company-wide structure that aimed to support games on a more consistent cadence. A couple years earlier, Blizzard had reorganized in a big way, shifting from teams based on games into teams based on franchises. Now, rather than have dedicated company leaders for each product, there were general managers (GMs) in charge of *Warcraft*, *Diablo*, and *Overwatch*. Each of these franchise departments would employ hundreds of developers to work on both ongoing content and new games. It was a structure that Kotick had been pushing for years, based on the success of the *Call of Duty* model, which relied on multiple teams working in parallel to create a predictable schedule.

The GM for the *Diablo* franchise was Rod Fergusson, a veteran producer who had worked on games like *Gears of War* and had a reputation for being a tenacious closer. Under Fergusson, *Diablo IV* had a plan for the next ten years: a live team would work on patches and seasons while others developed the next two expansions and even a new game, whatever that might look like. It wasn't a strict division, and people would shuffle around when a deadline was approaching, but they hoped the structure would allow for more efficiency and predictability.

Overwatch was led by Walter Kong, who oversaw the release of regular heroes and content for *Overwatch 2* as well as new projects, like a mobile version of the franchise. The *Warcraft* department was run by John Hight, who had been production director of *Reaper of Souls* before moving to the *World of Warcraft* team. Hight was aiming to achieve what Blizzard had been trying to pull off for more than a decade: make *World of Warcraft* expansions more quickly. In the summer of 2022, Blizzard had purchased a game studio in Boston, Massachusetts, called Proletariat that it absorbed into the *World of Warcraft* team, which now comprised hundreds of people. The most recent expansion, *Dragonflight*, was received well by players and critics. "I can't help but be impressed at how a handful of new ideas, along with major facelifts to some old ones, breathe new life into Blizzard's flagship title," wrote one reviewer.

Just after the release of *Dragonflight*, Blizzard saw the return of a beloved veteran: Chris Metzen, whose infectious, booming energy had played a key role in the creation of so many franchises over the years. Metzen had resigned in 2016, not long after the release of *Overwatch*, saying on a podcast that he was "having panic attacks left and right" and "nonstop anxiety," in part spurred by the failure of *Titan*. Although he didn't say it publicly, his turbulent relationship with Rob Pardo had also played a significant role in his departure, according to people familiar with his thinking. He'd spent the next few years working on board games and other lower-key creative projects, but he'd never truly cut ties with Blizzard, and he still returned occasionally to do voice acting for *World of Warcraft*'s Thrall and other key characters in the games.

Throughout 2022, he started talking to some former colleagues about potentially coming back in a limited capacity. That soon turned into a full-time job, and by the start of 2023, Metzen had become executive creative director of *World of Warcraft*, plotting out a story arc for the next decade of the game. Much of Blizzard's old culture had been washed away in recent years—for better or worse—but with Metzen back around, it wasn't all lost.

■　■　■

By the summer of 2023, dozens of countries had rubberstamped Microsoft's planned acquisition of Activision Blizzard. It would have already been official if not for two holdouts. One was the United States Federal Trade Commission, led by a firebrand named Lina Khan who preached about pursuing antitrust laws more aggressively. But during a July court battle, Khan's department failed to convince a judge that the deal was illegal, largely because of a commitment from Xbox to keep publishing *Call of Duty* games on rival PlayStation platforms for at least the next ten years. When the FTC lost, the second holdout, the United Kingdom, subsequently relented and agreed to approve the deal in exchange for a few insignificant concessions.

On the morning of October 13, 2023, it was official: Blizzard had joined the Xbox organization, where *Warcraft* and *Diablo* would now sit alongside the likes of *Halo*, *Fallout*, and *Doom*.[35] Shortly after the deal closed, Xbox boss Phil Spencer flew to Irvine as part of a global tour across Activision Blizzard. Leaders of the development teams had prepared presentations for Spencer, like they might have in the past for Kotick, but their new boss wasn't interested in slide decks. He wanted to get his hands on the products, like the new mobile game *Warcraft Rumble*, and talk to the staff, who lined up for hours to take selfies and ask questions. "What they were trying to communicate to us was really wanting to get to know us," John Hight said in a *Bloomberg* interview. "'We're not coming in with a master plan. How can we help you?' It was awesome."

A few weeks later, roughly twenty thousand Blizzard fans and employees convened in Anaheim, California, for BlizzCon—the first since COVID, the lawsuit, the acquisition, and the wounds that Blizzard had suffered in recent years. Blizzard announced new heroes for *Overwatch 2*, the first expansion for *Diablo IV*, and—in a surprise move—the next *three* expansions for *World of Warcraft*, a sign that the effort to release content more quickly might finally be getting close to the moon. Under newcomer Holly Longdale—the first female executive producer

---

35 One of the strangest twists of the deal was that a few years earlier, Xbox had also purchased a company called inXile that was started from the ruins of a company called Interplay. Decades after Brian Fargo had helped his old pal Allen Adham get Blizzard off the ground, they were now coworkers.

in Blizzard's history—the developers had already succeeded at speeding up the cadence of updates between each expansion.

The star of the show was Metzen, who took the stage to raucous applause. As he had done at so many BlizzCons in the past, he demanded cheers from the crowd based on their *Warcraft* faction. "Horde!" he shouted. "Alliance!" His absence at previous shows had been striking, and this felt, in many ways, like a return to normalcy.

On the second floor of the convention center, Allen Adham met up with his wife, son, and daughter—the family he had once quit Blizzard to raise—and took them around the show floor. Even he would have to admit that Blizzard wasn't the same place anymore. The company was no longer ranked among the industry's best workplaces or the world's favorite gaming brands. They would no longer be able to get away with stamping their logo on a box full of rocks. But as fans gathered to speculate about the future of *World of Warcraft*, there were good reasons to be hopeful. At Microsoft, Blizzard was a small cog in a trillion-dollar machine. Now, delaying the next *Overwatch* or *Diablo* wouldn't require board approval or sink the company's stock price. The company behind Office and Windows didn't need to rely on shipping new games every fall to hit its revenue targets, which meant there would no longer be demands for extreme predictability to ensure growth every year.

Under Phil Spencer, the Xbox division had become known for giving its studios autonomy to make their own calls, and he'd told Mike Ybarra that he wanted to do the same for Blizzard. "Sometimes, when you're part of Activision Blizzard, I'll be honest, there are certain things where I go, 'Huh, wonder why we have to run this by whoever,'" Ybarra said in a *Bloomberg* interview. "Here, I think the expectation—and I embrace it fully—is going to be to run the studio, keep the teams happy, keep them motivated, let them bring their visions to life, foster a culture that drives creativity. I'm all in on that."

Outside in Anaheim, some fans were seeing one another in person for the first time in four years, hugging as they met up with longtime *World of Warcraft* guildmates. Some attendees had grown up playing the likes of *Warcraft*, *StarCraft*, and *Diablo*. Others were newer fans who had perhaps been introduced to the company's library through *Hearthstone* or *Overwatch*. All were there because of what Blizzard had created over the last three decades—because they'd spent long, bleary-eyed nights raiding the Lich King or battling hordes of screaming zerglings. Allen Adham and Mike Morhaime had always believed that video games were unique in their ability to bring people together, and now, even after everything the company had been through, Blizz-Con continued to prove out that hypothesis.

Back in Irvine, workers were preparing to remove the bronze "company value" plaques that surrounded the iconic orc statue and replace them with new ones. For more than a year, a diverse committee of employees had worked to revise Blizzard's old values for a new age, whittling them down from eight to five:

1. For the Love of Play
2. Passion for Greatness
3. Better Together
4. Strength in Diversity
5. Boundless Curiosity

Bobby Kotick's last day as CEO of Activision Blizzard was December 29, 2023, nearly thirty-three years after he took over Mediagenic. The rest of his C-suite, including Armin Zerza, would step down in the months that followed. In a note to staff, Kotick wrote that he was "profoundly grateful to the people who contributed tirelessly to building this company and I am confident you will keep inspiring joy and uniting people through the power of play." On social media, the comments from his former staff were much less kind.

Blizzard was about to turn thirty-three years old. It had a new owner, a new suite of games to develop and update, and a new mission statement. As employees returned to work, energized by the excitement they'd felt at BlizzCon, ready to enter yet another era for the company, it was easy to feel an emotion that had been missing from Irvine for a very long time: hope.

Then it all came crashing down.

THIRTY-ONE

NINETEEN HUNDRED

On the evening of January 24, 2024, Blizzard producer Jeremy Monken was up late in the hospital, watching his wife go through a lengthy labor that ended in a midnight C-section. The next morning, his boss asked him to get on a call. Still exhausted and high on adrenaline, he was informed that he was being laid off. He looked back at his wife, holding his newborn baby, and found himself unable to come up with words. "Delivering that news was one of the hardest, most emotional struggles I've gone through," he said.

Monken was one of 1,900 Xbox employees—or 8.5 percent of total Xbox staff—who lost their jobs in a mass layoff that mainly targeted Activision Blizzard, not just in departments that might have been redundant, like legal and marketing, but deep into the development teams of games like *Overwatch 2* and *Diablo IV*. Some of the people who had lined up to take selfies with Phil Spencer during his Irvine visit were now looking for new jobs. "It just seemed like the new age: We were joining the Xbox Games family and everything was going to be great," Monken said. "This was completely blindsiding."

For months, Monken had cheered on Xbox's lawyers during every regulatory hurdle. He had been incubating a new game with a small team who were told by Blizzard higher-ups that it was unlikely to come to fruition under the Kotick regime. "All of the internal discussion was that the greenlight is completely dependent on the Microsoft acquisition coming through," Monken said. He was exhilarated when the deal was closed—and now, three months later, he had been rewarded with a layoff.

Others had relocated to Irvine because of Blizzard's stringent new return-to-office policy, like Brad Sierzega, a veteran artist who was asked to move from Texas to join Blizzard in the summer of 2023. Five months later, he woke up to a call from his brother asking if he had seen the news. He rushed into the office, where he was ushered into a meeting room and told that he and many of his colleagues were out of a job, effective immediately—they weren't even allowed to go back to their desks and collect their things. Now he was stuck in a long-term lease for an Irvine apartment that cost more per month than his mortgage payments. "I sacrificed a lot to be here, and I felt completely betrayed," Sierzega said.

At the start of 2024, the video game industry was in a rough place. Big game publishers had swelled to keep up with pandemic demand and now found themselves overstaffed, while rising interest rates put an end to a brief period of easy borrowing. Every major game company was cutting hundreds if not thousands of jobs, and Activision Blizzard was no exception—Kotick and his circle had been planning this layoff before the Microsoft deal even closed. Still, there was an optimistic if perhaps naive belief among Blizzard staff that their new owners were different—one that was squashed when Phil Spencer offered the same kind of cold business jargon that Blizzard had heard from previous executives. "Together, we've set priorities, identified areas of overlap, and ensured that we're all aligned on the best opportunities for growth," Spencer wrote to his employees.

Mike Ybarra, too, was asked to leave Blizzard after two and a half years at the wheel. His policies had been broadly unpopular with staff, and that disastrous February 2023 meeting still hung over him, but he had still hoped to be the company's president for years to come. "Someone will drag me out of Blizzard," he had told *Bloomberg* at BlizzCon two months earlier. Ybarra, an avid gamer who often offered his opinion to development teams (sometimes to their dismay), had been looking to pivot away from the live-service model. He had planned to cut down on microtransactions in *Diablo IV* and reboot *Overwatch*, which had underperformed throughout 2023. But he had made some enemies during the two decades he'd spent at Xbox before joining Blizzard, and now the company was moving on.

Blizzard's next president was Johanna Faries, who had spent five years at Activision Blizzard as an executive on *Call of Duty*—first in esports, then overseeing the games—and eleven years in the NFL before that. Faries had been meeting with top Blizzard staff for more than a year about joining the company as Chief Operating Officer to oversee the business under Ybarra, but instead, she was given his job. She had a good reputation as a manager, but some Blizzard staff worried that her gaming background was limited—and that she'd come from Activision, given everything they'd been through.

In her first few weeks, Faries held a series of meetings with Blizzard leaders and staff to take their questions, listen to their concerns, and try to win their trust. People asked where she planned to steer the company and if she planned to reverse many of the controversial policies that had been enacted over the years, like stack ranking, return to office, and the profit-sharing overhaul, which had recently led to the *Overwatch* development team getting zero percent of their bonus targets. Faries said she was evaluating it all.

Xbox executive Matt Booty, who oversaw all of the company's studios, told Blizzard that he wanted them to continue developing new franchises and that despite the layoff, he and Phil Spencer still wanted the company to retain its autonomy. If there was one big difference between Booty and his predecessors, it was that he had experience as a game developer. He told colleagues and subordinates that he understood that making games was as much an art as a science and that he didn't think that a company could simply throw hundreds of people at a game just to produce content more quickly. He said he believed in giving creative teams the freedom to fail.

Chris Metzen was still around, but the other Blizzard lifers had slowly trickled out—even those who had stuck around through recent bad times. Sam Didier, who had set the artistic vision for so many of the company's games, retired shortly after BlizzCon 2023. Bob Fitch, one of the company's first employees, also left during the layoff.

And, for the first time in Blizzard's thirty-three-year history, neither of the founders worked there anymore.

■ ■ ■

Old-timers at Blizzard used to joke that Allen Adham had a reality distortion field—the term infamously ascribed to Apple cofounder Steve Jobs, who could convince people around him to do just about anything. When he came back to Blizzard in 2016 following his twelve-year absence, Adham tried to take that same approach to his new initiative, incubation, by following the old playbook: identifying an exciting genre without too much competition and developing a slick, polished version that beat out the other contenders. But all these years later, he no longer had the same effect on the company he'd founded, and he was no longer able to get games finished through sheer will.

Adham had found some success overseeing *Diablo Immortal* and *Diablo IV* (before handing them off to other executive producers), but by 2024, his incubation projects had failed. One of the most significant was *Orbis*, the *Warcraft* version of *Pokémon Go*. It suffered from several big issues, including attrition, scope creep, and the pandemic throwing a massive wrench in the idea of a game that required players to go outside and visit new locations; but the biggest problem was combat, which the *Orbis* team was never able to nail down. "There was this internal debate constantly," said one developer on the game. "Is this *Warcraft* for casual players? Or is this a casual game for hardcore *Warcraft* players?" Ultimately, it was the reality of the market that put an end to *Orbis*: other games that had tried to ape *Pokémon Go*'s augmented reality gameplay, even in popular franchises like *Harry Potter*, failed to find an audience and were shut down shortly after they launched. *Pokémon Go* was a one-time cultural phenomenon that couldn't be replicated.

The other big project was the survival game *Odyssey*, which Adham believed should have been a layup for Blizzard. The genre was full of popular but janky games that Blizzard was well-positioned to surpass, and during the early years, director Craig Amai and his small team developed a slick prototype that allowed players to forage and battle in a vibrant world. They worked in the Unreal Engine, a toolset developed by the company Epic Games that had become ubiquitous in the video game industry because of its ease and accessibility. Executives and developers across the company were elated by the prototype, even Kotick, who said he thought it looked delightful and asked when it would come out. "If you'd put that game on Steam, it'd be a hit," said Jacob Repp, the engineering lead.

But Blizzard's goal wasn't to put out a game in early access and potentially bring in one or two million players, it was to launch a billion-dollar franchise. The Unreal Engine seemed incapable of supporting their ambitions, and there was anxiety among Blizzard's executives about relying on technology that was owned by a direct competitor. Their solution was an engine called Synapse, which had originally been planned as a companywide initiative but instead wound up folded into *Odyssey*. Adham was against the switch, arguing that it was too risky and would add too much time to the schedule, but several other executives pushed for it. "It had a lot of issues," said Repp. "A lot of really speculative, big-bet technical items they really wanted to do that had never been proven, just added risk."

Under pressure from Kotick and Zerza to expand the team and get *Odyssey* out the door in a timely fashion, Blizzard brought in Dan Hay, a Ubisoft veteran who had helmed games in the popular *Far Cry* shooter series. Ubisoft had a long history of developing massive games with teams comprising thousands of people, and the higher-ups hoped that Hay would bring that kind of structured rigor to the game's development timeline. Under Hay, the *Odyssey* team grew quickly, exceeding two hundred staff, but struggled to enter production due to unstable technology and unclear design.

By 2023, the project was floundering. Many of the original Synapse engineers had departed when the tech was attached to *Odyssey*, and Blizzard had trouble hiring senior programmers for all sorts of reasons (PR issues, unpopular policies, and so on). The new engine remained incapable of bringing *Odyssey* to completion, so some of the artists worked in Unreal, knowing that they'd probably have to throw away their work and redo it all again from scratch.

Then, as part of the mass layoff, *Odyssey* was canceled. A Blizzard spokesman told *Bloomberg* the move was made "as part of a focus on projects that hold the most promise for future growth." Most of the developers were laid off, while a few would remain with Hay to begin incubating, of all things, a new *StarCraft* shooter. Perhaps after *StarCraft: Ghost* and *Ares*, the third time would be the charm.

Adham had stepped back from direct supervision of *Odyssey* to take a new title: Chief Design Officer, which put him in charge of mentoring developers and bringing back a development ethos that he felt had been missing from Blizzard since Rob Pardo departed. He'd been giving talks at conferences and having lunch with designers across the company, trying to impart some of the old values that he thought had driven Blizzard's success over the years—chestnuts like "concentrate the cool" and, of course, the old donut theory. "The trick is to invite people in without losing your hardcore gamer soul," he said during one talk.

But now, at age fifty-seven, with his incubation projects dead and his responsibilities fuzzy, Adham was ready for another change. His kids were heading off to college, the company was about to enter a new era under Xbox, and as part of the layoff process, he decided to make his exit. Thirty-three years after he'd first assembled desks in a tiny office alongside Mike Morhaime and Frank Pearce, Allen Adham left Blizzard for the third and perhaps final time.

The impact of what they'd built was impossible to measure. Despite the recent struggles, Blizzard was still one of the most important video game developers on the planet. Few of its peers had created as many monumental franchises or changed as many lives. Few other game companies had mastered such a wide variety of genres: real-time strategy, RPGs, shooters, and even digital playing cards. Over the previous three decades, Blizzard had developed a Korean national sport and built a virtual world in which people met lifelong friends and found their soulmates. Blizzard had even made a game so good that it drove that one guy's wife to complain that they weren't having sex anymore.

Adham didn't see it as retirement. He planned to join a few boards, do consulting for game studios across the industry, and maybe give some speeches. He told colleagues that after taking some time to detox, he planned to embark upon another, possibly quixotic project, just like he had all those decades ago, when he was testing out games for Brian Fargo during high school summers, before there were boards to join or conferences to attend or even much of an industry at all.

He thought he might develop his own video game.

ACKNOWLEDGMENTS

This book would not exist without the hundreds of people who took hours out of their busy schedules—in some cases, many hours—to answer my questions. To every single person who spoke to me for this book, who joined me for coffees and lunches and video calls and put up with my endless calls and texts, whether you were on or off the record, I am grateful for your patience. Thank you.

A big thanks to my wonderful editor Jacqueline Young, a master at trimming the fat. Thanks to my agent Charlie Olsen, to Lyndsey Blessing, and the rest of the team at Inkwell Management. Thanks to Estefania Acquaviva, Leena Oropez, Jeff Holt, Rebecca Holland, Albert Tang, Ben Sevier, Colin Dickerman, and everyone else at Grand Central Publishing who brought this book to life.

Thanks to Matthew S. Burns, Nathaniel Chapman, Doug Creutz, Cecilia D'Anastasio, Kirk Hamilton, Stephen Totilo, and several others for early feedback. Thanks to my fantastic colleagues at *Bloomberg* including Brad Stone, Tom Giles, Molly Schuetz, Chris Palmeri, Lucas Shaw, Mark Milian, and Felix Gillette.

Much love and gratitude to my parents, to Safta, for everything, and to the rest of my family: Rita, Owen, Jonah, Pam, and David.

Thanks to Amanda, my best friend and partner in crime, the best mom in the world. And to Sophie and Noah, who never fail to crack me up.

NOTES

CHAPTER ONE

7   **During lunch breaks:** Dean Takahashi, "Cofounder Looks at Chaos in Early Stages and Future Challenges," *Los Angeles Times*, March 13, 1994.

8   **One day at the UCLA computer lab:** Allen Adham, BlizzCon All-Access, November 3, 2017.

9   **Morhaime, too, obsessed over video games:** gamedev things, "Warren Spector lecture 07—Mike Morhaime," YouTube, October 22, 2007, https://www.youtube.com/watch?v=MzpS7xYyjNw.

10   **But Morhaime, who had graduated a few months earlier:** Dean Takahashi, "Mike Morhaime: The highlights and lessons of nearly three decades at Blizzard," *VentureBeat*, June 30, 2019.

15   **"I just thought, 'Oh my God'":** Blizzard Entertainment, "The Lost Vikings And How We Learned To Love Multiplayer Puzzles," February 20, 2021, https://news.blizzard.com/en-us/blizzard/23609765/the-lost-vikings-and -how-we-learned-to-love-multiplayer-puzzles.

19   **The two founders were tens of thousands of dollars:** Tom Marks, "Inside the early office culture of Blizzard, in their own words," *PC Gamer*, December 9, 2016.

CHAPTER TWO

20   **"It's nice that I got rich":** "A Big Math Attack," *Los Angeles Times*, August 22, 1994.

21   **The two cofounders were baffled:** Kosta Andreadis, "The Early Days of Blizzard With Cofounder Allen Adham," IGN, January 13, 2019.

26   **It was geek Mecca:** Dan Brodnitz, "An Interview With Chris Metzen," *About Creativity* blog, April 21, 2008.

30 **"Blizzard Entertainment has outdone itself":** Ron Dulin, "Warcraft II: Tides of Darkness Review," GameSpot, May 1, 1996.

CHAPTER THREE

32 **His family had moved around a lot:** David L. Craddock, *Stay Awhile and Listen: How Two Blizzards Unleashed Diablo and Forged a Video-Game Empire* (Canton, Ohio: DM Press, 2017).

38 **"ten good reasons why this doesn't make sense":** Peter H. Lewis, "CUC Will Buy 2 Software Companies for $1.8 Billion," *New York Times*, February 21, 1996.

42 **"*Diablo* is the best game to come out in the past year":** Trent Ward, "Diablo Review," GameSpot, January 23, 1997.

CHAPTER FOUR

44 **Later, Morhaime would estimate that Blizzard:** Tom Phillips, "Ex-Blizzard boss Mike Morhaime on why the studio bins 50% of its projects," *Eurogamer*, June 26, 2019.

50 **At the end of 1997, South Korea had just one hundred PC bangs:** Mark Magnier, "'PC Bang' Helps S. Koreans Embrace Net," *Los Angeles Times*, July 19, 2000.

51 **The merger came with all sorts of weird quirks:** Peter Elkind, "A Merger Made In Hell," *Fortune* magazine, November 9, 1998.

CHAPTER FIVE

60 **It wasn't "really like a traditional real-time strategy game":** Moritz Ernst Jacob, "Warcraft 3 announcement at ECTS 1999," YouTube, March 4, 2012, https://www.youtube.com/watch?v=0esQtZ9s9Fk.

CHAPTER SIX

72 **In January, press reported that Microsoft:** Johnny Brookheart, "Microsoft buying Vivendi games?" *Ars Technica*, January 30, 2003.

CHAPTER SEVEN

76 **a goofy, lighthearted documentary:** BlizzardArchive, "Blizzard—Official 10th Anniversary Movie—2001," YouTube, August 22, 2018.

77 **The best-selling PC game of 1996 was *Myst*:** Greg Miller, "*Myst* Opportunities: Game Makers Narrow Their Focus to Search for the Next Blockbuster," *Los Angeles Times*, March 3, 1997.

78 **In 1984, 37 percent of computer science majors were women:** National Center for Education Statistics, "Degrees in computer and information sciences conferred by degree-granting institutions, by level of degree and sex of student: 1970-71 through 2010-11," https://nces.ed.gov/programs/digest/d12/tables/dt12_349.asp.

78 **An NPR report found that this decline:** Planet Money, "When Women Stopped Coding," October 21, 2014.

79 **A survey by the International Game Developers Association:** Simon Carless, "IGDA Releases Game Industry Demographics Survey," Game Developer, October 17, 2005.

CHAPTER EIGHT

89 *GameSpot* **reviewer Greg Kasavan wrote that:** Greg Kasavin, "EverQuest Review," GameSpot, May 1, 2000.

CHAPTER NINE

97 **At the same time, Vivendi was drowning in debt:** Jennifer Bayot, "Vivendi Pays $50 Million In Settlement With S.E.C.," *New York Times*, December 24, 2003.

98 **"We're used to having more control over our destiny":** Alex Pham, "Vivendi Leaving Blizzard in Cloud of Uncertainty," *Los Angeles Times*, September 1, 2003.

CHAPTER TEN

102 **"I parked like a mile away":** Seth Schiesel, "World of Warcraft Keeps Growing, Even as Players Test Its Limits," *New York Times*, February 10, 2005.

105 **"Normally when we ship a game it is basically done":** Ibid.

106 **"I had no idea that one day I would be standing up here":** Kalianos, "Blizzcon 2005 Intro," YouTube, October 2, 2014, https://www.youtube.com/watch?v=uNa4_GW_hkg.

CHAPTER TWELVE

125 **Kotick's mother, a teacher:** *Forbes*, "Activision's Unlikely Hero," January 15, 2009.

125 **Later, as a curly-haired teenager with an impish smile:** Ibid.

125 **He had never been a big fan of school:** Ibid.

127 **On the way, Wynn explained that two decades earlier:** Becky Quick, CNBC Evolve Conference, November 19, 2019, https://www.cnbc.com/2019/11/19

/cnbc-transcript-cnbcs-becky-quick-interviews-activision-blizzard-ceo-bobby
-kotick-from-the-cnbc-evolve-conference-in-los-angeles-today.html.

127 **"Like my dad":** Brian Crecente, "A Delightful Chat With the Most Hated Man in Video Games," *Kotaku*, June 14, 2010.

127 **"I think my talent is being able to get things done very quickly":** Gail Pellett, Software Productions, PBS, 1984, https://gailpellettproductions.com /software-entrepreneurs-84/.

128 **Activision found quick success**: Jimmy Maher, "Jim Levy and Activision," The Digital Antiquarian, November 5, 2014.

129 **Incredibly, the courts all ruled in Magnavox's favor:** David Kalat, "The Case of the Video Game Lawsuit Racket," Thinkset, July 11, 2019.

129 **He and his partners, including Marks and Wynn:** *Forbes*, "Activision's Unlikely Hero," January 15, 2009.

130 **As Kotick tells the story:** Betsy Cummings, "Private Sector; From Showdown to Good Times," *New York Times*, January 25, 2004.

130 **so Kotick took out his office keycard:** Ibid.

133 **He said he believed in letting game companies make their own strategic decisions:** *Forbes*, "Activision's Unlikely Hero," January 15, 2009.

133 **"If you want to run an institutional-level company":** Dan Gallagher, "Kotick changes the game at Activision Blizzard," *MarketWatch*, December 4, 2008.

133 **One comment to investors:** Brendan Sinclair, "Activision games to bypass consoles," GameSpot, February 18, 2010.

134 **"I was thinking it was mind-boggling":** Matt Casamassina, "Activision Passed on *The Sims*," IGN, February 18, 2010.

134 **Kotick, meanwhile, was enticed by the growing appeal of Blizzard in China:** *Forbes*, "Activision's Unlikely Hero," January 15, 2009.

135 **A decade earlier, Kotick had reluctantly moved Activision:** Steve Lohr, "Market Place; Home Software's Treasure Hunt," *New York Times*, December 28, 1993.

135 **In 2008, as the merger closed and he took his seat:** Dan Gallagher, "Kotick changes the game at Activision Blizzard," *MarketWatch*, December 4, 2008.

CHAPTER THIRTEEN

137 **The new campus was 240,000 square feet:** "Blizzard Entertainment moves into new campus," *Orange County Register*, March 10, 2008.

147 **Back in 1997, games generated around $5 billion in revenue:** Brendan Sinclair, "NPD: 2008 game sales reach $21 billion, *Wii Play* sells 5.28M," GameSpot, January 20, 2009.

CHAPTER FOURTEEN

153 **"Everyone expected Blizzard's 'when it's ready' philosophy to pay off":** Steve Butts, *"StarCraft 2 Beta Terran Impressions,"* IGN, February 18, 2010.

154 **But in 2007, the landscape changed:** Alec Meer, "Blizzard: Korean e-sports TV deprives devs of IP rights," Gamesindustry.biz, December 6, 2010.

155 **The two organizations entered a legal dispute:** Ibid.

CHAPTER FIFTEEN

159 **One internet petition, signed by some fifty thousand people:** Alec Meer, "Ain't No Pleasin' Some Folks," Rock Paper Shotgun, July 1, 2008.

164 **David Brevik spoke publicly about *Diablo III*:** Connor Sheridan, "Diablo dev's disappointment sparks disdain from *Diablo III* team," GameSpot, August 21, 2012.

CHAPTER SIXTEEN

172 **One reviewer wrote that:** Vince Ingenito, *"Diablo 3: Reaper of Souls* Review," IGN, March 28, 2014.

175 **"For $15, you're right to expect more":** Brett Todd, *"Diablo 3: Rise of the Necromancer* Review," GameSpot, July 11, 2017.

CHAPTER SEVENTEEN

184 **Wrote one previewer:** Cassandra Khaw, *"Hearthstone: Heroes of Warcraft* preview," *PC Gamer*, March 25, 2013.

CHAPTER NINETEEN

199 **A leaked slideshow even revealed the name *Titan* to the outside world:** Logan Westbrook, "Blizzard Admits that *Titan* Is Real," *The Escapist*, December 17, 2010.

201 **Rob Pardo first discovered the joys of game design:** Soren Johnson, *Designer Notes* podcast, 1: Rob Pardo, October 30, 2014.

201 **Growing up an only child in Southern California:** Ibid.

202 **In May 2006, a *TIME* magazine spread:** Lev Grossman, "The 2006 *TIME* 100: Rob Pardo," *TIME*, May 8, 2006.

203 **he even claimed responsibility for Adham's old donut theory:** Kristin Kalning, "Can Blizzard top itself with 'StarCraft II?,'" NBC News, May 29, 2007.

203 **Later, Pardo would say on a podcast:** Soren Johnson, *Designer Notes* podcast, 1: Rob Pardo, October 30, 2014.

CHAPTER TWENTY

207 **With its stock tanking, Vivendi ousted its CEO:** Cliff Edwards and Marie Mawad, "Vivendi Said to Seek Buyer for $8.1 Billion Stake in Activision," *Bloomberg*, June 30, 2012.

207 **At the beginning of 2013, Kotick and Kelly made a formal proposal:** Chancery Court filing, "IN RE Activision Blizzard, Inc. Stockholder Litigation," C.A. No. 8885-VCL.

208 **outside banking firm that subsequently opposed Kotick's offer:** Ibid.

208 **This was unacceptable to Kotick:** Ibid.

208 **The bank J.P. Morgan, which was underwriting the loan:** Ibid.

208 **In the tense weeks and months that followed:** Ibid.

208 **suggesting in emails:** Ibid.

208 **Kotick and Kelly personally netted:** Ibid.

212 **Kotick was once asked by a journalist:** Andrew Ross Sorkin, "How Leslie Moonves and Bobby Kotick Consistently Get Great Results," *Vanity Fair*, October 14, 2016.

212 **Kotick had spent decades betting:** Ross Miller, "Activision Blizzard CEO Kotick: Vivendi franchises lacked 'potential to be exploited,'" Engadget, November 6, 2008.

213 **"Activision's original mistake was probably in making the *Hawk* series annual":** Keza MacDonald, "Feature: What the hell happened to Tony Hawk?," *VG247*, December 15, 2010.

213 **Kotick thought the idea was absurd:** Andrew Ross Sorkin, "How Leslie Moonves and Bobby Kotick Consistently Get Great Results," *Vanity Fair*, October 14, 2016.

CHAPTER TWENTY-TWO

233 **By 2015, he was managing $50 million from nearly one hundred people:** SEC Filing, Tenfold Capital Partners LP, October 7, 2015.

237 **Although Bobby Kotick had originally dismissed mobile gaming as a fad:** Steve Peterson, "Activision's Kotick brushes aside the mobile market," Gamesindustry.biz, May 9, 2013.

CHAPTER TWENTY-THREE

247 **The first documented video game tournament took place in 1972:** Luke Winkie, "The story of the first esports champion, undefeated since 1972," *PC Gamer*, February 7, 2019.

253 **A few years earlier, Jeff Kaplan and his team had been reeling:** Tim Mulkerin, "Blizzard's Jeff Kaplan talked to us about 'Titan,' the yearslong game development failure that never saw the light of day," *Business Insider*, September 27, 2016.

CHAPTER TWENTY-FOUR

260 **Kotick maintained a private art collection:** Matt Richtel, "Activision's Chief Looks for Gaming's Next Moves," *New York Times*, December 5, 2007.

268 **"We continue to have multiple teams work on multiple unannounced *Diablo* projects":** Felicia Miranda, "Blizzard Cofounder Allen Adham says 'we have not forgotten' core *Diablo* fans," Digitaltrends, November 3, 2018.

271 **"We are troubled by the way the announcement was made":** Jason Schreier, "Blizzard Abruptly Kills Heroes of the Storm Esports, Leaving Players And Casters Fuming," *Kotaku*, December 14, 2018.

CHAPTER TWENTY-FIVE

272 **Rumors of layoffs had been swirling for months:** Christopher Palmeri, "Activision's Plan to Cut Hundreds of Jobs Caps Tumultuous Week," *Bloomberg*, February 7, 2019.

278 ***World of Warcraft* executive producer John Hight later told a reporter:** Eddie Makuch, "WoW Classic's Success 'Surprised' Blizzard, Dev Thought It Would Only Appeal To Core Fans," GameSpot, February 19, 2021.

279 **Protesters said the bill was just the latest symbol of encroachment from China:** Austin Ramzy, "Hong Kong March: Vast Protest of Extradition Bill Shows Fear of Eroding Freedoms," *New York Times*, June 9, 2019.

CHAPTER TWENTY-SIX

291 **Later, a Blizzard spokesperson told *Bloomberg*:** Jason Schreier, "Blizzard Botched *Warcraft III* Remake After Internal Fights, Pressure Over Costs," *Bloomberg*, July 22, 2021.

291 **"This is not the remaster that *Warcraft III* deserves":** Fraser Brown, "Warcraft III: Reforged," *PC Gamer*, May 1, 2020.

CHAPTER TWENTY-SEVEN

304 **When *Overwatch 2* was first announced:** Andy Chalk, "'I have no idea' when *Overwatch 2* will be out, Jeff Kaplan says," *PC Gamer*, November 1, 2019.

CHAPTER TWENTY-EIGHT

316 **A year later, in October 2014, a standup routine by comedian Hannibal Burress resurfaced old rape accusations:** Kevin Fallon, "When Hannibal Buress Called Bill Cosby a Rapist and Helped Topple an Icon," *The Daily Beast*, February 21, 2022.

317 **A subsequent article on the gaming website *Kotaku*:** Ethan Gach, "Inside Blizzard Developers' Infamous Bill 'Cosby Suite,'" *Kotaku*, July 28, 2021.

CHAPTER TWENTY-NINE

331 **Americans had grown up with consoles in their living rooms:** Eustance Huang, "Americans largely won't pay to win a video game—but Chinese gamers will," CNBC, May 30, 2018.

335 **In May 2023, Keller dropped the news:** Tamoor Hussain, "FEATURE ARTICLE: *Overwatch 2*'s PvE Hero Mode Is Being Scrapped, Blizzard Explains What Happened and Why," GameSpot, May 16, 2023.

CHAPTER THIRTY

346 **"I can't help but be impressed":** Cameron Koch, "*World of Warcraft: Dragonflight* Review," GameSpot, January 30, 2023.

346 **saying on a podcast:** Scott Johnson, "The Chris Metzen Interview," SoundCloud, November 15, 2016.

347 **"What they were trying to communicate to us":** Jason Schreier, "Blizzard Boss Is Optimistic About a More Independent Future Under Xbox," *Bloomberg*, November 6, 2023.

348 **he'd told Mike Ybarra that he wanted to do the same:** Ibid.

INDEX

INDEX

INDEX

INDEX

INDEX

INDEX

INDEX